Enhancing Learning, Teaching, Assessment and Curriculum in Higher Education

SRHE and Open University Press Imprint

Current titles include:

Catherine Bargh *et al.*: *University Leadership*
Ronald Barnett: *Beyond all Reason*
Ronald Barnett: *Higher Education: A Critical Business*
Ronald Barnett: *Realizing the University in an Age of Supercomplexity*
Ronald Barnett and Kelly Coate: *Engaging the Curriculum in Higher Education*
Tony Becher and Paul R. Trowler: *Academic Tribes and Territories (2nd edn)*
John Biggs: *Teaching for Quality Learning at University (2nd edn)*
Richard Blackwell and Paul Blackmore (eds): *Towards Strategic Staff Development in Higher Education*
David Boud *et al.* (eds): *Using Experience for Learning*
David Boud and Nicky Solomon (eds): *Work-based Learning*
Tom Bourner *et al.* (eds): *New Directions in Professional Higher Education*
Anne Brockbank and Ian McGill: *Facilitating Reflective Learning in Higher Education*
Stephen D. Brookfield and Stephen Preskill: *Discussion as a Way of Teaching*
Ann Brooks and Alison Mackinnon (eds): *Gender and the Restructured University*
Sally Brown and Angela Glasner (eds): *Assessment Matters in Higher Education*
Burton R. Clark: *Sustaining Change in Universities*
James Cornford and Neil Pollock: *Putting the University Online*
John Cowan: *On Becoming an Innovative University Teacher*
Sara Delamont, Paul Atkinson and Odette Parry: *Supervising the Doctorate 2/e*
Sara Delamont and Paul Atkinson: *Successful Research Careers*
Gerard Delanty: *Challenging Knowledge*
Chris Duke: *Managing the Learning University*
Heather Eggins (ed): *Globalization and Reform in Higher Education*
Heather Eggins and Ranald Macdonald (eds): *The Scholarship of Academic Development*
Gillian Evans: *Academics and the Real World*
Merle Jacob and Tomas Hellström (eds): *The Future of Knowledge Production in the Academy*
Peter Knight: *Being a Teacher in Higher Education*
Peter Knight and Paul Trowler: *Departmental Leadership in Higher Education*
Peter Knight and Mantz Yorke: *Assessment, Learning and Employability*
Ray Land: *Educational Development*
John Lea *et al.*: *Working in Post-Compulsory Education*
Mary Lea and Barry Stierer (eds): *Student Writing in Higher Education*
Dina Lewis and Barbara Allan: *Virtual Learning Communities*
Ian McNay (ed.): *Beyond Mass Higher Education*
Elaine Martin: *Changing Academic Work*
Louise Morley: *Quality and Power in Higher Education*
Lynne Pearce: *How to Examine a Thesis*
Moira Peelo and Terry Wareham (eds): *Failing Students in Higher Education*
Craig Prichard: *Making Managers in Universities and Colleges*
Stephen Rowland: *The Enquiring University Teacher*
Maggi Savin-Baden: *Problem-based Learning in Higher Education*
Maggi Savin-Baden: *Facilitating Problem-based Learning*
Maggi Savin-Baden and Kay Wilkie: *Challenging Research in Problem-based Learning*
David Scott *et al.*: *Professional Doctorates*
Peter Scott: *The Meanings of Mass Higher Education*
Michael L. Shattock: *Managing Successful Universities*
Maria Slowey and David Watson: *Higher Education and the Lifecourse*
Colin Symes and John McIntyre (eds): *Working Knowledge*
Richard Taylor, Jean Barr and Tom Steele: *For a Radical Higher Education*
Malcolm Tight: *Researching Higher Education*
Penny Tinkler and Carolyn Jackson: *The Doctoral Examination Process*
Susan Toohey: *Designing Courses for Higher Education*
Melanie Walker (ed.): *Reconstructing Professionalism in University Teaching*
Melanie Walker and Jon Nixon (eds): *Reclaiming Universities from a Runaway World*
Diana Woodward and Karen Ross: *Managing Equal Opportunities in Higher Education*
Mantz Yorke and Bernard Longden: *Retention and Student Success in Higher Education*

Enhancing Learning, Teaching, Assessment and Curriculum in Higher Education

Theory, Cases, Practices

Veronica Bamber,
Paul Trowler, Murray Saunders
and Peter Knight

 Society for Research into Higher Education
& Open University Press

Open University Press
McGraw-Hill Education
McGraw-Hill House
Shoppenhangers Road
Maidenhead
Berkshire
England
SL6 2QL

email: enquiries@openup.co.uk
world wide web: www.openup.co.uk

and Two Penn Plaza, New York, NY 10121–2289, USA

First published 2009

A catalogue record of this book is available from the British Library

ISBN-13: 978 0 335 23375 5 (pb)   978 0 335 23376 2 (hb)
ISBN-10 0 335 23375 9 (pb)   0 335 23376 7 (hb)

Library of Congress Cataloging-in-Publication Data
CIP data has been applied for

Typeset by RefineCatch Limited, Bungay, Suffolk
Printed in the UK by Bell and Bain Ltd., Glasgow

Fictitious names of companies, products, people, characters and/or data that may be used herein (in case studies or in examples) are not intended to represent any real individual company, product or event.

The **McGraw·Hill** Companies

This book is dedicated to the memory of Professor Peter Knight who made important contributions to it but passed away suddenly in the early stages of writing. Peter was a friend and colleague of the other editors and many of the contributors. He was widely known and respected by academics, university managers and educational developers around the world. His many publications on the enhancement of teaching, learning and assessment in higher education are a valuable and permanent legacy for the higher education community and to students everywhere. He is sadly missed by his many friends.

Contents

List of figures

List of tables

List of contributors

Professor Cliff Allan is Deputy Vice-Chancellor (Development) at the University of Teesside. Prior to this Cliff was Deputy Chief Executive of the UK Higher Education Academy. This followed his period as Director of the Learning and Teaching Support Network (LTSN) which he led from its inception in 2000.

Cliff worked for a decade developing HE funding policies at the Higher Education Funding Council for England (HEFCE), where he was Head of Teaching and Learning Policy. He has also worked as a management consultant, primarily in the further and higher education sectors.

Having started his working life as a lecturer in International Relations and Politics he moved into working for several third world development agencies. He is a visiting professor of Higher Education Policy and Practice at the University of Bradford and a fellow of the Royal Society of Arts.

Dr Veronica (Roni) Bamber is Director of the Centre for Academic Practice at Queen Margaret University, Edinburgh. Previously she was Director of Educational Development at Heriot-Watt University. The Centre for Academic Practice is responsible for enhancing learning, teaching and research at the university. She has worked as an educational developer for nine years, and has participated in numerous national initiatives, including the Scottish Enhancement Themes. Prior to this, Roni was a lecturer in Spanish for 18 years, teaching in four different universities around the UK. Roni has had significant experience in other academic activities, such as course leadership, curriculum consultancy, external examining and quality audit. Her current research is in the area of learning and teaching development through the development of staff, and in evaluation of development programmes.

Associate Professor Simon Barrie is Associate Director of the Institute for Teaching and Learning at the University of Sydney. Simon's research explores the nature of the student learning experience in universities as well as the academic experience, and the academic development processes associated with efforts to improve university teaching and learning. In particular his recent work has focused on the development of graduate attributes and the conceptual, structural and institutional barriers and enablers to curriculum renewal to achieve generic graduate attributes.

Scott Court is a senior policy manager in the Policy and Resources Directorate at the UK Economic and Social Research Council. Prior to joining ESRC he was based in the Department of Educational Research at Lancaster University, where he worked as a researcher and tutor.

Dr Alan Davidson, originally from Edinburgh, studied civil engineering at the University of Edinburgh. He then worked in the construction industry for several years before taking up a lecturer's post in civil engineering at the University of Dundee. He progressively developed a role in quality assurance and became Director of Quality Assurance in 1998.

He has had extensive involvements in quality assurance and enhancement at the national and international levels. He completed a part time PhD in educational research at Lancaster University in 2004 and joined RGU in November 2006.

Before becoming a lecturer **Dr Norrie Edward** worked in manufacturing industry as an engineer and rose to the position of manufacturing manager. He entered education some 20 years ago and is now a teaching fellow in the School of Engineering at the Robert Gordon University.

Norrie's research is in education where he is always looking for ways of improving the way we teach and students learn. He has constantly developed and evaluated educational resources and gained his PhD as a result of this work.

His interests cover the use of innovative methods to enhance the educational experience. A particular interest both in teaching and research is the application of student centred design and manufacture activities. Much of this work has been directed at attempting to establish the importance of different factors in the effectiveness of educational methodologies.

Professor Gareth Fisher was born in 1951 in Cumbria. Educated at Edinburgh College of Art in the early seventies, Fisher became a practising artist and visiting lecturer at several colleges. He became a full time lecturer at the Duncan of Jordanstone College of Art, now part of the University of Dundee, in 1985 and became a professor in the School of Fine Art in 2001. Alongside his artistic practice, Fisher became increasingly interested in the enhancement of the learning process in fine art education and subsequently became Associate Dean for Learning and Teaching for the college.

Marilyn Higgins is a senior lecturer in the School of the Built Environment, Heriot-Watt University, Edinburgh. Following 18 years in planning practice, she teaches and researches in Urban Design and People & Organizational

Management. Her keen interest in education developed during her Urban Studies degree at Brown University, Rhode Island, where she was included in the first intake to a radical 'New Curriculum' in 1969. She has published on creativity, personal development planning and work based learning in higher education. In 2007–08, she spent a year at the University of Auckland as Deputy Head of the School of Architecture and Planning.

Dr Gerry Humphris studied psychology at Reading University (1973–76) before going to Guy's Hospital to complete a PhD (1983). Gerry gained his clinical psychology qualification at Liverpool (1986) and after ten years of being involved in undergraduate teaching of dentists and medics (Director of Communication Skills) he moved to University of Manchester as Reader in the Clinical Psychology Department (2001) before taking up the post of Chair in Health Psychology at Bute Medical School, University of St Andrews (2003). Gerry studies the communication processes between clinician and patient in particular conditions, including the assessment and description of the processes involved. This work informs the teaching of medical students at St Andrews.

Dr Paul Kleiman is Deputy Director of PALATINE, the Higher Education Academy Subject Centre for Dance, Drama and Music. Trained as a theatre designer, he spent the first part of his career as a designer, director, performer and writer, touring political and community theatre around the UK. In 1995, after various spells of part time teaching, he joined the small team that established the Liverpool Institute for Performing Arts (LIPA) where he became Head of Design and also Head of Assessment. He joined PALATINE in 2001. His main research, writings, conference presentations and consultancies focus on creativity, curriculum design and assessment.

Professor Peter Knight started his professional life as a secondary school teacher, and then spent more than twenty years as a lecturer and researcher, first at Lancaster University and then at the Open University. From 2004 he was Director of the Institute of Educational Technology at the Open University, where he also became Founding Director of the Practice-based Professional Learning CETL (Centre for Excellence in Teaching and Learning). His research covered employability, assessment of student learning, and professional learning and development in higher education. Peter was also active in evaluation and consultancy, acting as one of the evaluation team, for example, of the Scottish Quality Enhancement Framework. Tragically, Peter died in 2007, in the early stages of writing this book.

Dr Anita Laidlaw studied biology at the University of Edinburgh (1993–97) before completing a PhD at Newcastle University (2001). After postdoctoral work in the School of Psychology, University of St Andrews, she moved to the Bute Medical School, also at St Andrews, in 2005. Anita's research investigates factors impacting on an individual's ability to communicate, the teaching of communication and the assessment of communication skills. This research is directly applied to the teaching of students at St Andrews.

Kirsten Hofgaard Lycke is Professor at the Institute for Educational Research, University of Oslo, Norway. Her current research is focused on quality of studies and learning environments in academia and in the workplace. As Professor at the University of Oslo, Kirsten is involved in educational innovations in general and in the university's adaptation to the current national quality reform in particular. This involves consultations with departments, running seminars and workshops for academic staff, and supervising master and doctoral students. Kirsten is Past President of the International Consortium for Educational Development (ICED).

Dr Colin Mason is currently Dean of Teaching and Learning at Unitec, Auckland, New Zealand, where he is leading development of a teaching led, research informed academic strategy. He was previously Director of Learning and Teaching Development at SALTIRE, University of St Andrews. Prior to that he was a lecturer and then senior lecturer at the University of Bradford, specializing in haematology.

He contributed extensively to the distinctive Scottish QAA Enhancement theme management, steering and consultation groups from 2003 to 2007. He was a workshop director for the assessment theme, 'Assessing Personal Transferable Skills', and together with Professor David Lines at Robert Gordon University, Aberdeen, he co-edited *Enhancing Practice: Assessment*, a summary of the main outcomes of all eight workshops. He also led a recent pilot project funded from the Scottish QAA enhancement theme on flexible delivery, SHEDLOADS (Scottish Higher Education: Learning Objects And Distributed Services).

Professor Kenneth Miller is Vice-Principal of the University of Strathclyde. He also chairs the Scottish Higher Education Enhancement Committee which has overall responsibility for the management of the enhancement themes in Scotland. He currently is responsible for staffing, equality and diversity issues and international policy at Strathclyde. Before that he was the senior officer with responsibility for learning and teaching and quality assurance.

Mike Molesworth is a senior lecturer in interactive marketing at Bournemouth Media School and a learning and teaching fellow at the Centre for Excellence in Media Practice. His research interests focus on the consumption of digital media, especially videogames and the Internet, and also on the use of such technologies in higher education. You can see examples of both his and his students' work at: http://www.CEMP.ac.uk/communities/interactivemedia/

Professor Rob Moore is Deputy Vice Chancellor at the University of the Witwatersrand (Wits) in Johannesburg. He spent 12 years at the University of Cape Town researching and teaching in higher education studies, before being appointed as Director of Institutional Audits for South Africa's Council on Higher Education. He then joined Wits in 2006 as Director of Strategic Planning. His research interests have focused on issues of institutional adaptation. In particular, he has published on issues of institutional responsiveness to policy, on curriculum reform and on the development of management capacity. He is a member of the Advisory Board of the journal, *Studies in Higher Education*.

Lizzie Nixon works as a researcher in the Centre for Excellence in Media Practice at Bournemouth University. Alongside a range of projects capturing the learner voice for the Centre, in areas such as personal development and the use of technology in HE, Lizzie has also co-authored several conference papers and journal articles which reflect her interest in understanding the student experience and engendering transformational learning. For the last three years she has also worked as a part time lecturer, facilitating undergraduate students' understanding of research methods in advertising, marketing, communication and PR.

Professor Anthony Rosie has worked in schools, colleges and higher education. He is currently Professor of Social Science Education at Sheffield Hallam University and a senior fellow of the Higher Education Academy. He was Director of the Subject Centre for Sociology, Anthropology and Politics (CSAP) from 2003 to 2005. His teaching and research interests are in historical-comparative sociology, supporting learners who find tasks difficult.

Professor Murray Saunders is Director of CSET (Centre for the Study of Education and Training at Lancaster University, UK) and Professor of Evaluation in Work and Education. He has acted as a consultant to, and has undertaken a wide range of evaluation projects for, UK based government organizations (DfID, HEFCE, ESRC, SfC, British Council). He has carried out evaluation and research projects in a wide range of cultural contexts, including China, Japan, Singapore, Tanzania, Kenya, Jordan, Russia and Ethiopia as well as in other member states of the EU. He is Past President and Council Member of the UK Evaluation Society, current President of the European Evaluation Society and Associate Editor of the only international multidisciplinary academic journal in the field, *Evaluation*. Murray has directed or co-directed some 40 separate evaluation and research projects over the last 25 years in areas of curriculum change, policy and strategic development and vocational education. Recently he has co-directed or directed evaluations of several policy and programme interventions in HE (national evaluation of the LTSN, national evaluations of the QEF strategy in Scotland, national evaluation of the CETL strategy in England, Scotland and Wales and has devised the evaluation strategy for Widening Participation funding).

As Director of QAA Scotland, **Norman Sharp** is responsible for the development and implementation of QAA's policy and practice in Scotland. In this
context he played a major role in the development and implementation of
the Scottish Quality Enhancement Framework (QEF).

Norman was previously an assistant director in the Higher Education
Quality Council. Originally an academic economist, Norman's interest in
quality assurance and enhancement was stimulated by his roles in curriculum
development and course management for 'traditional' higher education
students and also in the context of wider patterns of provision including part
time and work based provision. This led to his involvement in the creation
of SCOTCAT, the credit framework for higher education, and subsequently
to his role in the creation of the comprehensive credit and qualifications
framework in Scotland, the SCQF. In 2007, Norman became a founding
director of the SCQF Partnership, the company formed to manage the
SCQF.

Norman has had extensive international involvement in quality matters
including work in South Africa, Ireland, Namibia, Luxembourg, Serbia and
Albania. He has undertaken a range of assignments on behalf of the Council
of Europe to support countries involved in the Bologna process. In 2006,
Norman was elected to the Board of the International Network of Quality
Assurance Agencies in Higher Education (INQAAHE), and in 2007 was
appointed to the Board of the Higher Education Training and Awards
Council (HETAC) of Ireland.

In 2004 Norman was appointed to the Board of LEAD Scotland (Linking
Education And Disability). He has also been a consultant on quality matters
to a range of employers and Professional and Statutory Bodies. In 1999 he
was appointed to the Board of the Clinical Standards Board for Scotland and
subsequently to the Board of NHS Quality Improvement Scotland of which
he was Vice-Chairman and, in 2006, Chairman.

Norman was awarded the OBE for services to higher education in the 2006
Queen's New Year's Honours List.

Professor Lorraine Stefani is Director of the Centre for Academic Development at the University of Auckland, New Zealand. With over 20 years' experience in academic development, she has a strong record of scholarship gained
through academic positions and consultancy within universities across the
UK, South Africa, Hong Kong, Hungary, Switzerland and New Zealand. She
has particular expertise in developing sustainable partnerships linking academic development and developers with faculty and disciplinary based staff.
She is an advocate for blended learning strategies and provision of personal
learning spaces, with a research output on a range of topics including
e-learning, assessment of student learning and student engagement.

Professor Paul Trowler is Professor of Higher Education at Lancaster
University. He has written numerous book and journal articles around the
area of academics, change management, the enhancement of teaching and

learning and academic cultures. In addition he has been involved in numerous evaluative studies in the higher education sector, worked with Centres for Excellence in Teaching and Learning as a research adviser and critical friend as well as being asked to give numerous keynote talks and consultancy services on change and development issues in higher education systems around the world. He teaches about a range of higher education issues on postgraduate programmes in the Department of Educational Research.

Associate Professor **Dr Belinda Tynan** is Leader of the Academic Development Unit within the Teaching and Learning Centre at the University of New England, Australia. Her background is in the field of academic staff development, teacher education, distance education and arts education. She has worked internationally and received a range of internal and competitive funds. Her research background is in the area of academic development, distance education, social technologies and models of research collaboration. Belinda is an editor for *HERD*, which is a key journal relevant to teaching and learning in higher education, and Treasurer of the Open and Distance Learning Association of Australia.

Professor Sir David Watson is a historian and Professor of Higher Education Management at the Institute of Education, University of London. He was Vice-Chancellor of the University of Brighton (formerly Brighton Polytechnic) between 1990 and 2005. His academic interests are in the history of American ideas and in higher education policy. His books include *Lifelong Learning and the University* (1998), *Managing Strategy* (2000), *New Directions in Professional Higher Education* (2000), *Higher Education and the Lifecourse* (2003), *Managing Institutional Self-Study* (2005), *Managing Civic and Community Engagement* (2007) and *The Dearing Report: Ten Years On* (2007). He has recently been appointed Chair of the NIACE Commission of Inquiry on 'The Future for Lifelong Learning: A National Strategy'.

Preface

Enhancement and its relationship to innovation and change can be a challenging exploration. Educationalists are keen to help others learn from past and current experience but it is not easy to find an approach that is both useful and acceptably robust in an academic context. But times have changed and recently political will has focused on enhancement activity. In the UK there is widespread agreement on the need for professional development for teaching; there are funds to support innovations in pedagogy and national agencies to support collaboration and dissemination. A cadre of researchers and educational developers offer evidence and expertise and many conferences, workshops and seminar programmes foster debate. In comparison to the late twentieth century there is a benign context for those interested in developing their practice, innovating in teaching and changing their organizational systems to enhance learning, teaching, assessment and curriculum in higher education. This has come from a global frame within which education and universities in particular are recognized as agents of social and economic development. A second factor is the strong current of innovative pedagogy fuelled by information technology. Consequent on the previous two factors, managers and leaders nationally and within institutions have altered their perspective of educational development professionals from scepticism to endorsement as important agents for change.

Over a professional lifetime in higher education I have witnessed the move of a vulnerable group acting individually and on the very edge of their institutions to a powerful profession which transcends hierarchies and finds location within national agencies, at the very top of strategic management within institutions and within large and sustainable centres which attract external and internal funding streams. The work also increasingly pervades departments so that a focus on enhancement of teaching and learning is a natural part of academic life and a more frequently rewarded aspect of career development. National accolades are available for individuals, groups, departments and institutions in the form of grants and awards.

Success has also brought some negative consequences. Educational development has seen its fair share of in-fighting between sub-groups, squabbling over the 'proper' relationship of research to practice and rather too much self-conscious navel gazing. Any new professional area requires robust and critical analysis to progress. To take this endeavour beyond its early achievements, complacency and destructive in-fighting we need the kind of critical analysis offered by this text. The authors side-step jargon and rise above the temptation to labour the legitimacy of their approach. They simply state it, and the result is a text on enhancement offering a robust practicality.

This book is a welcome example of maturity in the field of educational development. In the past there would have been a tiny 'audience' for a book on enhancement that used sophisticated social scientific analysis. There might have been confusion about the way in which different case studies were presented as discreet and unique cases that create a backdrop for conceptual understanding. The idea that a book might stimulate an individual response towards the reader's own circumstance would have appeared altogether too much effort and yet here we have such a book. The authors balance simple language of presentation with a sophisticated theoretical dialogue. They walk a careful line between descriptive analysis of structural and organizational context and stressing the importance of action and agency. It is a book of its time; because the audience is better informed. We no longer need to be bashful about our interest in enhancement. The postmodern, relativist angst can be transcended and we can revel in the fascination of a meta cultural analysis that returns power to the thoughtful reader.

Dr Liz Beaty,
Director of Strategic
Academic Practice
and Partnership,
University of Cumbria

1

Introduction: continuities, enhancement and higher education

Veronica Bamber, Paul Trowler, Murray Saunders and Peter Knight

> Taking as a starting point 1530, when the Lutheran Church was founded, some 66 institutions that existed then still exist today in the Western World in recognizable form: the Catholic Church, the Lutheran Church, the parliaments of Iceland and the Isle of Man, and 62 universities
>
> (Kerr 1980: 9)

Change, innovation, enhancement

Change happens and continuities persist. Enhancement requires change. As educators our interest in enhancing the quality of learning, teaching, assessment and other aspects of curriculum (LTAC) in higher education faces us with the fact that while things change they also stay the same. One response, favoured by postmodernist accounts of the world, is to look with amusement on an unpredictable and uncontrollable world. Another, modernist response insists that people can steer change if only they properly understand how change happens and if they wisely use the resources at hand. Yet, regardless of the view taken, change happens in systems which are both resistant to change and which are also affected by the change.

Change can just happen without any deliberate actions, but whether deliberate or not, change can be interpreted as either positive or negative in its effects. *Innovation* by contrast is intentional and has certain goals in view which are desired and therefore seen as positive. Innovations also incorporate the idea of 'newness', whereas change can involve returning to older practices.

Enhancement, the subject of this book, also involves a deliberate move towards making things better. In one interpretation it is simply doing the same only a little better, in other words improvement on what already exists. Improving the quality of teaching materials might be an example of that. Another interpretation though can involve the addition of innovations into existing practices, for example adding an international dimension to a syllabus where no such dimension existed before, or a new teaching method to a repertoire. A final more radical understanding of enhancement involves a rethink of existing approaches, even fundamental purposes, and doing things differently. We consider examples of all three interpretations of enhancement in the case studies which follow.

Enhancement and universities

Innovations also often have unexpected effects, unintended outcomes (Fullan 2001). Universities are (still) loosely coupled organizations; loose linkages across the institution allow for substantial discretion and local adaptation (Weick 1995). Levers pulled in the university[1] top team's control room do not necessarily have the desired effects in the engine rooms at departmental level. Mechanisms for allocating responsibility, for getting and using feedback about achievement of targets and for giving rewards or sanctions are complex, messy and subject to constraints and influences that reduce university managers' and policymakers' power. Inertia and unexpected effects are just as likely as intended outcomes. Policy initiatives and the texts that describe them are usually the result of conflict, bargaining, alternative (even competing) understandings and compromise, even at the top of institutions or government. Policies and innovations are rarely simple and unambiguous. Rather they tend to be fuzzy and open to alternative readings. This is often beneficial because it allows for local adaptation, which we argue below is necessary. In university cultures, teachers at ground level always have room for manoeuvre – have discretion – even when innovations are very tightly defined and introduced in more tightly coupled managerial contexts. The outcomes can be characterized as provisional stabilities: stabilities in the sense that systems tend to settle into working patterns; provisional in the sense that these patterns are subject to change in resources, staff, expectations, organization, links with other systems, technologies and goals.

While we are arguing that it is important for change agents to have an explicit theory of change (i.e., an articulation of what is intended, the expected outcomes and the mechanisms by which one will translate into the other), their theory of change must recognize the dynamics of the context, and be adapted over the course of the enhancement effort. Where 'enhancement' is imposed by managers' power, with no accommodation of contextual factors, there is unlikely to be real change in values, attitudes or practices in the long term. Effective change is embedded in its context and comes when those involved make it their own through use and adaptation to local histories and contexts. Enhancements of practice are produced by a complex array of individually and collectively induced incentives, histories and values. A

---

[1] We talk about higher education in terms of universities here only for reasons of style and concision: we recognize that HE happens in other contexts too, of course.

measure of power and control at the ground level is a condition of success. The people who operate in them largely create local contexts. Backstage (where deals are done in private) and under-the-stage (where gossip is purveyed) views are adopted and transmitted and decisions are made. The knowledge, understandings and attitudes developed there have an important impact on innovation processes. These are largely dissociated from the explicit, official frontstage processes that more management driven models focus on.

So, we see enhancement as best arising from the 'bottom', 'middle' and 'top', with other change forces, such as resources, competing priorities and expertise, colouring the ways in which innovation efforts are translated into established practices. The location of power and control over change will also be different in different locations, so there is no one best place for power and control over change to lie – it will depend on time and place but will always be distributed between the 'top', 'middle' and 'bottom' in changing proportions. The exertion of brute power from the top of universities (or from government agencies) to achieve intended outcomes will fail. More subtle exercise of control is necessary in complex organizations in turbulent environments. A subtle understanding of the effective use of power and control requires a nuanced understanding of the history and context of locations in which change is desired. Agency on the ground is usually just as important as control from the top, so a fine-grained knowledge of the ground is necessary.

We argue, then, that there is no 'magic bullet', no 'magic feather' to enable Dumbo the Elephant to fly (Goodlad 1984). Some, who are committed to the modernist project of making a difference, say that the problem lies with the ways innovations are framed and that if we only understood better 'what works', or if we only identified and applied 'best practice', then change would follow. A refinement of this position says that 'what works' and 'best practice' will usually be a subtle blend of mutually reinforcing changes across the levels. Fullan (1999) saw the attempts to improve literacy in English schools in the late 1990s as a case in point, although his analysis was subtle in saying that multiple, aligned changes at different levels *increased the chances* of desired outcomes happening. Some years later improvement has stopped, and some ask whether test scores show 'real' improvements in literacy. There are also now plenty of complaints about unintended outcomes.

Whatever form change, innovation or enhancement takes, though, attempts to improve outcomes by changing only an element at one level may have limited, local and provisional success. The problem can be that because the rest of the system is not touched and established patterns prevail over the single change, there is little real change to the system's working. Some historians of education argue that schooling at the end of the twentieth century was little different from at its start (Tyack and Cuban 1995; Farrell 2000) despite waves of educational innovations over the decades. Clark Kerr (1980) makes a different point about continuity and stability, arguing that sometimes surface appearance belies real change below. Though universities appear to remain essentially the same over centuries, underneath there is a *constant* process of change and adaptation. We will shortly say more about the reasons why practices become set or ossified, but in the book as a whole we will be looking at ways in which enhancements can be encouraged.

Planned enhancements, wisely designed and implemented, may only improve the odds in favour of desired outcomes – but that, we say, is a project worth undertaking. Success is far from certain, but we consider the moral activity of using wisdom to try and improve social systems to be a good one. And, given the amount of energy that is, regardless of the standpoint of academics such as ourselves, invested in the neverending task of improving social practices, we argue that it is better for innovation to be based on understandings of how the probabilities of desired outcomes materialize than on the romanticism of policies that underestimate the sheer difficulty of making a difference.

Improving the odds of success

What we hope to achieve

While we intend this book to be useful, we reject the 'what works' approach of evidence based policy because it is based on a single and unconsidered value or vision of the educated graduate. We have an expansive notion of 'use' that accommodates and reconstructs the idea of a 'tip for Monday morning' as something that simultaneously offers a glimpse of what is possible, the basis on which it might be possible, the theories and concepts that enable us to understand what is possible and which help us to see the present differently, embodiments of examples of what is possible and, finally, who can make it possible. Part of our aspiration to be 'useful' through this book is by contributing to social and professional learning through encouraging readers to embark on sensemaking aided by both the case studies and the theoretical propositions to be found here.

Vision of what's possible

While the case studies form the main body of the book, the theoretical frameworks laid out in the next chapter may help you bridge the gap between what a case study author says about their situation, and how you might reconceptualize their example within your own context.

The book's approach

We offer a theoretical framework for understanding enhancement in Chapter 2. In the next section of the book, we present cases in thematic sections. The cases are organized by issue into Themes 1–4 and, as noted above, each of these four thematic sections is organized by level of origin: national, institutional, departmental and individual (see Table 1.1).

Each Theme is introduced and concluded by a 'Theme introduction' and a 'Theme commentary' respectively, which orient the reader to the cases

"embark on sensemaking"

Table 1.1 Themes

Theme 1: Influencing the disciplines	Theme 2: The Scottish way: a distinctive approach to enhancement	Theme 3: Developing frameworks for action	Theme 4: Challenging practices in learning, teaching, assessment and curriculum
National case	National case	National case	National case
Institutional case	Institutional case	Institutional case	Institutional case
Departmental case	Departmental case	Departmental case	Departmental case
Individual case	Individual case	Individual case	Individual case

and assist in thinking about their significance. The Theme introduction and Theme commentary are necessary because, as Eraut (2000) points out, it is important to recognize the situations in which one might appropriately apply ideas learned from cases. This is by no means simple:

> Most of the tacit knowledge lies in recognising the situation as one in which the maxim is appropriate – what Klein (1989) calls 'recognition-primed decision making' . . . [M]aking [maxims] explicit may help to draw attention to the context and conditions where it is appropriate to use them; and that is when the 'real' tacit knowledge begins to be disclosed and further learning is more likely to occur.
>
> (Eraut 2000: 124)

[margin handwriting: Recognizing situations]

There is a fairly small and almost entirely laudatory literature on the use of case studies for learning, usually in specific disciplinary areas (see for example Davis and Wilcock 2008 and Hassall et al. 1998). However, cases are by definition accounts of examples in specific contexts. What the cases show is that, no matter what the detail of the changes being attempted, the specifics of the context of enhancement and the approach adopted are very significant, and they interact in unique ways. We are very keen to stress the great significance of *context* in change processes. For these reasons we strongly caution against the fallacy of *secundum quid* – the mistake of attempting to learn direct, general, lessons from individual cases. Translation, reconstruction and bridging are more likely to succeed than attempts to transfer learning between contexts – and these notions are dealt with among the theoretical constructs in the next section.

So why use cases at all? Our aim in this is to illuminate change processes by offering different examples seen through our theoretical lens, as outlined below. Without explicit concepts and theory to illuminate, cases would simply be narratives, more-or-less interesting stories. With a theoretical lens they can help the reader to see enhancement initiatives in a new, more analytical way. Rather than just being narratives, the cases become both examples of and a test of a way of seeing, a framework of ideas (concepts, theories) through which both they and the real world can be understood and explained. With a good theory the particular can become an instance of

[margin handwriting: " "]

[bottom handwriting: Applying a theoretical lens to illuminate]

something more general, and apparently unrelated events and phenomena can be viewed anew, with the links between them made more apparent.

Of course, the lens we offer is only one of a multitude of possible ways of seeing. But, while all theories are wrong, some are more practical than others. Our topping and tailing of the cases is designed to draw out the usefulness of the theoretical approach we offer, as well as to offer readers a way of seeing which will help them to think about their own circumstances more clearly.

In the final chapter we conclude with our overarching analysis, and the learning which the cases offer to higher education professionals. We draw together some key ideas which have emerged from the cases. It does not offer practical advice in the form of 'tips', do's and don'ts: this would encourage a simplistic approach to interpreting and dealing with complex problems. Instead, we turn do's and don'ts into a tool set of conceptual and analytical ways of thinking about enhancement efforts: if we extend the notion of meta cognitive skills to the social and cultural arena, then this *meta cultural* approach will stand you in good stead in your enhancement efforts.

" meta cultural approach"
- conceptual and analytical ways of
  thinking about enhancement efforts

2

Enhancement theories

Paul Trowler, Murray Saunders and Veronica Bamber

Men [and women] make their own history, but they do not make it as they please; they do not make it under self-selected circumstances, but under circumstances existing already, given and transmitted from the past. The tradition of all dead generations weighs like an Alp on the brains of the living.

(Marx 1852: 1)

This chapter lays out our theoretical stall, with a brief overview of some of the conceptual underpinnings for our analysis of the cases. You will notice that we have not included classic change management theories – this is not an oversight, simply a desire to locate thinking about enhancement initiatives in universities within higher education cultural realities. The key concept is that of sociocultural theory, and that is our starting point, but sociocultural theory links to a number of related concepts which together offer a rich framework for understanding enhancement efforts.

Sociocultural theory

We argue that change agents should have an explicit theory of change if they want to increase their chances of success. Our own theoretical approach to change is firmly rooted in sociocultural theory. The key ideas in this understanding of the social world of universities are:

1 That people in universities, departments and work groups within them interact, and in so doing develop a particular set of meanings about the world they are dealing with, ones that are particular to their location. They also develop values, attitudes and practices which are, to some extent, unique to their social situation.
2 That in their interactions – perhaps in developing a new syllabus, preparing to teach a course, or engaging in quality enhancement activities – they

use artefacts and tools of various sorts which themselves influence the social reality in particular ways. Thus, for example, the use of PowerPoint can shape the way classes are taught and content is presented. Meanwhile the social context can, conversely, shape the ways in which tools and artefacts are used. Enhancements often involve changes in tool use, and so this interaction is significant for enhancement initiatives.

3 That discourses – the particular forms of production of 'text' (talk, writing, etc.) which are mediated by deeper social forces and social structures – express social reality and also operate to constrain and delimit it. Discourse and the social construction of reality (point 1) work together. Thus 'managerialist' discourse expresses a particular view of the nature of universities and works to bracket out other views and other discourses. In the end discourse can shape practices.

4 That individual identity, or subjectivity, is likewise both shaped by social context and itself can work to shape it. People interact at work and in so doing are also working to shape the identity of others and are themselves shaped, though they may also defend their identities from this process. However, identity is a lifetime project and people bring with them relatively permanent aspects of identities from previous contexts. Social characteristics such as cultural context are important in change processes, but so are individual people.

5 So, the historical background of individuals and also of the group are important, as Marx notes in the quote at the head of this chapter. History, and narratives about history, have significant influences on social life in the present. These may be stories about academics' disciplines, about the institution, about other institutions or about the higher education system as a whole. Whatever they are, these histories and stories about the past will impact on enhancement initiatives in the present.

6 A corollary of all of the above is that social context, and its particularities, is a very significant factor in enhancement. There are special features in every university, and every university department, every discipline, that mean that initiatives will be received, understood and implemented in ways which are, partly at least, unique. So, any attempt to generalize across social contexts is fraught with danger. Social research into phenomena related to social interaction must take contextual contingency into account.

Social practice

Perhaps the key aspect of sociocultural theory is that it takes as its unit of analysis *social practice*, instead of (for example) individual agency, individual cognition, or social structures. By social practice we mean the recurrent, usually unconsidered, sets of practices or 'constellations' that together constitute daily life (Huberman (1993) talks about 'engrooved' practices). Individuals participate in practices, as 'carriers' of 'routinized ways of understanding, knowing how and desiring' (Reckwitz 2002: 249–50). So, a social

I think it is both social and individual
– interaction between individual + environment

practice perspective leads us to direct our interest towards how a nexus of practices affects, for example, the way that learning and teaching is produced in a particular locale (Reckwitz 2002: 258). Moreover, a social practice viewpoint alerts us to the danger of a rational–purposive understanding of change, one which assumes that people on the ground will act in 'logical' ways to achieve well understood goals, or that managers and policymakers will have clear and stable goals in mind and be able to identify steps towards achieving them. This 'hyperrationalised and intellectualised' (Reckwitz 2002: 259) view of behaviour just does not stand up to scrutiny in university contexts.

Enhancement entails purposeful attempts to change constellations of practices for the better. This is not always easy because practices often become reified into systems, ossified. Examples are easily seen in individual organizations, in national systems and even internationally. They become set in stone in organizational architectures – documentation, pro forma, committee structures. More importantly however, the attribution of meaning, the knowledge resources they depend upon and the sense we make of practices are part of a cultural field that can likewise become ossified. While it is obvious that enhancement embodies the idea of learning, it also – and this is often forgotten – involves 'unlearning', by which we mean laying aside engrooved, established and familiar ways of understanding and doing. It is debatable which is the harder.

So, the social practice perspective of sociocultural theory sets into the foreground social practices and focuses on the way 'practice' itself yields knowledge and learning. Influenced by this stance, we see professional and organizational enhancement as the production and maintenance of knowledge through situated work practice. This perspective integrates a number of theories: those that explore professional learning processes (see Schön 1991; Eraut 2000), those that develop the idea of 'practice' itself (Giddens 1976; Lave and Wenger 1991; Wenger 1998 and 2000), along with the concept of the knowledge resources (formal, explicit and technical, on the one hand, informal, tacit, social, cultural and discursive on the other) that are produced and accessed, metaphorically as 'rules' (Blackler 1995; Bereiter and Scardemalia 1993) that frame our work behaviour.

What does a social practice perspective mean for thinking about the enhancement of teaching and learning in HE?

- That change, and specifically enhancement, involves changing social practices, in the sense set out above.
- That symbolic structures, particular orders of meaning in particular places, are very significant in conditioning practices, and in changing them.
- This involves implicit, tacit or unconscious layers of knowledge as well as explicit knowledge.
- Routinized ways of using the body are also involved – embodied knowledge, as Blackler (1995) calls it – and changes in these too are involved in enhancement processes. This includes ways of using and interacting with

'things' in general and 'tools' in particular; the challenge to 'traditional' learning and teaching approaches presented by the growth of e-learning tools such as virtual learning environments is a case in point.

• Emotions, feelings and desires are implicated in this. They will be affected by enhancement initiatives, implicated in them and perhaps changed by them.

Practices are inherently social and evolving. They are nested in cultures that form a major part of the intellectual, moral and material resources on which the practices themselves depend: cultures and practices constitute one another – they are not separable. Constellations and clusters of practices are bound together by social groupings, which are sometimes called communities of practice, sometimes called activity systems. We deal with these next.

Activity systems theory

Consider all the elements that are involved in an activity such as running an undergraduate degree programme. Taken together they could be called an 'activity system' (Engeström 1987) and include the elements enlisted in Table 2.1.

In fact a system for running an undergraduate programme has many levels, each of which has these elements. These levels might include the national level, the institutional level, the department, school or faculty level, and the individual level. While finer grained analysis is possible, it is not necessary in order to make two claims: first, that the system is more predictable when the

Table 2.1 Activity system elements

Elements	Illustrations
The subject	Depending on the point of view, this might be the teachers, the students, a university, i.e. the doer.
The objects	Depending on point of view, this might be student learning, getting a good degree, retaining almost all the students who enrolled . . .
Tools	Material and human resources; knowledge, processes, and practices that are to hand.
Rules	Formal rules, conventions, beliefs and taken-for-granteds.
The division of labour	Who does what.
The community of practice, or workgroup	The set of people involved in the activity. (They may not be much of a community in the usual sense of the word.)

different levels are aligned; second, that the levels are rarely well aligned and *Alignment* so the 'gears do not mesh'. Unsurprisingly, activity systems have a variety of outcomes, some intentional and many not, and attempts to enhance these outcomes can have unplanned consequences.

We can conceptualize practices and constellations of practices as parts of social systems. The value of using this soft systems thinking (Checkland 1981) is that it reminds us to look for connections, both horizontally and vertically. Soft systems thinking also recognizes that social systems are fluid and that their boundaries look different to different observers – in other words, they may have provisional stability in the eyes of one observer but have a different shape and stability to another.

Communities of practice theory

As noted above, social systems of practice are often described as communities of practice (Lave and Wenger 1991). Formal and non-formal learning within a community of practice (CoP) conventionally involves a cyclical process as a novice moves from the periphery to the centre in terms of experience and expertise (the phrase used to describe this in communities of practice theory is 'legitimate peripheral participation' (Lave and Wenger 1991)). The important dimension of this position is the way it involves a complex dynamic. This dynamic is constantly evolving as new and established members of a community of practice use the knowledge resources that are in place by following tacit and explicit rules but at the same time have the potential to create and add to the knowledge base at others' disposal. This is not to suggest that practice is the only source of knowledge resources, but that it has moved to centre stage in our understanding. It is an evocative frame of reference providing the theoretical base for many studies globally in which shared or collaborative learning is the central preoccupation, in professional groups (see for example Hilsdon 2004), in disciplines (for example Graven 2004), in online environments (for example Dewhurst et al. 2004).

While we draw on the idea of communities of practice to evoke how work groups learn, and how that might affect enhancement efforts, there are limits *Problems* to its descriptive and theoretical adequacy. Fuller and colleagues (Fuller *with* et al. 2005: 65) identify some problems. First, it cannot encompass all types *CoP* of workplace learning because 'experienced' staff clearly continue to learn despite leaving 'peripheral participation' (Lave and Wenger 1991) many years previously. In these cases, other types of continual non-formal learning are taking place. Second, the undervaluing of more conventional 'training' and out-of-work learning is not helpful. Third, the idea of 'peripheral' or 'novice' status, and the way in which an enculturation process takes place in the community of practice schema, makes invisible the way home and community identities combine to make a positive contribution to a new work–learning dynamic. Such identities are situated outside the community of practice yet are very significant to it.

A further issue arises when communities of practice are seen within activity system theory. In those terms, the idea of a community of practice privileges one of six elements – the community of practice or workgroup. If we use the communities of practice perspective as an enhancement lens, we also need to acknowledge the role of tools, rules, subject, object and division of labour. Furthermore, it is risky to assume that 'communities' are harmonious groups of like minded folk: CoP thinking lacks a theory of power and its operation – important components of the loose–tight, negotiated university workplace, as described in the preceding section. The sociology of knowledge, in other words its social location in differential power relations within the workplace, is crucial in understanding the way in which certain types of knowledge and understanding might be encouraged or inhibited, not on the basis of work practice knowledge but on the basis of status and power. While a critique of Wenger's notion of community might be that it fails to acknowledge this two-way process of knowledge creation at work, we are also interested in the extent to which the distribution of power in an organization or a community of practice precludes or enables the novice or expert in the production and legitimation of new knowledge. Knowledge (or a particular enhancement) is not legitimated (accepted) simply because it creates a useful new rule or way of doing something; it might depend on *who* created the rule rather than *what* the rule was.

Finally, some observe that there is a tendency for community of practice thinking to become a theory of everything. So, while we draw on the communities of practice strand of sociocultural theory, we do so cautiously.

The implementation staircase

The notion of the *implementation staircase* (Reynolds and Saunders 1987) is also helpful here. It highlights the significance of different levels of policy making and policy implementation by portraying the role played by those who are standing on the staircase: they implement enhancement strategies not as passive receivers, but as active agents who affect the process according to the agendas, meanings and values which they bring from their local circumstances and particular location on the staircase (there is a depiction of an implementation staircase in Chapter 10 by Davidson et al.). If social reality is partly socially constructed, as sociocultural theory says, then it will look different at different levels of the higher education system: so an enhancement will be seen differently by a government department, by the university top team, by heads of department and, at the ground level, in classrooms. Moreover, each level of the staircase will have multiple, but different, issues, changes and agendas, not just one initiative aimed at enhancement. So the enhancement 'ball' bounces up and down the staircase in sometimes unpredicted ways as it meets and is reshaped by these different realities. Any idea that the enhancement policy will look the same at the bottom of the staircase as it looked at the top would be naïve. Instead we find implementation gaps between the changes that are planned in policy, the changes that are enacted in practice, and the changes as they get constructed in the understandings of the students whose learning they were intended to affect. There are differences, invariably, between planned, enacted and constructed changes. Any change will be received, understood and consequently implemented differently in different contexts, so departments in the same subject area look quite different in different institutions. In a real sense, enhancements get localized, 'domesticated'.

Non-formal learning and tacit knowledge

Our theoretical understandings of learning and teaching enhancement must include some appreciation of learning theory. We noted above that enhancement involves learning and unlearning; that (un)learning is dependent on the staff and students who are the protagonists of enhancement. As sociocultural theory has developed so, in parallel, have ideas about learning. Formal learning, which is intentional and usually associated with some form of curriculum, is important, without question. Recent thinking about learning puts fresh emphasis on non-formal learning, which comes from the daily experience of practice, and may be more important at many points in a professional life. Eraut and colleagues (2004) say that professional learning is shaped by learning factors – confidence and commitment, the challenge and value of work, feedback and support – and by context factors – allocation and structuring of work, encounters and relationships with people at work, individual participation and progress, and performance expectations. Their research concentrated on professionals beginning their careers in the workplace, so the role of formal learning in a career lifetime has been undervalued. However, their findings are consistent with others (for example, Becher 1999) who point to the significance in teachers' professional formation of teaching environments or ecologies; in these ecologies they learn as they interact with colleagues and aspects of their physical environment, as they seek to sustain and improve what they understand and do.

A strong implication for those committed to enhancement, therefore, is that ways need to be found to evoke innovation through non-formal means. Rather than thinking solely of curricula for enhancement, innovators need to think about environments for enhancement. In the process, they accept that while outcomes of curricula may be uncertain, outcomes of environments are even less predictable.

A more subtle implication challenges a modernist view of enhancement. That view says that practices are changed by changing conceptions. Social practice theory, combined with evidence about the prevalence of non-formal learning, raises the interesting idea that to change practice we should change practices; thinking will follow behind. This challenges much HE educational development provision that is intended to enhance teachers' learning, teaching, assessment and curriculum practices. Our contention is that social and cultural factors are as powerful in encouraging enhancement in these areas as personal, cognitive factors.

For the sake of completeness at this stage, we observe that much professional knowledge is tacit, which means that it is not articulated or codified and then shared. Essential though it is (Sternberg and Grigorenko 2000), it is locked up in practices and being: in Blackler's terms (1995) it is embodied, embedded and encultured. Innovators face the challenge of fostering the unpredictable emergence of tacit knowledge – the catch being that, unlike explicit knowledge, tacit knowledge cannot be directly observed or measured, although its presence may be pragmatically inferred from its inferred effects. This is a real challenge to modernist measure-and-mend approaches to social improvement.

Translation and reconstruction *and boundary crossing*

We touched briefly in the previous chapter on the difficulty of 'transferring' learning from one site to another, or from one case to another. If this book seeks to improve our enhancement efforts, then we must address the question of how to tap our non-formal and tacit learning in one setting, and make it available in other settings. One thing is clear: that the metaphor of transfer, which is the default way of expressing the way learning is applied in other contexts, is misleading (see Beach 2003: 39). Instead we need concepts that stress the work involved in bringing knowledge to bear in novel settings; the metaphors of translation, reconstruction, boundary crossing and bridging are helpful here, since they recognize that work has to be done. They also imply that the original enhancement is liable to change as it crosses the 'boundary' between one setting and another, with its own cultural nuances.

This powerful metaphor of 'boundary' (Tuomi-Gröhn and Engeström 2003) acknowledges that when people in one social environment, such as a university or department, move ideas across a boundary to another institution or department, this entails a boundary crossing process. These concepts – translation, reconstruction and boundary crossing – have interesting implications for enhancement. If we depict educational organizations and the workplace as different activity systems, characterized by different communities of practice, then moving from one to another involves a form of brokerage in which a variety of tools might aid and develop learning – what we might call 'bridging' tools. When groups of teachers are asked to adopt one set of practices rather than another, brokerage and bridging tools are called for.

The term 'bridging' connotes the concept of a journey and a metaphorical connection between places in two senses: just as a bridge takes an individual or group from one point to another, it also joins one place to another. In the new location, the enhancement is *reconstructed*, so that practices emerge which are different from those envisaged during the planning process. Clearly, sometimes such reconstruction does not take place: intended practices are simply adopted. But this can never be assumed. There will be a need for a range of bridging tools to help teachers and those supporting them to navigate these transitions. Our approach seeks to provide precisely such 'bridging resources' (e.g. case studies) and in the last chapter of this book we return to how these resources can be used.

Empowering enhancement

In the preceding pages, we have presented a view of change and an accompanying set of theories that lead us to think afresh about the means by which learning, teaching, assessment and curriculum may be enhanced. Although cautious, our approach is not sceptical about the prospects for change. Rather, it argues that we have to accept uncertainty about what will emerge from enhancement efforts, and we need to base innovations on a new approach informed by the theories we have laid out.

What you, the reader, will take from this discussion will, of course, vary, according to your own context: we recognize that enhancement involves real people working on sets of practices that occur in real time and real places. At the end of the book, we extract from our cases ideas about how people engage in change processes, including what might be termed the 'enhancement identities' of key actors. What this refers to is the way colleagues involved in enhancement practice have predilections concerning change. We each have a history or biography of past experience of changes, a vision of how change should be brought about or, through our actions and discourse, an implicit assumption or orientation toward the change process. Enhancement identities refer to the mindsets, visions of the world and the sense of self in relation to bringing about change held by those engaged in change. It differs from implicit change theories which are to do with the connection between means and ends. Enhancement identities are more to do with underlying beliefs about how to behave, where to put energy, what is proper, and connects to what kind of person an individual might think they are. What we ask of the reader is that you reflect, while reading, on your own enhancement identity, and what this identity might mean for how you will tackle future enhancement initiatives. To help you along the way, you will find that each Theme has a Theme introduction and Theme commentary; the Theme introduction reminds you of some of the pertinent theoretical constructs related to the Theme, and the Theme commentary draws together key points from the four case studies within the Theme.

Theme 1

Influencing the disciplines

3

Theme 1 introduction

Paul Trowler

Influencing the disciplines

The first theme that our case studies address is _influencing the disciplines._ The case studies here all relate to the subject discipline based approach to enhancing teaching and learning which began in the UK in 2000 in the form of the Learning and Teaching Support Network (LTSN) and continues to the time of writing (2008) as the 24 subject centres of the Higher Education Academy.

The LTSN initiative marked a change in government resource allocation for higher education enhancement initiatives. It aimed to enhance teaching and learning through setting up subject centres responsible for particular groups of disciplines and able to speak to specialists in their own language and about their specific issues. Until that time resources tended to be allocated to institutions or to specific projects. But project based funding typically suffered from the effect of initiatives dying once the funds ran out (Elton 2002). The projects lacked sustainability.

The new approach was controversial. The Institute for Learning and Teaching in Higher Education (ILTHE), established in 1999, tended to take a generic approach to enhancement. Its advocates argued that there was very little that was specific about practices in or approaches to teaching, learning and assessment across the disciplines. Of course, there were some unique practices: object based teaching in archaeology; the 'public crit' assessment method and Atelier teaching method in art and design subjects; the consultant's ward rounds in medical training (_signature pedagogies_, as Shulman (2005a) calls them). But in the main there was a set of common skills and understandings required by a good teacher in any discipline. Partly as a result of this controversy, when the LTSN and the ILTHE merged into the new Higher Education Academy it was far from an easy process. Overlaying that debate were worries about personal careers and public identities too, as much had been invested in the LTSN and ILTHE by individuals and groups.

Meanwhile, inside universities, educational development courses aimed at training new staff for teaching in HE have tended to take a generic approach rather than being tailored for staff from different disciplines and the teaching and learning textbooks they rely on do likewise. This genericism has been criticized by some: '[Textbooks] examine only the generic processes of teaching and learning across disciplines. Indeed this is a deliberate attempt to shift attention away from a discipline-dominated curriculum towards learning and pedagogical questions' (McGuinness 1997: 19). However, advocates of the generic approach (including many educational developers) have argued that mixing different disciplinary specialists in these courses leads to fruitful learning across the disciplines. Comparing and sharing approaches was far more beneficial than destructively splitting the disciplines and building artificial walls between them.

So, the generic versus disciplinary debate has pervaded different areas of practice. Having conducted a three-year evaluation of the LTSN across the UK university sector, the Lancaster evaluation team asked and answered the fundamental question underpinning this debate: 'is this disciplinary-based approach a good one for enhancing teaching and learning in universities?' Their answer was:

> The policy of trying to enhance quality through using subject networks, which was tried in various ways before the inception of the LTSN, seems to us to be working. Importantly, it has 'buy-in' from teachers who are sceptical of other approaches to quality enhancement . . . Our first annual report . . . identified the most commonly deployed argument in favour of a subject-based approach as essentially a social or cultural one, emphasising the importance of disciplinary networks and peer groups
> (Saunders et al. 2002: 22)

These arguments suggested that academics seeking guidance about teaching will tend to give most credibility to peers from their discipline and are sceptical of what they may see as platitudinous generic educational advice. This view, held widely by subject centre staff, does not appear to rest on a belief that teaching and learning issues are fundamentally different in each subject area. We suggested that the arguments we heard for a subject centred approach were fundamentally about *method* (specifically, the desirability of naturalistic interactions with teaching colleagues) and not about *content* (what one might talk about in these interactions) (LTSN 2002).

So, the significant attraction of taking a disciplinary approach, at least at the national level if not at the institutional one, was not so much that there were objective differences in teaching, learning and assessment across the disciplines, but that subjectively, emotionally and discursively, subject specialists prefer to talk to other subject specialists about their practices in these areas.

However, UK government funding policy is probably correct not to put *all* its eggs in this one basket, the disciplinary (Trowler et al. 2005). The 1998 Department for Education and Science (DfES) consultation document had in fact proposed a new integrated approach to the funding of improvements in teaching quality: the Teaching Quality Enhancement Fund (TQEF). The TQEF would provide funding at three levels: the institution (through grants for achieving explicit enhancement strategies), the academic subject (through the LTSN) and the individual (through the National Teaching Fellowship Scheme, which rewarded excellence in teaching). It was recognized that together, in an integrated strategy, a combined approach like this would have the greatest chance of success in enhancing teaching and learning. As we shall see from the case studies within this Theme, this was a fruitful way to go.

The four authors in this Theme approach the topic of influencing teaching and learning through the disciplines from the four levels analysis which is the organizing structure of our case studies. Cliff Allan, who was Director of the LTSN organization, provides a brief overview of that scheme and offers an insightful analysis of both the policy principles involved and the impact of the scheme on the sector as it was actually implemented.

Anthony Rosie's case describes the operation of a subject centre within the institutional environment of its host university. The subject centre in question, like a number of other subject centres, is the hub for a range of subjects with different norms and expectations. The arrival of a new centre director and the decision to change centre strategy highlight the complex environment within which the subject centres work. The new strategy attempted to change an atomized, possibly unsustainable, approach to an approach based on strategic policy drivers. It also aimed to align the centre's strategy with that of the host institution. This brought success on one side, but dissatisfaction from those departments which felt that their individual agendas were not being met.

Paul Kleiman writes from inside one of the LTSN subject centres, a different perspective on the same scheme. He explores the different discourses which his own subject centre had to use in order to be successful in the different arenas in which it operated. Kleiman's piece illustrates the point made above, quoting the LTSN evaluation report, that in order to be successful it is necessary to speak the language of those whose practices are being addressed. The accommodation of sometimes contradictory agendas and discourses is a clever trick to pull off, but a necessary one, Kleiman argues. In the language of activity theory and communities of practice theory, each subject centre was acting as a boundary object, mediating different discourses and activity systems to find a way forward.

Scott Court's piece looks at an attempt at enhancement at the ground level supported by another of the 24 subject centres. He shows that no matter how supportive and effective the subject centre was, and the disciplinary approach in general might be, other factors are also involved. In this case institutional policy and departmental priorities operated to obstruct an innovation which might have been successful in enhancing teaching and learning within the institution. This illustrates the wisdom of the multifaceted approach to enhancement policy initiated in the TQEF discussion document in 1998, described above.

4

Changing the rules of engagement: down the disciplinary road

Cliff Allan
Deputy Vice-Chancellor, University of Teesside
(former Programme Director, The Learning
and Teaching Support Network)

Context

The Learning and Teaching Support Network (LTSN) was conceived in 1999 and launched in January 2000 by the UK higher education funding bodies to promote high quality learning and teaching in all subject disciplines and support the sharing of innovation and good practices in learning and teaching (L&T). It was a cornerstone of the funding bodies' response to the 1997 Dearing Committee of Enquiry's report (NCIHE 1997) into the future of higher education (HE), which recommended a new focus on the enhancement of L&T, and raising the profile and importance of teaching and learning in HE.

The LTSN was predated by a series of relatively short term and often loosely connected national funding initiatives which focused on developmental activity, primarily institution or discipline specific (including the Teaching and Learning Technology Programme, the Computers in Teaching Initiative, Enterprise in HE and the Fund for the Development of Teaching and Learning Programme). Throughout the 1990s a great deal had been invested by government through its funding bodies in educational development activity, but successive evaluations of these initiatives questioned how far the developments had been disseminated, translated, adopted and adapted beyond the limits of the departments and institutions involved in the actual development.

Policymakers began to realize that more effort was required in supporting effective forms of dissemination and embedding practice if the previous and ongoing investment in educational development was to be maximized. Moreover, the evaluations of previous initiatives presented clear evidence that within HE, strategies designed to support change in professional practice and professional development needed to align to the conventional cultures and structures of the sector. Therefore, a focus on dissemination, professional support and professional networking around academic subjects and disciplines was developed.

Following extensive consultation across the HE sector throughout early 1999, the UK funding bodies jointly launched the LTSN as a network of 24 subject centres and a single generic centre, both managed and coordinated by a central directorate. Universities were invited to tender to host one or more of the subject centres and develop a broad support strategy across the UK for the subject(s) covered by the centre. Tenders were expected to locate the subject centres within the context of a relevant subject community within the university and be led by respected and senior academics from the subject.

The identification of 24 subject centres was not without controversy. Part of the consultation exercise had been to tease out an effective mapping of disciplines into cognate subject centres. At the time a larger number of subject categories (42) was in use by the Quality Assurance Agency, and some felt that 24 meant that there were to be some rather strange disciplinary bedfellows within one centre. The constraint on the number of centres was the funding available and the desire of policymakers to ensure that each subject centre had sufficient critical mass and resource to deliver an effective range of services to its subject community. There was a reluctance to dilute the constrained resources across too many small and narrowly defined disciplines. A number of distinct, but relatively small disciplines argued for their separate subject centres with limited success. Indeed there was a tension, which in some cases continues today, between on the one hand a focus on discipline identity and on the other hand critical mass and operational efficiency. The result of the sector consultation was a mapping of the QAA's 42 standard subject units (and the 69 units of the then Research Assessment Exercise) into more broad cognate and manageable subject areas. This created a combination of single discipline subject centres, which covered sizeable communities (for example English, psychology, economics) and multidisciplinary subject centres (for example health science and practice; engineering; history, classics and archaeology). Some flexibility in the location of specific disciplines was allowed, but within a total number of 24 centres.

The concept of a subject focused initiative was challenged by some in educational development who claimed that most learning, teaching and assessment practice in HE was generic in nature, and they saw little to limited value in establishing a subject focus. Furthermore, it was argued that a strong subject focus would reinforce the inflexibility and relative conservatism of academic disciplines at a time when inter- and multidisciplinary innovations were necessary in a changing HE sector. The architecture of the LTSN provided a response to these perspectives. First, the subject focus of the network was complemented by a generic centre which was to work across and between the subject centres to promote the transfer of ideas, practice and innovations from the subject to the generic and from the generic to the subject specific. Second, the central management and coordination of the network facilitated active networking between subject centres to ensure inter- and multidisciplinary activity, thus reducing any danger of 'fixed territories' and solid subject boundaries.

The LTSN was funded initially for three years, with an expectation for a further two years subject to an evaluation of the network's effectiveness. It was the intention of policymakers to develop the network as a longstanding feature of the HE system if it proved to be successful, although the funding bodies' own funding regimes prevented any guarantee of long term funding. However, an outlook of a five-year funding horizon at this time was unusual, and helped generate a number of high quality proposals for subject centres. The initial budget of £6.2 million (£5.2 million of which was allocated across the subject centres) was soon complemented with an additional £2 million to support particular developments. Then, later in 2002–03, a 25 percent increase in subject centre funding was approved in recognition of the scale of work being undertaken by the centres. Two major evaluations of the network demonstrated that the concept of a subject based network to support L&T enhancement was highly valued and well used across the sector. The 2004 government white paper on HE brought wider policy changes, in response to a greater emphasis on quality enhancement (QE) in HE and the need to rationalize a number of various national initiatives and bodies concerned with aspects of QE. However, the subject centre network was relatively unfettered by this, as its concept and relative success were recognized by university leaders, subject communities and policymakers. While the LTSN came to an end at this time, its subject centres became the core and largest part of the newly formed Higher Education Academy in 2005. This ensured a further five-year period of funding, and thus embedded the subject centres as a key feature in the support infrastructure for the enhancement of L&T across the UK.

Analysis

While the subject nature of the network was widely welcomed, the subject centres had to develop a range of services and activities which would have some resonance and utility within their constituencies. Moreover, while being a centrally managed network, it was important that each subject centre retained its subject context and specificity and was sufficiently responsive to its disciplines' needs. This resulted in a range of common activities and services across subject centres – for example, websites/portals, information and resource databases and repositories, research and development project grants, publications and good practice guides – and some variation in other services depending on discipline needs and interests – for example, departmental visits and seminar programmes, conferences and joint developments with other discipline bodies. Moreover, the subject centres chose to focus on slightly different issues at different times over the years – for example employability, widening participation and student retention, pedagogic research, teaching and research relationships and e-learning – depending on the needs of and demands from their constituencies.

The need to be responsive and act responsively to their discipline became engrained in the subject centres, to the extent that many felt that they were owned primarily by their discipline, not by their host institution, the funders or latterly the HE Academy.

It is clear that as the subject centres built up greater awareness of their role and services within their subjects they were put to greater use and, increasingly, expectations were raised about what they should and could deliver. Policymakers and subject related bodies began to see the subject centres as the main vehicle to reach academic staff and disciplines. This put the centres under increasing pressure to moderate how they might be used, who they were for and whose priorities prevailed, given the continuing constrained resource available to them. All subject centres continued to retain support for L&T as their primary focus, but many branched into other areas as led by the interests of their discipline. For example, some began to support the promotion of the subject to schools and colleges to improve wider understanding of the subject. Several took on brokerage functions, managing large scale projects and initiatives for their subject community, often outside the L&T remit.

As universities began to realize the utility of the subject centres and their focused interaction with academics within their institution, a number began to harness the subject centres' work and departmental contacts within their institution to complement their own L&T strategies. This has worked well where the institution/subject centre links are loose and flexible, as any tighter coupling could erode the 'independence' and relative autonomy of the discipline focus of individual academics and subject centre.

Over the years, many of the subject centres have grown in stature as they have penetrated deep into their communities. In some cases they are now seen as an essential part of the subject landscape. In other cases their role has been more at a surface level, but nevertheless valued. At one stage there was a danger that they would be seen as 'agents of government' dictating or proselytizing on government priorities and change policies to their subject communities. The reality has been quite different; instead they have given a 'voice' to practitioners in the engagement with policymakers, sometimes shaping and influencing HE policy initiatives. Where they have acted on advancing policy issues they have often done so as 'active translators' where they put the policy change in the context of the discipline, facilitating the interpretation and adaptation of policy relevant to their discipline context.

Conclusions

The concept of a major sector-wide initiative based on the subject focus of higher education seems to have proven to be relatively successful. In conceiving the LTSN, policymakers looked at what type of intervention would achieve maximum 'buy-in' from the target audience and what would prove most sustainable in the long term. The subject focus of the LTSN was about 'going with the grain', as most academics communicated, shared practice, developed ideas, networked and responded to discipline and subject interests at this level, more so than at university level. The network was established to be responsive to professional development needs as articulated and located within the core academic structures, culture and communities of department, subject and discipline. There is a strong but implicit assumption here that change is incremental and can be best supported through a responsive, collaborative and contextual agency or method.

The evaluation report of the LTSN (2002: 21) summarized the outcomes after four years:

> The degree to which the LTSN has become embedded in the professional concerns of academics is clear from our data. The survey of Heads of Department and other staff showed very high levels of basic awareness, with 86% of those responding having heard of the LTSN, and 80% of the Subject Centre for their discipline. In addition to awareness, there was evidence of considerable impact, with 49% of respondents reporting that the Subject Centre had already made a contribution to the work of their department. More impact was expected over time, with 51% of respondents saying that it was still too early for full impact to have been achieved and 67% stating their belief that the LTSN has the potential to affect teaching and learning. There is therefore, a high level of awareness of the LTSN, there is a growing participation in activities sponsored or co-ordinated by the LTSN and there is now a small, but growing, evidential base that suggests that teaching and learning is being influenced by LTSN activity. This is a remarkable achievement in a sector so jealous of its autonomy, so strident in its desire to direct itself and so confident in its own capacity to produce solutions. It is also indicative of a sea change in the culture of HE, with the emergence of teaching and learning as a legitimate core professional concern for the academic community amid a series of systemic pressures on the quality of teaching and learning that should be taken seriously.

5

Layers of the onion: a subject centre in its institutional context

Anthony Rosie
Sheffield Hallam University, England

Introduction

In 2000, the Learning and Teaching Support Network (LTSN) introduced 24 subject centres, located in UK universities. Universities were awarded individual centres through a competitive bidding process. Most participating universities were able to appoint a senior member of academic staff to centre directorship at the outset. The host universities also recruited centre managers, either from within their own staff or through external recruitment. Centre managers might be members of academic staff or, sometimes, members of administrative staff. The centre directors reported directly to LTSN and were also required to report to appropriate levels within their institutions. This included direct reporting to the relevant pro-vice chancellor (P-VC), as might be expected with a sector-wide initiative, but such reporting could also include the relevant dean or equivalent. For some centres, the local subject department in the host university was also included in the reporting scheme. Each centre was required to appoint a steering committee, which had an independent chair, institutional representation and external membership. The steering committees did not report to LTSN, but they took an active role in the life of each subject centre, including receiving its financial, strategic and operational plans and accounts. It is perhaps a slight oversimplification to say that centre directors were responsible for strategic leadership and managers were responsible for operational leadership, but this division has come to characterize the life of the different centres.

Inevitably there was staff turnover at all levels in the subject centres. In 2003 the host university for the Centre for Sociology, Anthropology and Politics (CSAP) appointed a new Subject Centre Director. This was an external appointment and led to a refocus of work, led jointly by the newly appointed Director and the Centre Manager. This strategic refocus highlighted the substantial financial surplus which, by summer 2003, this particular Centre held a as a result of underspend over the previous three years. Its budget was committed to almost 100 mini projects (£300–£3,000 per project) in social science departments, with over 50 percent of the subject centre budget committed in this way, due to be paid out by 2005.

Key people and groups from in and around the subject centre were involved in working out a new overall strategy which would reduce the significance of mini project funding and introduce new priority areas. These were: the incoming Director, the Manager, the ongoing team of academics and administrators at the Centre, the representatives from different subject departments across the UK who formed reference groups, as well as the subject centre's Steering Group. These people and groups had different priorities and tasks.

For the Subject Centre Director and the Manager, who reviewed all the documentation surrounding the first three years of Centre activity, their concerns were:

1   Heavy mini project expenditure was restricting the overall output of the Centre.
2   The costs in terms of project oversight were high.
3   It was difficult to see how far such projects had achieved impact beyond the immediate beneficiaries and their students.

Their overall analysis showed that the Centre had relatively weak connections with social science departments across the UK. The emerging strategy and operational plan also sought to recognize the complex interlinkages between the three subject centre disciplines and relevant departmental activity in the institution in which they were hosted. This was a complex task. The host university had reorganized its social science provision. In brief, the subject centre had no direct link with anthropology in the institution, but there were some instances of development studies work spread across a number of departments. The sociology and politics subject areas were based in separate departments. This required coordination and the departments were not necessarily receptive to approaches by the subject centre.

The host university expected the Director to be a member of the institution's learning and teaching committee. This provided one forum for developing such linkages, through presentations to departmental representatives in the university. The Manager had worked for the Centre in different capacities since 2000 and was an employee of the host university. This meant she was able both to draw upon the university's staff development unit for a new programme of training for Centre staff and to contribute to the university's own staff development activity. For the Director and the Manager of the subject centre it seemed best to position the Centre as a broker in this staff development activity. On the one hand the university's staff development and information management service units contributed to training for administrative and academic staff in the Centre, thereby contributing to the requirements of an ambitious new Centre plan. On the other hand, both the Director and the Manager supported the host university's institution-wide learning and teaching programme through inputs to the institution's annual learning and teaching conference, lunchtime sessions for departmental staff, contribution to activities led by individual faculties, and invitations for staff undertaking the university's 'new staff course' to spend time in the Centre.

The Director and the Manager felt that the new strategy and operational plan should involve a move towards funding a much smaller number of projects each year (8–10 instead of 30+). Instead, particular individuals and groups funded as special initiatives would be required to take a lead on making an impact both within their own institutions and more widely through new networks. Some of the projects were also to be ringfenced for students to work on teaching and learning initiatives. Some of the resource saved from the mini project activity was shifted to working directly with the host university. This included specialist contributions to the university's planning for the Centres for Excellence in Teaching and Learning (CETL) initiative. The reduction on funding for project work was to be accompanied by an expansion of funding held and used by academic coordinators, funding for all day events, and increased funding for Centre staff development.

This change was proposed to the host university, to the subject centre's Steering Group, as well as to LTSN as part of a wider set of changes. Other changes proposed included:

1 Reforming the Steering Group into an Advisory Group with an expanded membership but with the host university moving from full membership to representation in an ex officio capacity.
2 Appointing new academic coordinators with secondments to the Centre of one or two days per week, to involve departments with little previous experience of working with the subject centre.
3 Developing support for subject departments which were planning to bid for external teaching and learning funds. The latter included departmental and institutional bids for funding under the CETL initiative, and 'Aim Higher'[1] funds for widening participation.

The proposal to move away from a steering group to an advisory group was recommended by the Head of LTSN. It was warmly supported by the Centre's external evaluator. Over time all subject centres took this step. CSAP used the opportunity afforded by a major strategic plan to rethink relations with all the groups it worked with. The overall Centre strategy was to establish the Centre as a source of support for teaching and learning with all social science departments, and to encourage the direct participation of students in teaching and learning activity.

The Steering Group had raised concerns over the ongoing underspend. The committee also felt the Centre needed to increase its work with departments across the sector. However, members of the Steering Group felt strongly that mini project funding provided opportunities and benefits to

---

[1] 'Aim Higher' was an HEFCE funded initiative to encourage closer collaboration between universities and schools and colleges.

departments with relatively little institutional support for their teaching and learning work. A move towards 'advisory' rather than 'steering' group status might compromise the independent scrutiny the group could make. In fact, the chair of the group not only accepted and supported the change to advisory status, but continued to provide robust support, ensuring that all members of the committee understood everything the Centre proposed and that the Director and Manager reported fully and transparently on the work of the Centre. This was an extremely valuable and welcome support.

The changes were made 'from above' by the two leaders of the Centre, but in making these proposals they addressed concerns expressed by members of the Centre's Advisory Group and by relevant subject departments in a number of different universities. Some departments had not found a satisfactory way of working with the Centre and wanted to explore new avenues. The Centre proposed (successfully) a joint cross-institution project to provide placements for undergraduate students in social science. Meanwhile the Centre's Advisory Group recognized that there were both discipline and LTSN agendas that the Centre had given less attention to hitherto, but, as indicated above, there was a strong case for mini projects too.

The changes were designed, in summary, to align the Centre's strategy more strongly with national LTSN strategy and also to meet the learning and teaching strategy of the host university.

Implementation: some problems

The new subject centre strategy was first proposed to the Centre's Advisory Group and the subject reference groups as well as the P-VC in the host university. All initiatives were discussed with the P-VC who also had oversight of the Centre's budget and staffing plans. The initiative was then disseminated through the subject centre's newsletter, in its mail-out, through contact with departmental representatives and through the efforts of a new team of academic coordinators. The latter were colleagues representing the Centre disciplines who were seconded by their institutions to the Centre for one or two days each week. Two new coordinators were appointed to join the existing academic coordinators and to strengthen work in politics and sociology. This was not unproblematic. Relations between one of the professional associations and the host university were poor. Nevertheless, several applicants from the affected discipline came forward whenever secondment (e.g. as an academic coordinator) was advertised. It was usually the case that the applicant either had little interest in the professional association, or that they were already a substantial contributor to the work of their institution on teaching and learning. As institutions sought available funding opportunities, so the work of the subject centre was seen to be a worthwhile addition to departmental and institutional portfolios. The academic coordinators who were appointed developed the special initiatives, including work on critical pedagogy, e-learning, undergraduate dissertation support, employability and work based placements, and race. They also oversaw the mini projects and organized departmental visits. A further important link was the administrative team at the Centre who were the first port of call for inquiries from academics in departments seeking to work with the Centre.

In one sense all social science departments formed the target group. The operationalization and implementation of the revised strategic plan included increased activity under the selected headings of e-learning, employability, race and critical pedagogy. This was a broad and ambitious plan. However, while members of the Advisory Group had a full picture of relations between elements, this did not necessarily translate outwards for all. At the level of individual departments with interests in one theme or area, only the wider work of the Centre was of little interest. This was particularly true for subject departments who had received mini project funding in the early years of the Centre and who had no interest in the broader strategic plan. They were interested in ongoing support for work which the subject centre had funded. This might include work on developing students' ethnographic skills, seminars on teaching social theory or supporting new doctoral students. These were quite specific initiatives and did not fit easily within the headings and themes now put forward by the subject centre.

The overall strategy was implemented from September 2003, then reviewed and adapted as necessary in 2004 and 2005. For the first time all funded projects reported at Centre conferences or similar events, which was a significant and welcome change from previous project practice. This proposed strategic change generated some areas of controversy and some problems. For subject centre administrative staff with special responsibility for the mini projects the change was potentially threatening. There was no suggestion that jobs were at risk, but a change away from a previously familiar way of doing things was perceived as a threat by some. As mentioned above, some subject departments which were only interested in bidding for project funds under their own control felt excluded. This was particularly true of anthropology departments. The first CSAP Subject Centre Director had led a major anthropology subject initiative supported by the Funding Council. She had successfully involved every anthropology department in the country in this work, and such involvement had been very much in terms of the issues of interest to the departments. Anthropology departments understandably found it difficult to move to a different approach where they had to work 'beyond their immediate horizons'. This had implications for the academic coordinators who had to secure the interest and commitment of colleagues used to running their own projects, who needed encouragement to link their departmental strategies to a wider agenda. Two examples of academic coordinator activity illustrate how some success was achieved. The sociology and politics coordinators worked together to involve departments who had been unsuccessful in bids to the Centre. They led a separate project to support these departments. This had some success and certainly raised the number of departments working with the Centre. However, some departments still felt that unless they had project funding or grants under their own control they would not participate in subject centre activity. The second example is based on the work of the Anthropology Coordinator and the Subject Centre Director to support a bid from the discipline of anthropology through the Royal Anthropology Institute (RAI) to secure widening participation funds under 'Aim Higher.' The successful bid was located in a single department, but other departments obtained funding through the initiative and thus gained something of the style of work to which they were accustomed in the early days of the subject centre.

Overall, what proved to be most difficult was encouraging project teams who were unsuccessful in bidding to nevertheless work as part of a broader coalition of interests when additional funding was provided to take forward the theme which they had identified. The examples given above of academic coordinator activity are indicative of small successes. Nevertheless, some departments remained annoyed and felt that their specific subject interests were being ignored by the subject centre. CSAP works with over 300 departments across the UK. There may be five or six disgruntled departments only, but dissatisfied departments report their concerns to others. Nonetheless, a subject centre cannot meet the needs of all individual departments and must do as much as possible to encourage departments to engage in wider strategic initiatives where it can.

Evaluation of the strategy

The strategy was analysed by the following methods:

- Standard data collection approaches, to measure take-up by departments, individuals and networks, to enable comparison with previous measures of Centre output. This was a continuation of the reporting mechanism for monitoring required by LTSN.
- A new measure of impact in order to trace how far, if at all, activity developed by individuals, departments or networks had led to take-up and achieved recognition within institutions. This included projects on teaching particular research methods which were taken up more widely. It also included personal and professional career development, including achievement of both institutional and national teaching fellowships. The work with the host university was also part of this measure.
- The interviews were conducted by the Centre's external evaluator.

The implicit theory of change underpinning these changes was one of multiple brokerage and the building of interconnections. The evidence collected suggests this overall strategy was successful. Relations with the host university also developed, because the Centre was now discussing with the host university a broader work plan focused on a wide range of learning and teaching policies. The Centre was a small but recognized contributor to the work of the university. Regular meetings between the Director, the Manager and the P-VC contributed to this work.

As indicated, some departments felt excluded by the new strategy. However, the decision to move to a smaller number of projects with loose coordination met the planned outcomes, and the change was well received by the Advisory Group. The majority of departments across the UK felt able to engage with the strategy. What attracted departments was the breadth of topics on offer. Departments might work with the Centre on a specific initiative or a project funded for a limited period of time. Thus, the linkage of Centre interests with national agendas meant departments could attract support which benefited their institution. There was also still room for support on topics of considerable interest to departments but which were not seen as priorities by institutions, including race and critical pedagogy.

Examples of new ideas and practices that were adopted by departments include enhanced employability work with greater student involvement, including student-led projects; revising departmental activity with CSAP assistance; developing resources trialled in more than one institution; and linking Centre-funded project activity to other departmental work. These can be seen to be part of an ongoing process of departmental reconstruction of pedagogic practice in the light of changing national and professional body perspectives. On the negative side were the few occasions when, following an unsuccessful application to the subject centre for funds for a very specific internal initiative, that was the end of the link between the department and the centre. This negative reconstruction was not common at all, but it was present.

New practices included cross-activity brokerage. The linking of a subject centre project with an ongoing departmental initiative, which is then taken forward through activity of the new CETLs, is one such example. The number and breadth of such linkages increased noticeably from 2003 and was an indicator of success in embedding for innovation. This work featured strongly on the second evaluation measure identified above.

The analysis of mini project activity, as well as other initiatives conducted by the Subject Centre Director and Manager in 2005 for the second strand of evaluation strategy, revealed that a number of the former mini projects with small amounts of funding had achieved institutional impact well beyond the funded department. One example is the development of filmed ethnographic interviews being applied on courses very different from the social science department that hosted them in the first place. This does raise the question as to whether the strengths and desired outcomes would have happened anyway without a change of strategy.

The subject centre activity became more geared towards students, with tutors as essential intermediaries. The obvious gains included the benefits of having student projects, and student presentations to the annual subject centre conference. The numbers involved were fairly modest, but it is unlikely they would have occurred without the change in strategy.

Conclusions

The model moved from strategy based on the analysis of materials to strategy developed through a mixture of discussion with interested parties and top–down initiative. However, the needs of a number of key people, particularly in subject centre administration, might have been better met early on. The bringing together of academic and administrative interests and roles was more complex than was realized.

The overall lesson is that the appreciation of a multilevel approach was appropriate, in that it helped achieve the aim of working with a wider range of departments, but is difficult to translate into practice. It would be helpful to really learn from the successes of the small-scale projects, which may have had far greater impact than anyone realized. One line of inquiry for which there is some supporting evidence is to look to see how some mini projects have been taken forward at a later date through other institutional initiatives. For instance, all institutions with mini projects which were successful in gaining CETL funds conducted some further work based on that mini project. The same is likely to be true in other cases of bidding for funds. However, successful project bids, whether for CETLs or CSAP mini projects do not in themselves improve student experience or tutor activity, and further evidence of this impact is needed. Anecdotal feedback does at least suggest that there is an increasing number of colleagues successfully seeking institutional recognition and promotion for teaching and learning, for which CSAP activity has at least played a part. This is itself part of the consequence of attempting to develop multilayered and multilevel interaction. What is clear is that the continuous development of Centre strategy, approach and activities will be an ongoing task for as long as the subject centre initiative lasts.

6

Talking the talk, walking the walk: the work of an LTSN subject centre

Paul Kleiman
PALATINE Subject Centre, England

Introduction

PALATINE (Performing Arts Learning and Teaching Innovation Network) is the Higher Education Academy Subject Centre for Dance, Drama and Music. The Subject Centre provides support, information, expertise and resources on good, successful and innovative learning and teaching practices. In October 2003, the PALATINE Subject Centre received its formal feedback letter on its annual performance from the Executive of the Learning and Teaching Support Network (LTSN). The LTSN – consisting of 24 subject centres and a generic centre – was established in 2000 by the four UK higher education funding councils following the publication of the report of the National Committee of Inquiry into Higher Education, chaired by Sir Ron Dearing (the 'Dearing Report'; NCIHE 1997). The need for support and, particularly, the improvement and enhancement of learning and teaching in higher education was one of Dearing's main recommendations, and the LTSN had been established to fulfil that role by undertaking and achieving three main objectives:

- Setting up, supporting and developing learning and teaching networks.
- Promoting and sharing good practices in learning, teaching and assessment.
- Brokering the transfer of knowledge between users, experts, developers and innovators.

The letter to the Subject Centre from the Executive began by commending it on its 'broad and impressive range of activities' and the delivery of those activities through an 'effectively run network'. The letter continued: 'You give the impression of a strong, experienced and stable team with a clear and coherent vision for the role of the subject network'.

Along with the satisfaction, after three years of operation, of receiving a good 'end-of-year report', there were some wry smiles among the senior staff at the comment about 'giving a good impression'. Though the Subject

Centre was clearly working successfully, meeting its targets, etc., the phrase captured the sense that while the success was explicit, the manner as to how that success had been achieved was not.

Discourses and practices

In order to achieve the LTSN's objectives, the Subject Centre recognized that it had to be perceived, by its academic communities, as a credible and valued source of support for learning and teaching, and that it gained and retained the acceptance, trust and respect of those communities.

An important feature of the Subject Centre, and one that was shared by the other 23 LTSN subject centres, was that its entire senior staff came from and were based in the subject disciplines associated with the Centre. The idea, inherent in the establishment of the LTSN, of enhancing learning and teaching via discipline based subject centres with discipline based staff, represented a significant departure from the prevailing situation in which support for learning and teaching in universities normally was provided by staff based in central educational development units.

The creation of the subject centre network was premised on the recognition that the key to 'getting through' to university teaching staff was through the disciplines themselves. Most university teachers identified first with their discipline and its community of practice, then with their department and then finally with their institution and the wider higher education system (Henkel 2000; Becher and Trowler 2001). These three components – the discipline, the collegiate and the institutional – each represented a different and distinct discourse that the Subject Centre had to engage with.

The Subject Centre, in its role as an 'agent of change', set out to fulfil the LTSN's objectives by undertaking a range of activities. These included running workshops, seminars and conferences on issues and themes of concern and interest to its various subject communities; making direct formal and informal links with individuals, departments, institutions and subject associations in the subject areas covered by the Centre; developing a website of useful resources for learning and teaching; providing small-scale funding to individuals to undertake research and development in learning and teaching; funding small-scale pedagogically focused projects; and producing publications.

The source of the perceptual gap between how the Subject Centre was perceived by its subject communities and how it was perceived by the LTSN Executive lay in the nature of the various discourses within which the Subject Centre operated. Duke (2001: 103) depicts the modern university as 'pulled' between the discourses of managerialism and networking, and he provides a useful list of the characteristics that group around each of the terms (see Table 6.1).

The Subject Centre realized from its inception that, in order to succeed in working with its communities of academic practice, it had to situate its own

Table 6.1 Characteristics grouped around the terms 'managerialism' and 'networking'

Managerialism	*Networking*
Hierarchical	Participatory
Corporatist	Clusters
Vertical	Horizontal
Bureaucratic	Entrepreneurial
Controlling	Enabling
Risk-averse	Innovative
Clients	Partners
Multiple managers	Multiple boundary-spanners
Executives and managers	Leaders, administrators, facilitators
Bosses and workers	Colleagues
Mode I* (discipline-based)	Mode II (issue-based)

Note: * See Chapter 22 for more detail on the significance of Mode I and Mode II approaches in higher education.

Source: Based on Duke 2001: 107.

discourse and practices within the networking discourse. However, it was not a case of having to adopt an alien discourse, but rather a matter of recognizing that through their involvement in and familiarity with the 'cultural undergrowth' (Trowler and Knight 1999) of the disciplines, those attributes and dispositions were already 'hard-wired' into the Subject Centre through the pedagogic and professional experiences and values of its staff.

At the same time, the Subject Centre's mission, which was also that of the whole LTSN, was set within the context of the UK higher education funding bodies' core objective to achieve coherence and coordination within their learning and teaching support strategies, and to ensure effective dissemination and transfer of good practice. The LTSN – through its subject centres – would 'play a central role in driving forward the UK's higher education agenda' by maintaining 'a high profile position at the leading edge' and 'delivering a first class service' (Allan 2000: section 2).

This was language, particularly the emphasis on delivering a service, which unequivocally situated the LTSN within the managerialist and corporatist discourse of higher education. It made it clear that the LTSN was to be an intrinsic part of the policy and organizational framework that embodied the drive towards quality assurance and quality enhancement in higher education and the delivery of government policy in the relevant areas of HE.

The Subject Centre was caught between discourses, and it needed to negotiate a careful path between the various and potentially contra-directional values, demands and expectations of its primary stakeholders on the one hand, and its academic communities on the other. Those communities, despite the perceived threat from and mistrust of the increasingly managerialist trends within HE, still placed great value on implicit, shared assumptions;

informal networks and procedures; individual autonomy; professional judgement, collegiality, democracy and trust. The senior staff of the Subject Centre, though they shared a strong identification with those values, had to adopt a 'Janus-like' role, facing the networking and disciplinary discourse and practices of its academic communities in one direction, and the managerialist discourse and practices of the LTSN executive, funding councils and government in the other.

Despite some serious reservations about and, in some cases, antipathy to the managerialist discourse that emanated from the LTSN executive, the Subject Centre's senior staff felt it was worth accepting and responding positively to it, and adapting some of their organizational practices, in order to gain and exploit the opportunity to make a genuine contribution to the enhancement of learning and teaching in its subject areas.

A key factor in enabling the Subject Centre to maintain a balance between the two positions was its ability, when necessary, to speak and, particularly, to write in the managerialist discourse of the LTSN executive. Gewirtz et al. (1995) refer to the importance of 'bi-lingualism' in higher education: maintaining side by side both the discourse of managerialism and the professional discourse of the discipline, and adopting each in the appropriate context. This tension between managerialism and networking was, and remains, an important factor in the development and work of the Subject Centre.

Although it appeared obvious that the Subject Centre had to engage effectively and successfully with both the managerialist discourse of the funding and executive 'stakeholders' and the networking discourse of its academic communities of practice, experience revealed a more complex picture. For example, while any form of communication with academics that utilized the language of the managerialist discourse had a low or non-existent level of acceptability, there was also some resistance to the networking discourse, as it was perceived by some as the 'other side of the managerialist coin', utilizing a different but similarly alien form of discourse. This resistance appeared particularly acute in the 'old' pre-1992 universities, and went some way to explaining the noticeable lack of interest in the work of the Subject Centre from that sector.

The third discourse

It became clear that, alongside the managerial and networking discourses, there existed a 'third' discourse that the Subject Centre had to engage with in order to enter properly into the interaction between the individual, the discipline and the higher education institution that Henkel (2000) describes as the 'critical dynamic in the lives of individual academics'. The third discourse – the '*discourse of the discipline*' or the '*scholarly-craft discourse*' is specific to the cultures and ethos of particular communities of academic practice. While both managerialism and networking tend to be 'broad-brush' discourses, it is the often finely grained nuances and subtleties of discipline specific discourses and practices that play a significant role in defining the distinct identity, culture and values of a particular community of practice (Lave and Wenger 1991). Examples such as the forms and style of language, communication and nomenclature may seem trivial or insignificant, but such nuances are critical to an understanding of the factors that would encourage or dissuade individuals within a particular discipline or community of academic practice to engage with the work of 'their' subject centre.

The Subject Centre had to choose and use language very carefully in order not to alienate, or alienate further, its various academic communities. An example of how this worked in practice centred on the use of the word 'workshop'. One of the difficulties is that the term has become so ubiquitous that almost any gathering together of a (not too large) group of people to discuss or explore a topic can be called a 'workshop'. Some disciplines are far more familiar and comfortable with the term 'workshop' than other disciplines. Also the connotation of 'workshop' with a practical, pragmatic, roll-your-sleeves-up-and-get-going approach is perceived (by some disciplines and a number of the older, more traditional universities) as an activity that is not particularly appropriate to the more cerebral, discursive and intellectually rigorous approaches that 'proper' academic investigations and pursuits require.

In order to fulfil its obligation to share good practice, the Subject Centre had run a series of workshops that, though generally successful and well received, attracted colleagues mainly from the 'new' universities and mainly from two of the three major disciplines represented by the Subject Centre. The other discipline, or certainly a significant section of that discipline, was characterized by terms such as '*traditional*', '*historically rooted*' and '*very serious*'.

'These people wouldn't be seen dead at a **workshop**!' was how a senior and eminent academic from within that discipline described it. The solution, for the Subject Centre, lay in adapting its discourse and practice. 'These people' may not have considered attending workshops, but they certainly went to seminars, colloquia, conferences, forums, etc. So when the Subject Centre expanded its range of events to include seminars, which were described on the Centre's website as 'high level discussions among a relatively small but very experienced group of colleagues', then there was a noticeable increase in engagement with and by academics who previously had exhibited little or no interest in the Subject Centre's work.

Talking the talk, walking the walk

The work of the subject centres can be aligned closely with the theory of change at the centre of this book, and with the activity systems and social practice theories that inform that theory of change. Both the Subject Centre that is the focus of this case study and the other LTSN subject centres operated at a point where the various strands or activity systems of higher education policy, institutional and organizational structures, subject disciplines and individual academics intersected in an amalgam of coexistence, coercion, compliance and confrontation. The subject centres had to work with the contradictions between the potential for networks to be more productive and dynamic and the fact that the political–institutional context in which they operated was, and remains,[1] rooted in vertical organizational systems and bureaucratic logic (Castells 2001).

The subject centres occupied a dynamic and fluid operational space that not only contained the tensions and contradictions between the managerialist and networking discourses but also the specific discourses of the various disciplines and subjects. Located among constellations and clusters of specific academic and discipline based practices, each with their shared meanings and socially accepted sets of rules, the 'bi-lingualism' of Gewirtz et al. (1995) became – for the subject centres – a need for *multi*-lingualism where the centre covered several subject or discipline areas.

However, the key to understanding the effectiveness of the subject centres lies beyond language (i.e., 'talking the talk'), in the realm of practice, and the social and cultural factors that linked the subject centres with their respective communities of practice. Whereas the LTSN executive could only engage at a macro level with the relatively broad-brush discourses of managerialism and networking, the fact that the subject centres were discipline based and staffed, on the whole, by academic and pedagogic practitioners from within those disciplines enabled them to gain the trust of and achieve credibility within their respective academic communities of practice by utilizing and engaging properly, at a micro level, with the discourses, practices and cultural memes of those communities.

---

[1] In April 2004, following a review of the support infrastructure for higher education in the UK, the LTSN, including all 24 subject centres, was absorbed into the newly established Higher Education Academy, alongside a number of other HE support organizations and agencies.

7

Against the grain: e-assessment in the physical sciences

Scott Court
Economic and Social Research Council, England

Veronica Bamber
Queen Margaret University, Scotland

Context

This case study is based on interviews undertaken as part of the evaluation of the Subject Centre Network commissioned by HEFCE. It explores an innovation introduced by academics working in a traditional university, in a discipline in which, it could be argued, the competing agendas of teaching and research serve to inhibit the development of reflective networks in relation to teaching and learning issues. Interviews with academics working within the discipline suggest that although there is much high quality teaching within the disciplines, historically much of this is 'down to the professionalism of the staff involved rather than any incentive', as one teacher of physics in a pre-1992 university said. In the physical sciences particularly conservatism prevails, as is typical in subjects with strong paradigms as to what is studied and the teaching methods used (Biglan 1973: 195). This can be contrasted with non-paradigmatic subjects in, for example, the humanities, where the curriculum and teaching approaches are much more open to flexibility and negotiation. In the physical sciences, it is more difficult to push forward initiatives which might be seen to develop students' generic skills or learning approaches at the expense of what is considered key disciplinary knowledge. Innovators have to be able to provide strong justifications for diluting the curriculum with what Gibbons et al. (1994) refer to as Mode II type knowledge production, with its greater emphasis on generic skills development. These tendencies also correspond to the profile of a highly classified and framed curriculum area identified by Bernstein in his classic work (Bernstein 1971). In this profile, a highly classified curricular area is one in which domain knowledge is very stable and highly valued with clear boundaries. The physical sciences also retain the notion of high 'teacher fidelity' (framing) in which teachers tend to perceive themselves as 'discipline gatekeepers' in a way that militates against absorption of non-discipline-specific activity. With these theoretical issues in mind, this case will examine the way in which a more generically derived intervention plays out within this discipline profile.

As will be explained below, the innovation in question was sponsored by the Higher Education Academy (HEA) Subject Centre for Physical Sciences, whose approach is rooted in the notion of 'colleagues working with colleagues', with a particular emphasis on disciplinary credibility as a means of facilitating engagement with the subject community. This is a particularly important approach in the physical sciences, given the paradigmatic and conservative nature of learning and teaching in the subjects involved.

Prior to the innovation, science teaching at the case study institution was typically characterized by traditional forms of teacher/student contact such as the lecture and laboratory, although there was an increasing drive at the institutional level towards the use of modern technology to support and enhance traditional teaching methods, as well as an increase in awareness of assessment issues. This institutional drive had limited impact on the physical sciences area, however, since research pressures and an ethos of not investing significant time in teaching improvement prevailed. Although three lecturers in the department were interested in less traditional approaches, they were not supported by the other 15 members of staff, and a culture of innovation was not present. For example, the regular research seminars held in the department were not mirrored in similar attempts to share ideas in teaching. Furthermore, any central university initiative tended to be generic and was not considered relevant to the specific needs of the physical sciences discipline.

The innovation

Doctors Cox, Davies and Hallett (pseudonyms) were teaching undergraduate modules in science subjects to groups of students possessing a very broad range of educational achievements. Lattuca and Stark (1994) have commented that inclusiveness, in other words acknowledgement of the (increasingly) diverse backgrounds of students, is a particular challenge in the sciences, where curricula may not have changed significantly over the last few decades. Students in the UK are often criticized for not having sufficient mathematical ability to study science subjects, and the three physical sciences lecturers felt that something had to be done in their institution. In the modules in question, students were required to attend lectures and labs, and undertake summative assessments at the end of their course. Student results in these assessments were not particularly good, and there were no formative assessments during the modules. The three lecturers decided to introduce computer aided assessment (CAA) as one way of providing students with interim feedback on their progress without, perhaps, placing an onerous burden on staff.

In the first stage of introducing CAA, the lecturers explored the use of online course material for facilitating formative assessment and generally enhancing the student learning experience. They were inspired by a project initiated in the physical sciences in another university, with the help of subject centre funding. Assessment software had been developed which catered for disciplinary needs, such as the ability to work with very large and small numbers. This also made the initiative more cost effective, since much of the time intensive development work had already been funded elsewhere. The three lecturers started to build their CAA from the software developed by colleagues at the other university, but after months of frustration the collaboration was abandoned.

The main barriers to this original project were the fact that the software was difficult to learn to use, but more significantly, that their own university would not agree to support another institution's software on its server. The three colleagues did not give up, however, and, in the second stage of trying to introduce CAA, they started to explore the possibility of using commercially available software which would be acceptable to the institution.

A number of systems were considered, but several were rejected because they were complicated, time intensive in terms of learning to use or lacked the degree of versatility required. Finally, one was chosen that met the team's requirements in that it offered various wizards to assist teachers in developing questions, and assessments could be modified and expanded with relative ease. Additionally, the university was prepared to support the software on the central server.

At this point, the HEA Subject Centre for Physical Sciences sent out a call for projects in the area of computer aided assessment. The team applied for, and were awarded, funding to develop online formative and summative assessment materials. Their aim was to use the Subject Centre sponsorship to cover the costs of their time in developing the materials. From the Subject Centre's point of view, they would then make the resources available to the wider subject community. The majority of the development work was undertaken by Doctors Cox, Davies and Hallett, although they received some assistance from students undertaking research projects in the department. This process was not problem-free, since each of the academics had significant research responsibilities, and were subject to the pressure of preparing for the national Research Assessment Exercise. In the end, Dr Hallett had to withdraw from the initiative. Nonetheless, within six months the team had developed enough material to begin web based trials. The development process gathered momentum as students began using material and the team were able to evaluate the assessments and iron out serious problems. Students taking the team's modules would receive a lecture on a topic, followed by a short online formative assessment. Summative assessment at the end of the module was also undertaken online. The weighting of formative/summative assessment was 50/50 percent.

Impact of the innovation within the institution

The impact of the innovation was readily identifiable at both the departmental and institutional levels. In the department, students taking the module in question were generally enthusiastic about the change in assessment practice, and the students' initial assessment results indicated that the new method of assessment improved results. It was felt by the team that this was because the formative assessments provided additional focus for the students, as well as a degree of flexibility that was of benefit to all students, but especially those with lower levels of achievement on entry. At the level of individual teaching practice, Dr Cox commented that the experience of using and being able to analyse online formative assessment material provided real insight into the difficulties experienced by students when getting to grips with the course material, and highlighted areas which needed more attention. He felt he was reflecting much more than previously on how he taught his subject, and had definitely developed a more 'student friendly' approach to teaching it. This reflective insight has provided additional motivation that has resulted in Dr Cox broadening the scope of the initiative, so that dissemination is not limited to academics working within the physical sciences, but has also been extended into other subject areas. Within physical sciences, colleagues were appreciative of what seemed to be an improvement in student engagement and achievement in the student year group – although there was a lack of good data on the effects of CAA. However, while most colleagues in the department itself were happy to passively accept the innovation, they felt unable to invest time in extending its use to their own teaching. They were prepared to let Dr Cox set up assessments and administer them for their students, since this was a time-saver for them. Dr Cox suffered from the 'lone ranger' syndrome (Trowler 2008), which often prevents a particular innovation from going further than the initial champions. The innovators were anchored in an 'underlabouring' role with respect to their colleagues, where their inertia supported by the disciplinary profile acted as a disincentive to becoming proactive.

In an attempt to buck this trend, dissemination was undertaken at the institutional level, via peer-led lunchtime seminars. The team was then invited by colleagues in other departments to assist in developing online assessment material for both science and non-science subjects, illustrating the value of networks as a means by which to engage fellow academics in enhancing learning and teaching practices within the institution. However, as colleagues who have made use of the online assessment material moved to posts at other institutions or left higher education, the use of the material diminished. Elton (2002: 12) describes this issue in his analysis of the effectiveness of the Enterprise in Higher Education (EHE) initiative in the UK, which he describes as successful in the unfreezing (pre-adoption) phase, but not in the refreezing (implementation) phase. This meant that EHE did not become institutionalized, since EHE staff in some institutions were unable to transfer the ideas to colleagues, while in other universities continuation policies (e.g., continued funding) failed. Unless attitudes are changed in the process of introducing an innovation (Elton 1987: 174), then existing 'ways of doing things around here' are likely to prevail.

In the CAA innovation in question, the attempts to introduce the change and make it sustainable beyond a single module were not helped by an institutional push to standardize online assessment and move over wholly to a rival software package, which the team regarded as being less versatile in terms of both question types offered and its capability to provide nuanced online feedback to students undertaking formative assessment in their subject. There now remains a core group of half a dozen users of the original material who have resisted the institutional push for standardization; as Dr Cox commented – 'because we're working with the software, we're sticking with it'. The institutional view was that there were a number of reasons for insisting on staff using one single assessment platform. For instance, at the technical level, if the university computing service was to use its resources well and be efficient, then a multiplicity of assessment packages could not be supported, since computing staff could not maintain expertise in too many programmes. Also, as a learning and teaching principle, it was felt that students should not have to move between different assessment packages if they were taught by a range of lecturers with individual preferences. Dr Cox and colleagues felt that these were rationalizations of a tendency to centralize computing and other services, at the expense of academic autonomy. The innovators were also displaying characteristics of an 'enclave' culture (see Saunders et al. 2006) in which an introspection and protectionism sets in once a 'siege' state is in existence. This can result in innovators protecting their original innovation rather than celebrating small wins.

Impact beyond the institution

The online assessment material produced using Subject Centre funding by Dr Cox and the team has been widely distributed among the subject community in CD format and has also been made available on the Subject Centre website. However, rather than simply offering good practice in the form of 'off the peg' ideas or products, the Subject Centre has worked hard to provide opportunities for dialogue and two-way flow, with the project team being asked to act as sounding boards for ideas and play a role in advising other departments in their discipline on CAA. The project team has presented the results at Subject Centre conferences and other events hosted by interested university departments, and the material has been enthusiastically received by those attending events. This could be because the online assessment material is presented by academics working within the discipline and is grounded in the scientific principles upon which the discipline is based, thus facilitating engagement on the part of academics who may be wary of pedagogic decision making on the basis of generic approaches to enhancing learning and teaching. This illustrates the apparent effectiveness of the strategy for change employed by the Physical Sciences Subject Centre. The strategy is represented by a mix of activities that prioritizes the development and dissemination of subject based pedagogic knowledge, research and experience, and relies on the development of informed, reflective networks as a means by which academics can make decisions – on information based grounds – about ideas and new approaches intended to improve the quality of teaching and learning within the disciplines. However, what is not clear is to what extent the enthusiasm for the software which colleagues showed when attending events was then converted to practical application of the software in their own departments and teaching: it is notoriously difficult to transfer practice, as indicated in Chapter 2 of this book. Furthermore, academic staff increasingly lack time to spend discussing new practices, in what appears to be a forced 'loss of collegiality' in increasingly pressurized departments (Trowler and Knight 2000: 72).

Impact of the project has not been limited to the team's own institution and subject community. For example, Dr Cox now teaches statistics to undergraduate students on non-science courses, and has been awarded funding by a second subject centre to develop online assessment materials for students undertaking training in the use of statistical methods, thus providing a means by which to promote the use of computer aided assessment to a much wider subject community. In the teaching of statistics – a subject in which learning can be compromised by students' 'fear of numbers' – Dr Cox believes CAA offers a learner friendly means by which to consolidate material provided in lectures and provide formative feedback to build students' confidence in using statistical methods. In his own teaching incorporating online assessment, Dr Cox comments that although there is often antipathy and resistance to the new material at the time the lecture is delivered, at later stages of the module students often return to the online material to assist them in undertaking, for example, project work or lab reports. As with the original project, the online assessment material will be made available on CD for use by the wider subject community within the UK. Dr Cox hopes that the project will serve as a means by which to promote the use of online assessment to support students' development in the use of statistical methods – a 'problem' subject that crosses subject/disciplinary boundaries – within a much wider range of academic subjects, using general interest questions to appeal to a wider audience of both academics and students.

Conclusions

Although the innovation in question could be seen as having a significant impact at the individual, institutional and subject levels, there is a real danger, as discussed above, that much of the assessment material developed will become redundant over time, as individual champions move on. From the perspective of academic practice as culturally rooted patterns of behaviour regarding learning and teaching, the core group of staff involved in the innovation can be seen as 'carriers' (Reckwitz 2002: 256) of an academic practice that is misaligned with the reified practices advocated by the framework of their institution's teaching and learning policy. It has also been seen that it is difficult for 'lone rangers' to sustain innovations if unsupported by colleagues and institutional policies.

As such, this illustrates an important lesson for those involved in the teaching and learning policymaking process at the institutional level. If academic staff are to comply with the direction of change advocated by institutional policy, it is important that the policymaking process is consultative and that institutional policymakers do not stifle innovation by imposing a 'top–down' vision of change – in this case, by limiting the software that academics working within the institution are allowed to use. If the strategic priorities of institutional policy are not aligned with the practices of the staff responsible for implementing changes in learning and teaching activity, then the outcomes will be at the expense of creativity and innovation. However, Lattuca and Stark (1994) tell us that contextual factors (such as institutional policies) are less influential than the disciplinary and educational beliefs of academic staff. In this case, while institutional constraints were important, they were perhaps less of an inhibitor of change than the attitudes of colleagues to teaching and learning in the discipline.

The major lessons from this experience fall into two groups: factors which facilitated the innovation, and factors which inhibited it. The introduction of CAA was helped by funding from the HEA Subject Centre, and the discipline specific focus of the change effort was important to those involved. However, the efforts of the subject centres on their own are not enough, and other factors have to be in place for sustainable change to happen. In this case, champions (Dr Cox and colleagues) were very important, but, again, it is difficult for champions to extend or sustain change longer term. In this case, the 'lone rangers' involved found it impossible to resist institutional policy, although this might have been possible if all users of the software had made a sufficiently strong, evidence based case for continued use of their preferred solution. Not only were the innovators facing resistance from the institution, but also from their own colleagues who were not prepared to invest their own time in an extension of the CAA. This was not a simple case, therefore, of academic autonomy versus central opposition, but an example of the complexity of trying to innovate at discipline level in a multilevel environment.

While the institutional effects of this innovation may have been limited, it is an interesting example of 'leap frogging' where we have the effects of the project 'jumping' the confines of the host institution to having wider influences because of the networking infrastructure offered by the subject centre network. It demonstrates the complex and uneven character of change where a linear model involving micro, meso and macro progress falls short of making sense of the change process on the ground.

8

Theme 1 commentary

Paul Trowler

These case studies, all related to the subject centre initiative, raise five significant issues in relation to enhancement initiatives and implementation strategies:

1 *Transferability*: The issue of transferability of initiatives that have worked in one place to a different place. This raises general questions about the relationship between ideas, tools and artefacts, and the cultural context in which they are used.

2 *Origin*: The issue of the source of an initiative, whether from institutional or national policy or from the ground level, raises potential contrasts between coherent policy and resourcing on the one hand and ownership and fitness for purpose on the other.

3 *Target*: The issue of where to direct attention in trying to bring about change. The significance of disciplinary networks receives considerable attention. Other, complementary targets include universities, individual members of staff, departments or ad hoc project groups.

4 *Discourses*: The ways in which an initiative is framed discursively is an issue both explicitly and implicitly. Discursive positioning has an impact on how initiatives are framed and how they are received on the ground.

5 *Alignment*: If change initiatives are congruent with previous practices and sets of values found on the ground their chances of success are greater. Going against the grain can be extremely counterproductive.

Transferability

We discussed in Chapter 2 the problematic nature of the metaphor of 'transfer' when applied to innovations in higher education, and suggested that 'translation' would be better because it implies that *activity* is required when crossing boundaries, whether of language or of social context. This issue arises with regard to the use of software described by Court and Bamber in Chapter 7. In attempting to use software developed by colleagues at another university as well as commercially available packages, the academics at the centre of this case study encountered a number of difficulties: their own university would not agree to support the software on its server; the learning curve involved was too steep; the software lacked the versatility required for their students.

By contrast the software package they chose 'could be modified and expanded with relative ease'. This also had the very important advantage that the finished product which could be employed in their context was also to some extent at least 'owned' by the academics involved. As well as the very practical problems about transferability outlined above, this issue of owner-ship is also important. The phrase 'reinventing the wheel' has come to signify a pointless waste of effort. And yet there are merits in reinventing wheels. The resultant wheel might be slightly different from the standard one, adapted to local ground conditions. But at least as important is the fact that it becomes 'our' wheel: one that was invented here, or at least adapted here.

So, transferability issues have to do with innovations which do or do not conform to local conditions (and those conditions might be practical ones, or they may be to do with discourse, values, assumptions and practices), but they also have to do with ownership.

The relevant subject centre was clearly aware of this issue, being sceptical about 'off-the-peg' ideas and practices, and working to provide for dialogue about the use of such software and appropriate applications in different contexts. In the early days of the subject centre network there was some talk of subject centres acting as brokers, providing a central point where practitioners and departments in the same discipline could access good ideas, 'best practice', tools and so on. Experience has taught, however, that the broker-age concept is not an appropriate one, because it is a model based on the metaphor of transfer.

Sociocultural theory generally stresses the interrelationship between 'tools' and their social context. Each influences the other, according for example to Latour (2000). While Latour acknowledges that technologies and artefacts can 'script' their users, affecting movement and behaviour and sometimes also shaping goals and aspirations, he also notes that artefacts are appropri-ated into established patterns of the social order: there is a dialectic at work here. To give an example, PowerPoint technology can configure teacher and student practices in the classroom because of the underlying assumptions software designers built into its code (Adams 2006). 'PowerPoint karaoke' has become the dominant mode of pedagogy throughout the world. And yet there is still space for innovation and localized adaptation, even using that software. The innovative use of graphics, video and the developing awareness of the dangers of sleepwalking into PowerPoint karaoke has meant, in some cases, new and interesting practices have developed, often based on previous practices or on theories of teaching and learning which were already in place. Such dynamics of appropriation mean that 'domestication' of practices and tool use occur even where there is quite heavy scripting.

Sociocultural theory

Origin

The second issue but with very clear links to the first is the question of the source of an innovation. Court and Bamber in Chapter 7 describe how online assessment practices 'grew' from the ground up with the assistance of the relevant subject centre. However, an alternative innovation in the same area was initiated by the institution, and there was a push from the institution for standardization using a rival software package. This tension between the framework of university policy on the one hand and practice on the ground on the other led to a diminution of the use of the original software and to a change in practice.

This conflict highlights the significance of the origin of an innovation. Enhancements in teaching and learning very often do come from individual academics or small groups who can see a better way of doing things and are motivated to change their practices and to tell others about what they are doing. Enthusiasm, motivation and fitness-for-purpose are huge advantages in these cases. However a major disadvantage, frequently seen, is the Balkanization of innovation. The innovator is a 'lone ranger' who makes no discernible impact on practices more broadly.

Alternative sources of changes in teaching and learning are: the top team of the institution; outcomes of quality review processes; external bodies such as a quality assurance agency; central government; and, indirectly, changing funding mechanisms. Each of these has its advantages and disadvantages, many of which are threaded through the stories in this book. The broader point is to distinguish between top–down and bottom–up approaches to enhancement. As we have argued in the Chapter 2, we suggest that a middle–out approach is best. Here broad guidelines are set, fuzzy goals are articulated and low-res innovations are proposed. Thus space is left for local interpretation and domestication. In this way the advantages of providing clear direction and adequate resourcing conferred by the best top–down approaches is combined with those of fitness-for-context and local ownership associated with bottom–up approaches to change.

Target

These case studies each emphasize the significance of the discipline in efforts to enhance teaching and learning practices. The subject centre network was founded on the principle that disciplines are a very significant organizing framework. As Kleiman in Chapter 6 says: 'the idea, inherent in the establishment of the LTSN, of enhancing learning and teaching via discipline-based Subject Centres with discipline-based staff, represented a significant departure from the prevailing situation [which focused on] central educational development units'. As Kleiman notes, most academics first identify with their discipline (sometimes at a global level), then with their

department and only finally with the institution and the wider higher education system. Cliff Allan, the original Director of the LTSN, also highlights the
significance of a discipline based approach to change. As noted above, Court
and Bamber also consider it significant in the particular case they examined
that there was alignment between the characteristics of the innovation and   *Discipline*
the disciplinary character of the context of implementation.   *as*
   The national evaluation of the whole Learning and Teaching Support   *primary*
Network concurred that the decision to target the disciplinary communities   *community*
in this way was a good one, though not because there are necessarily significant disciplinary differences in teaching and learning. More important was
the point that Kleiman makes: that academics primarily identify themselves
as disciplinary specialists.

   Yet this choice of target represents a choice, and choices always exclude
other options, and other people. Cliff Allan notes how some educational
developers challenged this whole approach, claiming that most learning,
teaching and assessment practices in higher education were generic and not
disciplinary in nature. They argued that separating the disciplines would lose
the beneficial effects of synergies and cross-fertilization often seen in educational development courses and other activities. There was a danger of
inflexibility and conservatism if disciplines were simply allowed to reinforce
old practices by looking inwards. Finally, it was argued that, in the contemporary situation, cross-disciplinary and multidisciplinary approaches are
particularly significant and the LTSN approach thus represented an out-
moded model. Behind the principled arguments also probably lay a political
motivation: funding and other resources were being shifted away from educational development centres towards these new subject centres. Power relations, resources, identities were being reconfigured and such a situation
involves winners and losers. Cliff Allan's chapter argues that these concerns
of principle were effectively taken into account; however, the extent to
which this happened is debatable. Moreover, the political concerns are much
harder to address.

   We argue that it is important that there is a joined-up approach to targeting
enhancement. Although the discipline may be important, it is only one
potential target for implementation efforts. Funding mechanisms at the
institutional level, the activities of educational development units, work at
departmental level, policies and practices throughout the sector, and so on
are all important. The process of aligning these different levels in a roughly
similar direction is really important if higher education is to move away
from its loosely coupled, garbage can past. In this, the Teaching Quality
Enhancement Fund approach was exemplary. As Trowler et al. (2005: 429)
put it: 'The 1998 consultation document proposed a new integrated approach
to the funding of improvements in teaching quality: the Teaching Quality
Enhancement Fund (TQEF). The TQEF would provide funding at three
levels: the institution, the academic subject and the individual'.

Integrated approach –
– targeting institution, subject area,
and individual

Discourses

Paul Kleiman's chapter explicitly addresses the issue and significance of discourse in relation to change initiatives. For Kleiman the discursive repertoires in use by the central LTSN organization could be located within managerialist discourse linked with the drive towards quality assurance and the delivery of government policy. (Though Kleiman's argument is debatable. Cliff Allan, Director of the LTSN at the time, notes in his chapter in this book that there is great danger in being seen as 'agents of government' because that undermines credibility among the very practitioners one seeks to influence; see Chapter 4).

The discourse of managerialism tends to draw on other discursive repertoires, especially financial, commercial and engineering ones. Thus 'clients', 'franchised programmes', 'credit accumulation', 'unique selling point', 'market niche' are terms often mobilized when discussing the curriculum and its 'delivery' (Trowler 2001). 'Core skills' which can be 'audited', 'acquired' and 'accumulated' are very significant parts of learning and teaching, and learning generally is about the acquisition and accumulation of sets of 'learning outcomes'. 'Disciplines' become 'subjects' and 'academics' become 'teachers'. This is in contrast to a more personalized, student centred discourse which positions learning and the learner at the centre of attention.

The Lancaster project on managerialism[1] collected interview data which illustrates managerialist discourse in use:

> We talk about this as an educational business and we don't talk about courses in a sense, we talk about products which we have to sell to students and to industry. Now, that's a cultural shift . . . the days when you were just delivering to students and they liked it or not have gone. You're delivering to clients now. And you've got to deliver on time, to quality or walk away. And if they walk away there's no income and if there's no income there's no business. If there's no business, there's no job.
>
> (HoD, Applied Science, post-1992 university, in Deem and
> Brehony 2005: 229)

Yet as Kleiman points out, on the ground the networking discourse and the disciplinary discourse were more prevalently in use. Situated between these levels of the LTSN as a central organization and academics on the ground, the subject centre, from this account, was caught between discourses. As a result its managers effectively had to learn to be 'bilingual' (Gewirtz et al. 1995) or even trilingual, speaking managerialism in contexts where that was

---

[1] An ESRC funded project on managerialism in higher education, 1998–2000. There were focus group discussions and 137 semistructured interviews with manager–academics (HoD-VC) in 16 UK universities. Four case study institutions were researched more intensively using a variety of methods.

appropriate and the discourse of networking and the discipline where that worked.

The Lancaster managerialism project also found that most HoDs acquired this skill. They were not uniquely monolingual in terms of managerialist discourse even while forced to operate the technologies of managerialism: devolved budgets, sometimes robust staffing and other strategies, and the rest (Deem 2004). Deem and Brehony (2005) also make the point, based on the data from that project, that academic managers become bilingual or trilingual. Thus managers, like subject centre staff, draw on discursive resources rooted not only in managerialist ideology but also those which flow from their disciplinary background as well as from an earlier humanist, collegial set of understandings of higher education.

Prichard (2000) agrees with this analysis, pointing out that many managers can shift between 'stations' discursively and in their thinking – between the 'managerial station' and the 'locale', the latter rooted in localized understandings of what works, how to get things done, what is acceptable and so on. Localized knowledges both address and draw on professional and academic expertise. Prichard's (2000: 90) interview based study of new managerialism in further and higher education suggests that: 'The manager is not a coherent distinct human being, but a multiple of subject positions within various discursive practices, which in this case sit uncomfortably together'. The manager's professional identity, and the discourses he or she draws on, is dynamic and protean. He or she will move between the managerial station, drawing on managerialist discourse – constituting students as 'funding units' and colleagues as 'their staff', for example – and more authentic 'locales', situated in specific contexts of professional practice. These are 'localized cultures of practices which produce other relations to the self – that is individualized identities, which variably resist and subvert managerially individuated identities . . .' (Prichard 2000: 41).

The significance of all this for the implementation of change is precisely in the careful selection of language; going with the grain, discursively.

Alignment

This issue of 'going with the grain' arises in Cliff Allan's chapter, but in terms this time of the match between current and past practices on the one hand and the implementation strategy on the other. As noted above, he points out that for academics the discipline is the key feature with which they identify, rather than the institution or the higher education system more broadly. This was noted in Lancaster's evaluation of the Learning and Teaching Support Network:

> Academics seeking guidance about teaching will tend to give most credibility to peers from their discipline and are sceptical of what they may see as platitudinous generic educational advice. This view, held widely

by Subject Centre staff, does not appear to rest on a belief that teaching and learning issues are fundamentally different in each subject area. We suggested that the arguments we heard for a subject-centred approach were fundamentally about *method* (specifically, the desirability of naturalistic interactions with teaching colleagues) and not about *content* (what one might talk about in these interactions).

(Saunders et al. 2002: 22)

Court and Bamber also make the point that the subject of their case study, online assessment, found fertile ground within the scientific discipline which was the context of the case because it was 'grounded in the scientific principles' with which they were familiar and which they respected. This innovation goes with the grain of the context, this time between current and past practices on the one hand and the practices encouraged by the innovation on the other. This is a very significant point, as Lewis Elton (2002) has pointed out. Elton's study showed that the widespread adoption of problem based learning in medical and health related disciplines could be accounted for in terms of its alignment with professional practices in that area. This point takes us back to the issue of transferability: PBL would probably not find such fertile ground in other disciplinary areas.

Theme 2

The Scottish way: a distinctive approach to enhancement

9

Theme 2 introduction

Murray Saunders

The case studies within this theme are drawn from the experience of a policy intervention across a whole university system in Scotland aimed at enhancing learning, teaching, assessment and curriculum there. This intervention has had some unique characteristics that were rooted in an emerging HE sector identity, intentionally nurtured and encouraged as part of a devolved educational and social policy culture. From its inception in 2003, the Quality Enhancement Framework (QEF), coordinated by the Scottish Funding Council with the participation of the Scottish universities themselves, attempted an integrated approach in which 'enhancement' rather than 'assurance' was emphasized in its approach to the quality of university teaching and learning. This approach was welcomed by the sector as an improvement on the previous, assurance based engagement between the Scottish universities and their national sponsors.

The dimensions of the policy or the policy mechanisms have been:

- Enhancement Led Institutional Review (ELIR) (external estimations of institutional quality processes).
- Internal review processes (an institutionally based, self-diagnostic process).
- Student involvement (a range of participatory activities in which students are helped to participate in developmental processes).
- Enhancement themes (activities involving enrichment, alternatives, new frameworks in targeted areas, e.g. employability, flexible learning, the student experience).
- New approaches to public information (engaging and using communicative devices that inform external audiences of university achievements).

We have in the QEF then a complex policy *instrument* designed to shift a culture to embrace enhancement rather than assurance, as the driving force to improve the quality of teaching and learning in Scottish higher education. It is characterized by some distinctive policy *mechanisms* that embody an inventive expression of a national higher education system.

The QEF aspired to a clear break with the emphasis of previous quality

Enhancement Themes

approaches (assurance based) within the Scottish system and still prevalent in other parts of the UK and associated, in the eyes of the HE sector at least, with the role of the Quality Assurance Agency (QAA). It would be a mistake, however, to imply an oppositional relationship between the aspirations of the new framework and the QAA in Scotland. The QAA were fully incorporated into the new initiative as members, even if sometimes uncomfortably, of all key steering groups. The QEF is distinctive, the creation of the sector and sponsoring agencies. There is a sense that it is owned by the higher education 'community', or at least by senior education managers.

Evaluations of the mechanisms suggest they have had uneven effects. Overall, however, the combination of a more developmental approach to institutional review, greater student involvement, a focus on teaching and learning themes and responsiveness to feedback and experience has resulted in a step-change in the way quality processes are understood and practised within the sector. However, the significance of the step-change differs according to the stakeholding group, as we will show in these case studies. Despite this caveat, and given the traditional and sometimes fierce resistance to central initiatives in higher education within the UK, particularly in the teaching and learning domain, the trajectory of the QEF has broad legitimacy for the sector as a whole. Needless to say, this is not always reflected in outcomes which exactly meet the desired intentions, but as an *approach* the QEF is generally welcomed.

Theory of change in action

As a 'theory in action', the QEF rests on a cultural and sectoral analysis that attempts to set itself apart from an overly managerial approach to quality management and development and build on a strong sense of appropriateness, pragmatism and collegiality. The Scottish higher education system is of a size that has allowed the formation of a higher education 'community'. While appreciating distinctiveness, rivalries and differences, evaluations have suggested a relatively high degree of collaboration and discussion among Scottish higher education institutions.

When we look at the strategies the QEF has embodied, we can see that there have been some 'change theory' themes running through the approach. These change theory themes are based on an understanding of the higher education sector in Scotland, of the kind of 'entity' it was, and how it might respond to the thrust of the broad approach to quality being promoted.

Most importantly, unlike many policies or programmes, the QEF in Scotland has had a built-in implementation reality that set it apart from its international neighbours. The policy was an interesting hybrid of ideas of and from the sector itself, from analogous experience elsewhere and a good knowledge of the current research and evaluative literature. That is to say, that it drew on ideas and influences from far and wide, but that there were strong local influences that gave it a distinctive 'Scottishness'. This means

[handwritten margin note: Developmental approach]

that in any turf war over legitimation or credibility, the promoters of policy could (and have) drawn attention to the fact that the main architects were from the sector itself. This is not to say that there is such a thing as a homogeneous higher education 'sector' in Scotland; there are many and – as in any national university sector – rather contrasting experiences and priorities, but the aspirations and interests in the approach were, in an important sense, known and shared.

So, the most obvious strategy or change theory theme within the QEF was to use the expertise in Scotland, informed by international experience, to create a Scottish solution. This characteristic has been an important part of the 'uniqueness' of the QEF as a policy 'instrument' and has been a core dimension of the way in which the approach has been 'home-grown', managed and developed. This enabled a familiarity, an ownership and a legitimation that other forms of implementation strategy might find hard to emulate. We term this a theory of *'consensual development'*.

From the start of the QEF there was awareness that disgruntlement with quality assurance processes, which was quite common in the UK (Saunders et al. 2006: 5), and the wish to do something different, was no guarantee that a feasible and better approach could be created. However, in Scotland there was the priceless advantage that their self-governing system comprised just 20 higher education institutions. This made it possible to assemble a distinctively Scottish alternative to current quality assurance practices. Since control of higher education was located with the Scottish Assembly (now the Scottish government) and since there was considerable interest among officials and agencies in the creation of a distinctively Scottish approach to quality, the scene was set for new thinking.

What emerged was 'home-grown' but not 'home-spun'. Scottish, certainly, but based on the pooling of expertise and knowledge of literatures on teaching, learning, change and quality from a wide range of sources, all shot through with a commitment to enhancing students' experiences as learners. In other words, QEF brought right to the fore the simple and powerful idea that the purpose of quality systems in higher education is to improve student experiences and, consequently, their learning.

Distinctively, the QEF has had a commitment to:

- Students and the continuing enhancement of their learning in higher education.
- Partnerships between agencies (such as the Scottish Funding Council, the Quality Assurance Agency and the Higher Education Academy), higher education institutions (as can be seen by the formation of the Scottish Higher Education Enhancement Committee, a self-organizing operation with a continued commitment to working QEF through the system), and other stakeholders (most distinctively seen in the active involvement of students and student bodies in QEF).
- A theory of educational change that placed far more weight on consensual approaches than on the more coercive stances embedded in some

quality assurance regimes. The approach emerged from serious discussion and thinking.

- A culture shift – away from top–down compliance inducing processes to participative and critical supported self-evaluation; away from audit and towards improvement; away from ruffling the surface of higher education practices and towards permeating the system with practices compatible with the QEF; away from metrics driven judgements of achievement and towards more sensitive forms of evidence of cultural change.
- Reflexivity, in the sense of exposing QEF itself to evaluation from the very beginning.

Evaluation was valued for the contributions it could make to the enhancement of QEF itself, even as QEF was working out what it would mean to have a higher education system committed to quality *enhancement*.

This raises questions about the degree to which stakeholders in Scotland will make QEF central to the further development of a distinctively Scottish approach to higher education in general and to organic, self-sustaining approaches to teaching, learning, assessment and other aspects of curriculum. Our case studies address this 'realization' process directly.

Permeation and change on the ground

The permeation of a new approach means a shift in day-to-day practices, using different knowledge resources within a different set of priorities. It may well be the case that the step-change is beginning to enrich day-to-day practices but the evidence from middle managers is uncertain.

Complex change of this sort cannot be reduced to a simple or easily identifiable line of determination. We refer here to quality of the humdrum, daily practice based kind, which is yet to be proved a prominent feature. Epidemiological or environmental metaphors of 'contagion' or 'climate change' might be more apt in this kind of context. That the QEF depends on creating 'affordances' is pertinent, which is to say a general climate and specific environmental features that are sympathetic to proposed changes and allowing the situated creativity of teaching groups, departments, schools and institutions to make of it what they will.

We do know from the evaluations (e.g. Saunders et al. 2006), however, that senior managers are positive and accept the legitimacy of the QEF. Those working with a specific brief to support teaching and learning are similarly positive; middle managers are overall aware of the approach and the qualitative data suggests many are seeing some positive effects. The student experience suggests overall an inclusive and productive relationship with departments in which they consider their voice is heard and more importantly, acted upon. The evaluations also suggest that, in general, students believe that they are experiencing positive teaching and learning experiences.

There is a gap in our understanding (apart from the experiential professional intuitions we all share) of how engagement with an enhancement-led culture of teaching and learning at the 'frontline' might be encouraged. Evaluations point to some 'disablers': the competing demands made on university teachers; uncertain rewards for a commitment to teaching; a view that the frontline already knows how to teach creatively; and the uncertain relationship between the enhancement themes and daily practices. It is likely that QEF will continue to consider ways in which teachers may be supported in enhancing their everyday practices.

The way forward

As we noted in Theme 1, the UK-wide framework of support for teaching and learning through the subject centre network embodies a strong theory of change which involves exerting influence through the disciplines with relatively high autonomy of action at the level of the individual subject centre. Within Scotland, the subject centre network and the HE Academy are aware of the QEF approach, and are evolving their work in Scotland to take account of specific national circumstances and differences. We suggest that the positive moves to connect the various UK-wide opportunities for support in Scotland have increased the possibilities of a joined-up approach, while still embodying a 'Scottish' feel, and have gone some way to address some of the 'dislocations' which can happen in a multiagency environment. Among the possibilities suggested in evaluations of the QEF (Saunders et al. 2006, 2007) has been the idea of subject 'nodes' within Scotland, still within the overall Enhancement framework but building on geographical accessibility and interchange between groups of practitioners that arise from HEA events or enhancement activities within Scotland. This is an interesting example of how a clear national orientation can offer an 'affordance' for further local developments which draws in a range of other initiatives.

The case studies within this second theme in the book express the experience of this theory of consensual development from different perspectives. It is easy to be seduced by the warm glow suggested by a discourse of consensus in Scotland. What our cases show is that stakeholder experience of complex interventions of this kind is hugely variable depending on where they sit within the system. In recognizing this maxim, we have contributions (Davidson, Sharpe and Miller, Chapter 10) which depict the QEF from a national perspective, where architects of the approach reflect on their experience and emphasize the consensual dimension. Moving to the way in which institutions have negotiated the meaning of the QEF, and its implications for the way systemic practice in quality procedures might be adjusted, we have the contribution by Mason et al. (Chapter 11). This case demonstrates the approach which one university took to using the QEF to promote the institutional enhancement of learning and teaching, with varied results. We argue elsewhere in the book that a locus of consideration for change in

HE should always circulate around how departments respond to internal and external dynamics, pressures and influences. This level of negotiation and accommodation and, again, the variety of results, is explored in Chapter 12 by Edward. It is interesting to note that the capacity of departments to adapt and reinterpret remains high and is the key unit of influence or mediating force for individual practice. How the QEF (as a policy instrument), through its various mechanisms which are mediated by institutional and departmental processes, is finally played out in terms of individual experience is analysed by Fisher (Chapter 13) in his case.

10

Up and down the implementation staircase: a focus on thematic approaches to change

Alan Davidson
Robert Gordon University, Aberdeen, and Convener of
Universities Scotland Teaching Quality Forum

Norman Sharp
Director, Quality Assurance Agency Scotland

Kenneth Miller
University of Strathclyde, and Convener of the Scottish Higher
Education Enhancement Committee

Genesis and context of the enhancement initiative

The Quality Enhancement Themes is a national-level initiative, intended to support staff in Scottish higher education institutions (HEIs) in enhancing the learning experience of students. It was started by the Scottish Higher Education Funding Council (SHEFC), and implemented in partnership with the sector. The Quality Assurance Agency Scotland (QAAS) administers the initiative, directed by the Scottish Higher Education Enhancement Committee (SHEEC) which includes representatives from higher education institutions and other national organizations.

The Themes are part of a wider approach to quality in Scottish HE. The abandonment in 2001 of the proposed UK-wide approach to external quality review provided an opportunity for the Scottish HE sector to take stock and consider the way forward. SHEFC led a process of reflection and consultation on the outcomes from previous assurance-led approaches to quality and possible models for the future (SHEFC 2001). There was a strong consensus in favour of a shift of emphasis from assurance to enhancement, and this led to the development of a strategic national approach, comprising five elements that became known as the Quality Enhancement Framework, summarized in Table 10.1.

SHEFC went out to consultation (SHEFC 2002a), highlighting the proposed features of the Quality Enhancement Themes initiative:

- Annual themes in both curriculum and cross-curriculum areas.
- Identification and dissemination of good practice from Scotland and beyond, and encouragement of embedding this in Scottish HE.
- Opportunity for professional development and activity by practitioners at the 'chalkface'.
- Outcomes in the form of reports and active engagement by institutions.
- Operation in partnership with the sector, including UK-wide development bodies and an international dimension.

Responses to this consultation (SHEFC 2002b) were diverse; there was general support for the principle and objectives, but also a number of concerns. It was felt that the initiative might be overambitious. There were worries that the initiative might be launched without proper funding or effective planning. Respondents also wished to influence the scope and definition of themes, with a preference for generic themes which encouraged the engagement of subject practitioners.

Controversies

Apart from the concerns noted above, there is little reported evidence of controversy within the sector; the initiative does however relate to a number of issues that are identified in the literature as controversial or potential points of tension. The first of these was an overall approach to quality that attempted to combine both assurance, for accountability, with enhancement. Second, and following from this, a single agency, QAA Scotland, would have responsibility for leading and administering both external institutional review and the Quality Enhancement Themes. Third, there was some concern about possible 'compliance' responses by institutions, in which

Table 10.1 The Scottish Quality Enhancement Framework

A comprehensive programme of subject reviews, to be run by institutions themselves.

Enhancement-led Institution level Review (ELIR) which involved all Scottish HE institutions over a four-year cycle.

Improved forms of public information about quality, based on addressing the different needs of a range of stakeholders, including students and employers.

A greater voice for student representatives in institutional quality systems, supported by a new national development service.

A national programme of quality enhancement themes, aimed at developing and sharing good practice in learning and teaching in higher education.

---

engagement with the Themes would be targeted and calculated to benefit external review outcomes. Fourth, there were tensions regarding the ownership of enhancement; at the national level, the LTSN was involved from the start, but there is evidence of some early tensions with the newly formed successor organization, the Higher Education Academy. Similarly, within institutions, there were potential tensions among those with responsibilities for quality assurance, educational development, educational research and staff development.

Policy trajectory

The policy trajectory for the Themes initiative over time is presented in Table 10.2.

Milestones in this trajectory were in three categories: the genesis and start-up of the initiative, the working periods of each of the individual themes,

Table 10.2 Policy trajectory timeline

2001	Abandonment of the proposed UK-wide approach to quality review. SHEFC publishes thoughts on a future approach for Scotland (SHEFC HE55/01).
	Formation of the Quality Working Group representing sector stakeholders, SHEFC, Universities-Scotland, QAA Scotland, LTSN and student representation.
2002	SHEFC consultation on the proposed new approach to quality (SHEFC HEC 2002/03) and responses to this consultation (SHEFC HE29/02).
2003	SHEFC update on quality issues, including announcement of first two Themes.
	Year 1 of Theme working, with the launch of two Themes: Assessment and Responding to Student Needs.
	First Enhancement Themes National Conference.
2004	Year 2 of Theme working, with the launch of two Themes: Employability and Flexible Delivery.
	Second Enhancement Themes National Conference.
2005	Sector discussion about the future of the Themes, leading to the development of a Five Year Rolling Plan and the formation of the Scottish Higher Education Enhancement Committee (SHEEC) to direct the Themes initiative.
	Year 3 of Theme working, with launch of three Themes, the First Year, Research–Teaching Linkages and Integrative Assessment.
2006	Third Enhancement Themes National Conference.
2007	Fourth Enhancement Themes National Conference.
2007	Publication of final report of external evaluation of the Quality Enhancement Framework.

and developments in the implementation and management of the initiative. A very significant feature of the initiative is the way in which the management of implementation, and the working of individual themes has evolved, and continues to evolve, informed by evaluation and reflection. This is discussed below.

The Policy intentions at a macro level are illustrated using an 'implementation staircase' model in Figure 10.1, and the steps in a typical individual theme are illustrated in Figure 10.2. These models provide references for the analysis and conclusions, below.

Systematic evaluation was built into the approach, in two broad forms. First, there was routine evaluation of individual elements of the QEF by the organization(s) responsible, which informed ongoing dialogue between the partners. Second, a longitudinal independent evaluation was commissioned from a research team at the start of the new approach. The reports from this inform discussion of outcomes in this chapter.

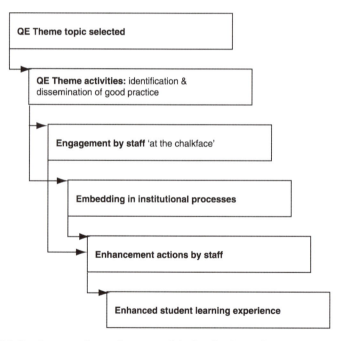

Figure 10.1 Implementation staircase model of policy intention

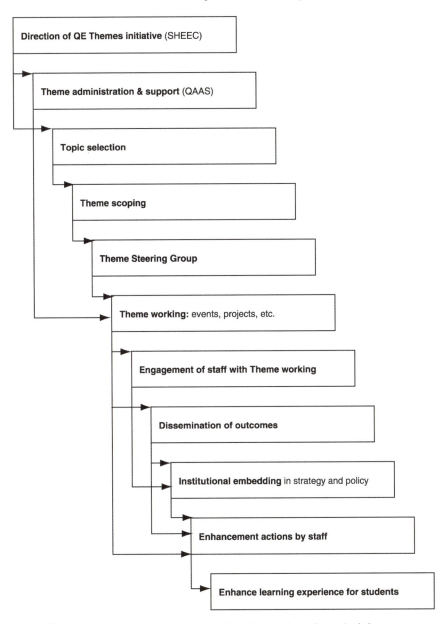

Figure 10.2 Implementation staircase model of operation of a typical theme

Analysis

Analysis of the strategy highlights factors at two levels. At the general level of the Quality Enhancement Framework, a number of factors are significant in the strategic approach. The first factor is a concept of quality, and the purpose of quality systems, that emphasized improvement (or enhancement). This concept of enhancement was about change, involving managed risk-taking. Another factor was an evaluative, reflexive approach: evaluation was built-in from the start, outcomes were discussed critically and openly, and led to progress in the development. Finally, there was recognition of the national context, a diverse, compact and collaborative HE sector, but with an international outlook. At the more specific level of the Themes initiative, the following factors are significant. There was a pragmatic view that the focus was on students and their learning, through the actions of staff who teach and support them. There was, again, recognition of the national context, and that themes are about common problems and shared approaches, but with recognition of, and space to reflect, institutional diversity.

The external evaluation explored the strategic approach, and the factors described above can be recognized within the general approach summarized as 'home grown' and 'consensual development':

> So, the most obvious strategy or theory theme within the QEF was to use the expertise in Scotland, informed by international experience, to create a Scottish solution. This, as we point out above, enabled a familiarity, an ownership and a legitimation that other forms of implementation strategy might find hard to emulate. We term this a theory of 'consensual development.'
>
> Secondly, and linked to the first point above, a series of steering arrangements was put into place that embedded advice on strategy in the sector. Voices could be heard, disgruntlement could be given a platform and the tentacles of informal representation and sounding went deep into the sector. Through these arrangements, a way of operating emerged that had a tone, a discourse and some professional networks that were distinctively Scottish.
>
> (Saunders et al. 2006: 10)

With specific reference to the Themes, the external evaluation found that the approach was not contentious, but that there had been problems of detail, and, particularly in the early stages, issues of timescale and outputs. It noted specific aspects of consensual development, highlighting evaluative and collegiate feedback, steering arrangements that enabled local voices to be heard, and responsive management.

A simple interpretation of the implementation staircase model would suggest a specific sequence of intended outcomes: academic staff interact with a theme, then change their practice, in ways that enhance the student learning experience.

The external evaluation reports practitioner engagement, but acknowledges that institutions are better placed to evaluate this. There is a focus on ongoing work, with longer engagement with the themes, guided in part by the recommendations of the Joint Quality Review Group (SFC 2007). It acknowledges also realities of timescale for change in HE, and attribution – academic staff may use ideas from an initiative such as the Themes, but neither know nor need to know the origin of these ideas within the Themes.

The external evaluation reflects on some of the problematic aspects, particularly in the early stages of the initiative, highlighting concerns about the number of themes and speed of roll out. However, it notes how the overall strategy has evolved, shaped by evaluative and collegiate feedback, and a willingness of the agencies to listen to the sector. These strategic responses included a shift from an initial model of two new themes each year, to a rolling plan, and the formation of a new committee to oversee the evolution and implementation of the Themes. The wider significance of this new group was noted:

> Another key development is that the quality enhancement themes are now planned and directed through SHEEC (the Scottish Higher Education Enhancement Committee) rather than directly by QAA or SFC. This committee was established in 2005 and is made up of senior institutional staff with responsibility for teaching and learning, with support provided by QAA Scotland. This body has signalled a step change in the approach to how quality processes within institutions might be supported and developed with a wide ranging set of resources and advice based on the institution as the unit of analysis.
>
> (Saunders et al. 2007: 20)

Reflection on ways in which the management and working of Themes has progressively changed provides further evidence of the 'consensual development' noted above. The most recent themes have included more systematic linkages to institutions, with each institution being asked to identify an institutional coordinator for each theme. There have also been development projects on specific topics, or associated with specific subject discipline groups.

Our learning

The themes are continuing, and 'learning to do it better' informed by evaluation and dialogue has been a hallmark of the initiative. The following learning points and shifts in practice are significant from a strategic change perspective. First, concerns from institutions about enhancement overload; this led to a reduction in the speed and extent of rollout of new themes, and changes to directing the initiative, discussed below. Second, introduction of a more systematic, structured means of directing the programme and individual themes, through the formation of SHEEC. This has promoted more systematic engagement by institutions, and embedding the themes in institutional strategic agendas. Third, benefits and shifts in ways of working of individual themes. Early themes tended to focus on events and reports; later teams have moved towards project working, at institutional level, and by subject or topic groups of practitioners.

The language and concepts of social practice theory can be used to analyse the initiative. A typical theme is directed at communities of practice, with the objective of promoting changes within those communities of practice. These ideas are illustrated in Figure 10.3 and discussed below.

Engaging with communities of practice, both existing and new

A typical early stage of working of a Theme involved engaging with the literature, and with a range of communities; within HEIs in Scotland, the wider UK, and internationally. Objectives were to find out what was going on

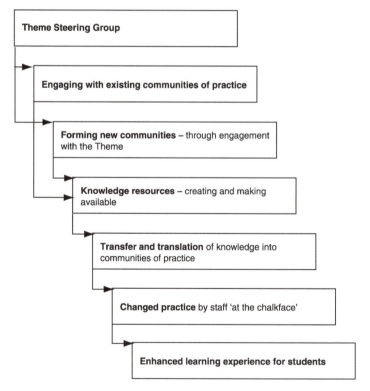

Figure 10.3 Implementation staircase model illustrating engagement with communities of practice concepts

around the topic of the Theme, and more specifically to identify experts, examples of good practice, trends and directions of travel and common problems. Besides starting to create a knowledge resource, this engagement typically helped define the shape of the Theme and the approach to engaging with Scottish HEIs.

The working of a Theme led to the creation of new, sometimes temporary, communities of practice. The Scottish Higher Education Enhancement Committee (SHEEC) could itself be considered a new community of practice that came into being to support and direct the working of the Themes initiative; it was not imposed, it evolved. The group of people involved in leading the Theme, the steering group and other key players, themselves constituted a national level community that progressively built up shared knowledge and experience relating to the Theme topic. This could be mirrored in sub-teams leading projects within the Theme, also within institutions through groups of staff who engaged with the work of the Theme, for example a group of staff with specific roles and interests in teaching the first year. A team could also trigger off-shoot communities through linked organizations. For example, the Employability Theme triggered additional funding and the creation of a new group, the Scottish Higher Education Employability Network, to continue work following the formal completion of the Employability Theme.

Knowledge resources, transfer, translation and changed practice

The product of a Theme could be considered as the creation of knowledge resources and making these available to potential users. These took a hard form in reports and conference communications, and a softer, more tacit form in learning by those who engaged with the Theme. The intention was to transfer these knowledge resources into local communities of practice, such as an academic department or a group of teachers in a subject. This was either encouraged or managed through institutional policy, or more informally and voluntarily, through individual enthusiasm, word of mouth or browsing. It seems likely that there was a process of translation, making the knowledge meaningful in the context. This contextual application of the new knowledge could stimulate and shape changes in practice by staff within the local community. The intended objective would be enhancement of the learning experience of students associated with that staff community.

Conclusions

At this stage, four key messages stand out. First, the importance of clarity of focus and purpose, in this case on students and their learning. Second, the holistic joined-up approach; the Themes are part of a bigger whole, the Quality Enhancement Framework, which is underpinned by a clear conceptual view of quality. Third, continuing development informed by systematic evaluation and dialogue with stakeholders. The way that themes are managed and work has progressively evolved, shaped by reflection on experience. There has been no prescriptive template, each theme has had its own character, reflecting the scoping and the views of its steering committee. Finally, the significance of context. The compact and collaborative nature of the Scottish HE sector, and the commitment to partnership working are significant features of the initiative.

11

Carrots but no sticks: resource-led enhancement

Colin Mason
Unitec, New Zealand

Anita Laidlaw and Gerry Humphris
University of St Andrews, Scotland

Veronica Bamber
Queen Margaret University

Introduction

This chapter explains how a particular institution has used the Enhancement Theme initiative to complement its internal L&T improvement processes. The case explains the institutional mechanism (a carefully thought through system of project grants) and gives an example of how these project grants have helped to develop the curriculum in medicine. Groups of staff who apply for grants tend to reapply in future bids, building on what has been achieved with the first grant. Synergies with subject centre initiatives can also be exploited. The result is that the small amounts of money available for project funding produce greater results than the initial money might suggest.

The context: the educational developer's view

SALTIRE is the University of St Andrews' learning and teaching support unit. It provides guidance, advice, training courses and funding opportunities for the development of innovative teaching strategies in learning and teaching for staff, as well as supporting students across the whole university.

In 2004–05, SALTIRE introduced a new funding initiative, the Strategic Enhancement of Learning Fund (SELF) specifically designed to promote innovation addressing the Scottish Enhancement Themes, as part of the Quality Enhancement Framework approach to quality assurance for teaching.

SELF submissions are invited from all staff within the university and competitive bids are submitted for evaluation by an expert panel. Criteria encourage collaboration across schools, as well as projects which are student centred, or which exploit research and research findings.

Role of the enhancement themes

The change of approach to quality assurance inherent in the Enhancement Themes promoted a more proactive attitude to improving student learning experiences in higher education in Scotland. At the time the first SELF bids were invited, all four of the initial themes (Responding to Student Needs; Assessment; Employability; and Flexible Delivery) addressed in the first two years of the new Enhancement-Led Institutional Review (ELIR) approach, focused on the issue of improving learning experiences. However, inevitably this depends upon redesign of all aspects of 'teaching' in order for students to realize benefits, and thus requires staff to seize the initiative.

In subsequent rounds of SELF project bids, additional criteria were added, to exploit the ongoing and new Enhancement Themes: the First Year, Integrative Assessment and Research–Teaching Linkages. So, members of staff were constrained by the criteria for successful bids to target their innovative ideas for teaching redesign to meet aspects of these Themes. This was not simply an instrumental approach by SALTIRE but one founded upon the understanding that the Enhancement Themes were not only worthy in themselves, but also key pedagogic aspects of good curriculum design. Introducing the SELF project funding was not controversial, since previous small grant projects, unrelated to the Enhancement Themes, had already become well established. SELF was a further extension, albeit with more constraints, for funding teaching innovation ideas.

Issues and successes

A feature of the SELF funded projects was that a relatively restricted group of staff was successfully seeking funding. The *dissemination* of projects was further restricted to mainly the same group, despite efforts to attract wider audiences through extensive advertising. In addition, some individuals and groups were establishing a pattern of successful bidding. This is perhaps reminiscent of the positive cycle of successful research grant writing, where it is vital to gain an initial grant, however small, that subsequently facilitates being successful in future, often larger, grant proposals: 'To they that hath, more shall be given'.

SALTIRE was keen to widen the group of staff and schools that were actively engaging with the Enhancement initiative. One key issue was the way in which dissemination of project outcomes was to be organized. It was decided to add a series of project dissemination activities to the programme for newly appointed staff, 'Introduction to Teaching in Higher Education in a Research-Intensive University', arranged at the beginning of the academic year, a key event in providing support for teaching. In addition to academic staff, teaching fellows, research fellows and part time tutors are invited to this event. Members of staff who had been successful in their SELF project bids were invited to give presentations to illustrate innovative approaches to teaching and learning to new colleagues. This would fulfil their obligation for disseminating the findings of their projects. Presentations were either by poster (project work in progress or still at an early stage) or by oral communication (for completed or substantially completed projects). Subsequent to this new process of dissemination, more newly appointed staff submitted project bids that were successful. They have then gone on to bid for further project funding for slightly different aspects of the first project or a completely different idea altogether.

One aspect that is worth commenting upon is the small sums of money (maximum £2500) awarded to successful bids, and how staff chose to spend the money. Many projects have used the funding to pay students, predominantly postgraduates, though more recently, undergraduates too, as 'research assistants' on the projects. Perhaps they ought to be re-entitled 'teaching development assistants', reflecting their functional role. This has created not only paid employment to assist in the funding of their degree programmes but has also contributed substantially to the development of the students' technical skills (especially for those projects involving e-learning approaches) and a range of other transferable skills such as team working, collaborating, taking initiative, leadership and presentation skills. Also, members of staff gain opportunities to develop their project management skills, supervisor skills and report writing as well as increasing their repertoire of technical skills (e.g. e-learning) and are forced to consider pedagogical issues in their redesigned teaching.

One of the greatest successes has been the collaborative projects established between schools (e.g. classics and computer science, psychology and medicine). Established staff with a successful track record continue to apply for more funding, but a substantial majority of established staff (and some schools) have, to date, still not become involved. This group remains a challenge for engagement.

The medicine case example: the academics' view

Communication skills teaching within the medical school is a relatively recent addition, which provides an opportunity to build teaching practice with comparative ease, without the constraint of previous traditional approaches. Hence we can improve our methods and attempt to provide new learning experiences for our students. However, to develop new techniques or novel delivery methods sometimes requires more resources than are available within a limited teaching budget. Although ideas were not limited, funding to implement these ideas was not readily available. Centrally, the university advertised a call for bids for the first round of the Scottish Enhancement themes based teaching and learning funding. This provided us with the opportunity to apply for funding to instigate some of our proposals.

After an initial successful bid, and because we had several other projects we were keen to implement, we thereafter kept up to date with other funding calls. If one of our projects fitted the call we submitted a bid. We now have a small programme of teaching and learning enhancement projects focusing on communication skills development, which is being rolled out within our skills teaching curriculum. Over the past three years, these projects have instigated a considered approach to gain indepth understanding of students who are underperforming. The medical skills curriculum has gradually been improved by building on project funding.

The projects

To date we have three main projects based on three of the Scottish Enhancement Themes: Flexible Delivery, Assessment and the First Year Experience. These projects are now in varying stages of completion from planning to completed and implemented.

The first project was based on the theme of Flexible Delivery. We wanted to introduce a new method of facilitation within our second year communication skills simulated patient workshops. During such workshops, actors play the role of a patient while a student interacts with them. Workshops run with groups of 8–10 students and while one student is interacting with the simulated patient the rest of the students and the facilitator watch the performance. When a student cannot proceed with the interaction they pause and a discussion takes place before a second student takes over the interviewing of the simulated patient. This type of workshop can cause anxiety in some students who find being watched while interacting with the simulated patient difficult. We wanted to introduce the reflection-on-action facilitation method with the aim of allowing these workshops to be run with larger groups of students (up to 20). The reflection-on-action method was developed originally by Professor Anders Baerheim from the University of Bergen (Baerheim and Alraek 2005: 1–3). It works by focusing discussion during these workshops on how to proceed with the interaction rather than on a student's performance. Students therefore know they will not be openly criticized and should feel more comfortable performing in front of peers. To evaluate the introduction of this teaching method the workshops were video recorded and the student simulated patient interaction was analysed. A questionnaire was also completed. Results were very promising, with students wholeheartedly supporting the workshops and the teaching methods.

This project was extended by a second successful application for funding the following year. Our introduction of the reflection-on-action method had been successful with a cohort of students inexperienced in methods of communication skills learning. But in the intervening year the curriculum had changed, with the new second year cohort experiencing small group communication skills teaching methods during their first year. We wanted to examine whether the reflection-on-action method would allow us to successfully teach these experienced students in larger groups using similar techniques. This project has also been completed, and although students who had previous experience of small group teaching were not as enthusiastic as inexperienced students, they did still prefer such workshops to other non-simulated patient teaching methods and appreciated that they learned more from them. Interestingly, this was the case even though students admitted to becoming apprehensive prior to a simulated patient workshop, but not prior to student role play workshops. Overall funding allowed us to introduce this innovative teaching method and, importantly, produced the evidence base to ensure we felt confident that it was achieving its aims.

Our second project was based on the Theme of Assessment. Currently we assess communication skills in practical exams where students interact with a simulated patient in front of an examiner. This gives us a good estimate of their practical skills level, but not why they interact as they do. This is particularly important in students who are having difficulty with their practical skills.

A method of assessing students' theoretical knowledge and cognitive approach to communication skills (the Objective Structured Video Exam (OSVE)) was originally developed in Liverpool by Humphris and Kaney (2000). Students congregated in a lecture theatre, watched a communication skills interaction on video and then answered a variety of questions relating to the clip and to communication skills theory. Different types of questions probed different aspects of the student's communicative abilities, such as the critical evaluation of the skills they had observed and projection of how they would respond in a similar communicative scenario. Unfortunately, the OSVE proved to be very labour intensive to administer and there were also difficulties with ensuring each student experienced similar audio/visual levels. A group from Amsterdam Medical School developed a computerized version of this assessment method called ACT (Hulsman et al., 2004), which solved several of the problems of the lecture theatre based version. We applied for funding to purchase this software and, in collaboration with Amsterdam, to develop it for use in the UK. This involved the production of two short video clips of doctor–patient interactions, and the linking of transcripts to the clips. Questions could also be written, linking these to both the video clip and the transcripts such that assessments could be compiled.

This software has now been piloted with several of our third year students, who have previously only experienced practical examination of their communication skills. Thus far the assessment method and the software itself have been favourably received, drawing comments such as 'I think the video sections definitely keep your attention and it makes you think more about how you would say something' and 'I think it's a good way of making you think about communication skills. Often these are skills that you develop and use without actually thinking about, so this aids in that respect'. This project has since attracted external funding from the Higher Education Academy Subject Centre for Medicine, Dentistry and Veterinary Medicine to produce more video clips for use within this software. In the future we aim to introduce this software to provide formative assessment to all students to complement our existing practical, summative assessment. This should provide a method of determining where problems arise for students who are having difficulties with their practical communication skills. In addition we are interested in the longer term to test some theoretical ideas about the basis of cognitive schemas informing communication behaviour.

Our third project was based on the Theme of the First Year Experience. Our first year medical undergraduate students have their communication skills assessed during a practical examination, as described above. Currently we have no way of assessing what aspect in their approach to communication skills students who fail this exam are having difficulties with. We applied for funding to purchase the Micro-expression Training Tool (METT) to help such students (Ekman 2004a). The recognition of facial micro expressions (rather than the more obvious major expressions) is thought to be important in a doctor–patient interaction (Ekman 2004b). The METT software assesses a person's ability to recognize micro expressions and also provides a training tool to improve their capabilities. This project is yet to be completed but we aim to run a pilot project for the use of the software with our first year students after their first practical communication skills exam. Students who fail this exam will complete a METT assessment and training session, and then complete a second assessment to determine any improvement. Comparisons between these students and those who received high scores in their practical assessment will also be made.

Analysis

The internal central funding programme enabled us to implement this series of research projects designed to improve our current teaching, assessment and learning opportunities for medical undergraduate students. This allowed us to instigate a review of how students learn communication skills and how we can help those students who are experiencing difficulties in improving their communication skills.

The funding calls focused our bids around the Enhancement Themes. The learning and teaching support unit behind the funding calls, SALTIRE, also provided the opportunity for successful grant holders to disseminate information about their individual projects to each other and also to the wider university audience by the organization of a day of seminars.

Discussion about the projects was widespread and useful. As many projects were not yet complete, helpful comments and suggestions were taken on board and incorporated or new ideas for future improvement generated.

This improved communication and provided opportunity for collaboration between different schools within the university.

Our learning

The introduction of SELF, with a focus specifically on the QAA Enhancement Themes, was based on the same fundamental principle – utilizing an incentive driven process (competitively funded project initiatives) – to encourage staff to redesign their teaching at the module or sub-module level. This strategy has emerged from practice and experience. The initial use of voluntary attendance at dissemination workshops or conferences was avoided because of experience of poor sign-up and attendance at similar events. Tying dissemination presentations to an induction programme for new staff provided a captive audience. Further, as the senior management team in the institution became increasingly aware of the Enhancement Themes, greater kudos was attached to these funded project initiatives, for example in the annual progress review as part of probation. Further, these activities were increasingly being used by staff to highlight a case for promotion (at least to senior lecturer level) based upon innovative teaching. Finally, the senior management group decided to showcase the project funding initiatives both in the reflective account and at the first of two visits by an external team when the university was reviewed as part of the Enhancement-Led Institutional Review process in 2006.

The major lessons from the strategy of linking grant funding to the Enhancement Themes are that:

- The instigation of a resource to allow ideas of enhancement to be brought to fruition has worked very well as a change incentive.
- Further changes of social practice then occurred, building on the initial impetus.
- Once funding was discovered by an individual or group within the university, they did this knowing that future funding calls would also be occurring. Therefore ideas that had previously been dormant (due to difficulty of instigation, lack of resource) could be worked up into a project proposal. The awareness level was boosted, and ideas were turned into proposals where previously they would not have developed further than ideas.
- A more comprehensive programme of change becomes possible if the scheme allows for applicants to return with further ideas to promulgate in the area of work. However, there is a danger that a narrower range of innovative ideas, albeit with greater depth within a particular subject or discipline, is promulgated. And success breeds success, so the possibility of the whole scheme evolving into an ongoing mini research exercise for one staff group lurks ominously below the horizon. Should a limit be placed upon the number of related project bids a particular teaching

team may make? Should we compromise high standards in favour of making additional improvements to teaching across more, so far not engaged parts of the institution?

- Through the seminar days where different projects were presented it was possible to discover what projects were being funded and discuss with other grant holders particular problems/issues/new ideas. This informs and encourages cross-department collaborations and exchange of ideas as well as of good practice.
- Innovations in other institutions may not be directly transferable to another university and course, but innovations can be translated to a different context. Small amounts of funding building on work done elsewhere, especially where expensive technology development is concerned, can be highly productive.

12

PASS the word

Norrie S. Edward
Robert Gordon University, Aberdeen, Scotland

Introduction: the scheme

One of the early Scottish enhancement Themes related to 'Responding to Student Needs', including pastoral and academic support. A major focus was on meeting the needs of first year students, including via 'the use and implementation of peer support' (QAA 2005: 9). The Peer-Assisted Study Scheme (PASS) arose from this initiative, as colleagues at Robert Gordon University considered specific actions to improve academic support, without placing excessive additional burden on academic staff. PASS brings trained senior student tutors together with first year students in the same course. The term 'peer tutoring' has described many different types of arrangement, but here it implies student tutors guiding tutees to their own understanding. They do not teach. Three schools in the university, engineering (SE), nursing (SN) and art (SA), introduced PASS in session 2004/05. The school ethos and the objectives of the schemes differ fundamentally in the three schools, and these differences illustrate how enhancement Theme outcomes are enacted differently in different settings.

Why PASS?

Peer tutoring has featured in education from the days of the ancient Greeks and was widely used in medieval universities. In today's universities, however, it has largely been supplanted by teacher-led education, although there is a resurgence of interest in its use. For students, the key is interaction on academic issues, whether it be with peers or with teachers (Harvey et al. 2006: 116), but analysis of the interaction in *peer* tutoring has shown qualitative differences in the interactions between teacher and learner. The small group of RGU staff involved in introducing peer tutoring felt that it might help students develop their problem solving skills: Larkin et al. (1980), have termed expert problem solving the 'knowledge-development' (KD) approach, working forward from the given information into the unknown. Novice problem solvers, in contrast, use the means–end (ME) approach, working from the unknown to the given information. The novice, in effect, reads the problem and selects what appears to be a related answer; typically, they try to answer an equation before considering what is given and what must be derived. Research indicates (e.g. Owen and Sweller 1989) that experts use principles rather than detail to classify problem types, work from data to goal rather than the reverse, have a better memory for relevant problem details, and are versed in problem solving routines. This makes problem solving both more systematic and more reliable. The contention of advocates of peer tutoring is that closer alignment in the problem solving approach of tutor and tutee may resolve misunderstandings more effectively than expert to novice tutoring.

Another reason for considering the potential of peer tutoring was the idea that students might be more likely to engage in group discussion with peers rather than with lecturers. The methodology of pursuing learning by group discussion derives fundamentally from socioconstructivist theory. Not only is learning seen to be a socially constructed phenomenon, but by using tutors who have only recently passed through a stage of development the interaction is maintained within what Vygotsky (1962) termed the learner's 'zone of proximal development'. In this mode, students can be helped to learn by collaborating with more advanced peers (Vygotsky 1978: 86).

Evaluations of peer tutoring (e.g., Kalkowsi 1995) often report that the tutor's gain is as great as that of the tutees. That they should develop communications skills and become more confident might be predicted, but the studies also report gains in domain knowledge comprehension. In the tutoring process, tutors will adopt meta cognitive strategies not only to structuring knowledge but also in probing the learner's difficulties with understanding, comparing this with their own comprehension (cf. Hartman 1990). They may too, perhaps for the first time, pause to consider their own learning processes.

A further advantage of peer tutoring is the prospect that students will be more comfortable in a peer environment. Although Schein (2002) asserts that learning a new topic starts with dissatisfaction generated by facts which conflict with existing beliefs, Schein (2002) also identifies learning anxiety as a restraining force militating against learning. There is ample evidence of the misconceptions of physical principles and their effects which are held by lay people (Edward 2002). These misconceptions are instinctively held, and challenging them may indeed engender acute discomfort. Similarly, semantic redefinition is needed, both in broadening the meanings of familiar words and in attaching more rigid definitions to them. All of this may engender loss of face, which an individual may feel in accepting either that a prior concept is wrong or that their knowledge is deficient. The peer tutoring environment is less threatening than the formal classroom and so this anxiety is lessened. Not only are the tutors more able to explain concepts in a way the novice understands, but they may act as role models and as sources of psychological safety. Of course, there is an inherent danger in the creation of role models, which is that the learner does not take ownership of the new knowledge and that their concepts do not become 'refrozen' (Lewin 1951). There is arguably less danger of this with a peer than with a learned professor. Another danger is that the tutors themselves have misconceptions and transmit these to the tutees. On introducing peer tutoring, those involved were intuitively aware of some of this conceptual background, but were largely carried by conviction rather than theoretical notions. As the project developed over time and staff took a more research informed approach, conviction and theory both came to be questioned in the light of experience.

Implementation of PASS

To start the process, it was felt that a coordinator was needed, and a keen academic from nursing duly volunteered. This provided an organizational hub. Then, with the coordinator's help, engineering recruited seven second year students as tutors for the mechanical engineering (ME) and six third years for the artificial intelligence and robotics (AIR) degree courses. Nursing recruited the coordinator's tutor group which consisted of the 12 students pursuing the paediatric nursing option. These students were trained by a professional consultant over two days, using role playing and other group based activities to help students gain skill in tutoring. Two of the applicants decided to drop out after the training, due to concerns about loss of study time. Art obtained seven third and six second year volunteers and undertook the training independently.

In engineering, the objective was that the student tutors assist the tutees with academic subjects. It was intended that each tutor would be allocated a group and would work on a specified topic each week. In practice, the tutors worked collectively with all students and on any topic they wished to raise. The scheme has run for three years, but uptake by first year students, particularly in mechanical engineering, has been disappointing throughout.

Nursing first year students often find their first clinical placements daunting. So the scheme here was primarily aimed at helping students to understand the requirements and to know what would be expected of them. The nursing course uses alternating eight week blocks of theory and clinical practice. An online discussion forum was set up which allowed communications to continue when the students were on placement. The tutors, in groups of four, each took on a group of about six students.

Since art courses are predominantly studio based and the tutors share one-to-one exploration of first year students' work, the Art School called the scheme 'Peer-Assisted Learning' (PAL), which reflected the concentration on one-to-one studio contact between tutors and tutees, and the emphasis on exploring the ethos and contextuality of study in art. Staff of the school attended the engineering and nursing tutor training and then operated their own tutor training.

Review of experiences in the three schools

Despite repeated exhortations from staff, the anticipated high participation by first years did not materialize. The artificial intelligence and robotics course is relatively small, and here between 40 and 50 percent attended quite regularly. However, only around 10 percent of the mechanical engineering course attended, rather sporadically. The student tutors themselves were the greatest proselytes for the scheme and continually encouraged first year students to participate. Accommodation and timetabling difficulties certainly did not facilitate the running of PASS. For example, lunch breaks and other unpopular times were allocated. This is seen as a priority issue for the future, as logistical obstacles compound students' concerns over the value of the scheme.

Nursing, despite focusing on a clinical component of their course, experienced low tutee participation. The tutors, buoyed by their enjoyment of training, were positive from the outset. Tutors worked with any students who appeared, rather than the intended grouping of tutors with tutees. Here too difficulties around rooming and timetables got the process off to a slow start and impacted on the attendance of tutees. Although the tutors were enthusiastic about the *online* discussion group, first years did not truly engage with it. However, in view of the school's problems with rooming and timetables it is an option worthy of greater consideration in order to achieve some of the putative benefits of a peer support system. The scheme ran for one session only in nursing, but the coordinator is planning to resurrect it.

Art recognized that there were some benefits accruing from PAL, but they decided that the intimate staff to student relationship in the studio served similar functions. The benefits did not justify the investment of staff and student resources in the scheme, and it has been discontinued.

The tutors

In first operation, the recruited tutors in all schools were mainly UK nationals, but in subsequent years in engineering, the only school to have continued the scheme, more applicants have been from overseas – an interesting development which perhaps reflects the wish of overseas students to make the most of their educational opportunities in the university.

Nineteen tutors completed pre-experience questionnaires and 11 of these came from nursing. Eight engineering students completed post-tutoring questionnaires. While statistical analysis is limited by the small scale of data, some tentative patterns appear to have emerged. Indications are that, while recognizing the employability benefits, tutors also genuinely wished to help the junior students. They did not expect their studies to suffer, and indeed the majority expected their subject knowledge to increase. Before they started, tutors felt nervous about their role but the nervousness evaporated during the experience. Almost without exception the respondents said that their communication skills were good, but that they expected to improve them. Post-tutoring questionnaires indicated that respondents confirmed this had been achieved. Tutors were known to be 'lobbying' students to attend, with some success in nursing and in AIR. Interviews revealed great enthusiasm for the scheme among tutors. They believed students had gained and that it had been at worst a qualified success.

The tutees

Informal interviews with engineering and nursing students indicated that logistical issues were the major obstacle to their participation. They had no strong inclinations to participate and so unsuitable times or accommodation were enough to deter them. Otherwise, the most common observation was that a student 'preferred to work on my own'. Suggestions to encourage participation included arrangements such that students would not have to move from one room to another and that tutoring would immediately follow a scheduled class. Times close to lunch or late afternoon would be avoided. It has also been suggested that the tutors should accompany the coordinator when the scheme was being explained to the first year students, and that this should be followed by an informal discussion of the tutors' perceptions of the course. Given these arrangements, students would commence participation in their first week and, if benefits accrued, would continue to participate.

Wins and losses: An analysis

Students have proved reticent in explaining their low participation. Opinions have been equivocal. There are advantages, but not with sufficient value to justify devoting time. Student tutors believed that the meeting time should appear on the timetable from the outset so that it was not seen by students as an add-on, that tutors should join the coordinator in explaining the scheme and that a 'useful' exercise be introduced for the first meeting. This last might be a discussion of assessment expectations and how to gain good grades.

The enduring feature in all schools has been the enthusiasm of the tutors. Their perceptions of the level of success have been much more sanguine than those of the learners on the one hand and the coordinators on the other. The nurse-tutors, for example, talked of good participation in both live and online discussions, whereas the coordinator believed, and students confirm, that attendance was sporadic at best and the VLE served mainly as a chatroom for the tutors.

While none of the schools was overwhelmed with applications, it proved relatively easy to obtain an adequate number of applications from students wishing to be trained as tutors. They were readily convinced of its developmental aspects and of the saleability of the skills gained in the employment market. The training sessions were lively and captured the imagination of the participants. Once trained, they became genuine converts and it was not their own development which then drove them. Rather, the more altruistic motivation to help junior students acquired an almost crusade-like nature.

Chapter 1 maintains that 'power and control at the ground level is a condition of success'. The tutors did not have the power, other than by persuasion, to require the students to attend. It may be that the keys to enhancing attendance are not just to persuade students that the tutors will facilitate their learning, but to persuade them also of the value of enhancing their grades. This may be far from the ideals of the 'community of learners' which Garrison and Anderson (2003: 23) suggest can help to construct and validate new knowledge and to develop capabilities leading to further learning. Critically they maintain that 'such a community encourages cognitive independence'. The community of learners requires social, cognitive and teaching presence. The challenges in peer tutoring are to establish the credentials of the tutors as being the teaching presence, and then to move learners beyond their focus on simply improving their grades.

Recruiting tutors takes planning and some effort, but students are relatively easily convinced of potential employability gains. A presentation and a question and answer handout were prepared and the student tutors responded well to this face-to-face invitation to apply. Good training created a sense of community and ownership of the scheme. The training benefited from having a professional trainer, a mix of nurses and engineers but above all from being group orientated and participative. Tutors are the greatest asset and will vigorously lobby for the scheme. Our aim is to capitalize on this sooner by splitting training into two sessions. In the first, applicants will explore obstacles to participation and develop plans to overcome these, while the second will develop tutoring skills. The mix of female nurses and male engineers facilitated exploration of ethos, learning styles and needs differences among individuals. If a cross-disciplinary mix of trainees can be assembled it is likely to enhance the benefits to the trainees.

Logistics clearly militated against success in both schools. This was the biggest single factor identified as the reason for non-participation by students. Ideally peer tutoring will appear on timetables and should follow a scheduled class. The first meeting might well explore the tutors' experiences rather than academic tutoring, and the importance of what might appear minor detail should not be underestimated; for example, students should be encouraged to arrange furniture to facilitate discussion. Chapter 2 uses the term 'environments for enhancement' in a much broader sense than simply the physical environment. Nevertheless, the lack of suitable premises and inconvenient timings clearly hindered success.

An online discussion forum has appeal, but in this and other contexts where it has been tried participation has been low. This is not surprising, as it is not the obvious place for first year students to seek help. It might be better used after successful classroom tutoring, particularly if a synchronous meeting is initially introduced.

The somewhat disappointing response of students suggests, in change theory terms, that we should seek misalignments in the levels of the system. The aims were similar for the parties involved. Staff, students and to an extent the peer tutors wished to enhance the students' learning. Staff also sought enhanced student achievement rates. Tutors valued the professional development. In terms of the implementation staircase, recruitment and training were readily achieved. Advertising patently failed to convince many of the potential tutees that the benefits justified the sacrifice of their time. This will be tackled by having the peer tutors act as assistants to academic staff tutors in normal scheduled classes. Not only will tutors be more familiar with the current topics, but it will help tutees to understand the type of help which tutors can offer. It is hoped that students will then see the value of peer tutor sessions.

Advice for next time

So what have been the most positive outcomes of PASS? Recruiting motivated applicants has been relatively easy in all schools. All of them attended training and proved to have the skills needed to be good tutors. Their enthusiasm has been the best advertisement for the scheme. Neither the introduction to first year students by a lecturer nor paper and electronic publicity have proved as effective as the lobbying by the tutors. Tutors persisted in promoting the scheme, whatever student numbers they encountered.

Peer tutoring schemes require considerable investment of time by staff and tutors. That the student tutors' investment is repaid in their professional development and so in their employability seems beyond question. The minority of potential tutees who attended tutoring reported benefits. It is clear from our experiences that first year students require convincing that the investment of their time will be worthwhile. Those contemplating introducing schemes should give at least as much attention to how they will 'sell' their scheme to tutees as to tutor training. Peer tutors are enthusiastic champions but similar promotion by academic staff and if possible employers will reinforce the message. Finally, it is paramount to success that the logistics of operation positively promote attendance.

13

Exchange and art: intradisciplinary learning

Gary Fisher
University of Dundee, Scotland

A new era

When a senior colleague, who was a member of the Scottish Higher Education Funding Council,[1] handed me a draft copy of the proposed enhancement document, its significance was immediately evident. As the Associate
Dean of Learning and Teaching in my institution, a Scottish art and design
college, my colleague was interested to have my thoughts and feedback prior
to a consultation response being sent to QAA Scotland. The document
was entirely rational and persuasive, but above all else, clever. Very clever in
the way that institutions would be evaluated on quality from the perspective
of enhancing the student experience. There was the whiff of a moral imperative that quality was no longer a retrospective audit trail, but an assessment of
how you were investing in the experience for your customers, the students.
The enhancement framework would keep institutions on the front foot,
continually trying to move forward.

Two qualms accompanied my general approval. First, would the push to
enhance perpetually induce change for change's sake, with traditional good
practice being branded static? Second, how on earth were they going to put
together the panels of reviewers, including student representation, and train
them for the lengthy ELIR engagements? I will return to these issues later.

The tools of enhancement

This case submission tracks my own individual introduction to enhancement
and a personal journey using the tools of enhancement and incorporating
the introduction of enhancement in my own subject, involvement in institutional review, external reviewing, international reviewing and bringing
an entire sector together to embed enhancement at a national level. In

---

[1] Now the Scottish Funding Council.

particular, the implication of enhancement for the art and design sector is addressed

With the final enhancement document approved and adopted at national level we set about the task of internally reviewing our four courses, architecture, design, television and fine art. I have no doubt that we approached this with a vigour that would not have existed under the old audit trail system. There is uniqueness to art and design education. It stems from the ethos of creativity which underpins most of our courses. If creativity is the core as opposed to the accumulation of knowledge, it stands to reason that a tutor's relationship with a student is different. There is an emphasis on one-to-one dialogue during which the individual's progression and development is given singular attention. It is from this perspective that I maintain that the student experience has always been at the forefront of delivery. Therefore, we immediately connected and identified with the idea of enhancement.

With this tutor–student contact comes a dialogue that allows an immediate responsiveness to student needs and aspirations. Some of the key themes and issues of focus within the enhancement debate were relatively accepted norms within the art and design sector: close mentoring in first year with resulting good retention; ongoing assessment as opposed to large end of year unseen exam papers; flexible delivery; blended assessment; the use of portfolios. However, an ongoing imperative for improvement and larger student numbers, more international students, fewer staff, estate and facilities increasingly not fit for purpose and most critically the changing needs of students and their patterns of learning all add up to a need for change to ensure enhancement can continue to happen.

Of course, any review situation, especially with the enhancement ethos, will not find favour with many academics who cite getting on with the job as the crucial factor, not pandering to external monitoring forces. Cynicism was particularly reserved for the emphasis on student representation on both internal reviews and institutional review. Time spent on review is continually questioned in terms of real long term value to the institution. As previously mentioned, I had reservations about the enormity of training institutional reviewers. The experience of review in my institution proved reservations unfounded. The review panel was rigorous but diplomatic in their probing. At internal subject review the introduction of student reps was a revelation. Original caution about the students' ability to contribute and be critically aware on panels with staff was also unfounded. The perceptive contribution made by student reps was constructive and pivotal in securing an enhanced perspective.

All internal reviews of our four courses happened over a two-year cycle and in prior preparation for the institutional review. We were therefore, as an art and design faculty in the university, able to contribute from a position of strength, having already carried out our own review. A main problem during this lengthy process was shifting staff attention from the collation of facts and defence of current practice to one of an enhancement perspective where improvement is celebrated and a forward thinking strategy articulated.

There was a reluctance to have student voices heard from the beginning. Experience taught us that open dialogue at an early stage was crucial in setting a positive framework for the review document.

Taking enhancement abroad

The confidence gained from the internal and institutional reviews was put to good effect when we began the process of validating two courses with two partner institutions at international level, a postgraduate course in Vancouver and an undergraduate course in Dublin. These would be the first external validations carried out by my university for several years. The experience of enhancement allowed us to approach the rigours of external validation with the knowledge that our own provision and standards had been reviewed with positive outcomes. We carried out the international validations continually looking not only for opportunities to encourage an enhancement ethos abroad, but to further enhance what we do by learning from the strengths evident in our foreign partners. In essence the process of validating these courses was primarily to broaden our knowledge of international practice and bring best practice for students to bear for our partners and us.

As we continued to take our deliberate steps toward improved provision, the question I continually asked was to what extent the national art and design sector was engaging with enhancement – and surely it was time to have a sector-wide debate? The true test of an effective national policy is the degree to which it permeates the sector and embeds itself into the operational workings of all institutions from top to bottom. To test the effectiveness of enhancement in the art and design sector and to share best practice, I organized a conference in Dundee for all nine institutions in Scotland that have art, design and media courses.

Subject level awareness

To support this initiative we approached the Art, Design and Media Subject Centre, part of the Higher Education Academy. Their strong interest was not only to help develop enhancement in the Scottish sector but to encourage institutions in England, Wales and Northern Ireland to attend, given the advanced state of enhancement in Scotland, compared to other countries. Fifty-five delegates came to the conference. Every art, design and media department was represented. Most had attended enhancement events but crucially there had been no subject/discipline specific forum for enhancement. Given the specific nature of our creative education sector, there were undoubtedly ways in which we could contribute to and gain from the national debate. Three keynotes were delivered on the three enhancement Themes of Assessment, Employability and the Learning Environment. The workshops thereafter discussed the wider ramifications of these three areas. Enthusiastic debate ensued between lecturers of graphics, fine art, textiles, history, theory, drama, media, etc. Sharing of issues produced a revelatory outpouring of similar situations with possible solutions, and strategies for future improvement. It was evident that similar issues and concerns existed across the sector, and there was a thirst to find and share best practice. The intention now is to meet annually with three different themes and grow a cohesive enhancement trajectory.

Hindsight and change

Greater awareness and confidence has stemmed from the range of enhancement activities. The apprehension that perpetual change for change's sake would lead to the loss of traditional good practice has been unfounded. Rather, the ongoing financial pressures in higher education demand change and with an enhancement framework there is the possibility that we try to make change advantageous, and greater emphasis is placed on student perceptions. We need to take the negativity out of change. Increasingly we will need to react spontaneously to a world which changes with every new technical advance. Ongoing curriculum adjustments/enhancement are a yearly reality, hence a new mindset. Twenty years ago you could return to an academic year without any change for periods of three years or more. The proactivity implicit in this new scenario should not only reside with the usual suspects who regularly turn up at conferences and try to preach new thinking back at home. While recognizing the important part that students played in our enhancement review activities, there is a strong need to develop ideas on how this involvement becomes an everyday norm. Too often after formal review activities people return to their 'real' jobs, and the ongoing debate between staff and students gets lost until problems arise. Similarly the constructive sharing of best practice between disciplines when preparing for enhancement review can so easily fade. Communication and information is a big issue in increasingly informal learning structures.

What was learned

- Ongoing change is a reality: make sure that change enhances provision wherever possible. In many ways what happens in higher education institutions is and should be a mirror of professional life, which is in constant flux due to market forces.
- Do not underestimate the power and relevance of student involvement and opinions. A sector like art, design and media can be more effective by working together to find best practice for effective delivery.
- The enhancement process is not a mechanical tool that you bring out and apply at times of audit. Rather it is an ongoing way of continuous appraisal

that should imbue all decisions and actions. There should be ongoing documentation of enhancement through annual reporting, and time linked plans should be in place as an enhancement ladder of expectation for development.

- While flexible and informal learning become more prevalent and structured contact less so, new lines of communication and information management need to be considered.

14

Theme 2 commentary

Murray Saunders

As we note in the introduction, the case studies within the Theme are drawn from the experience of a policy intervention aimed at enhancement across the whole Scottish university system. The cases refer to the early days of the Quality Enhancement Framework (QEF) approach and exemplify the way in which a drive to *enhancement* rather than simply assurance provided the impetus for a range of mechanisms to support the improvement of teaching and learning within an institution, a group of disciplines and in a single discipline.

The QEF policy was part of an emerging distinctively Scottish identity in the HE sector, part of a push for a new Scottish policy culture. The QEF aimed for an integrated approach in which (Scottish) 'teaching quality enhancement' superseded (English) 'teaching quality assurance'. However, the approach to change via the QEF was complex, involving several areas of tension and challenges to successful implementation.

As a complex policy *instrument* designed to shift a culture to embrace enhancement, the QEF is characterized by some distinctive policy *mechanisms* that embody an inventive expression of a national higher education system. These cases have shown the way in which broad brush policies like the QEF raised several interrelated issues in connection with change initiatives and implementation realities. These are summarized next and we elaborate on them in the rest of this chapter.

1 *Shared visions and alignment*: the QEF is premised on an approach to change that attempted to build on a collegiate and shared vision. This raises the issue of the extent to which it genuinely reflected or expressed a 'Scottish way'. The cases suggest that while broad identification with this approach existed within the universities, the devil was in the detail and several key 'tensions' were occluded in the name of consensus. We discuss below whether such tensions build to become pathological to the aims of the policy or whether they are accommodated, co-existing in a form of mutual adaptation.

2　*Beyond enclaves of interesting practice*: a consistent problem in change processes, particularly those that involve enhancement, concerns the mechanisms for moving from the interesting case to changing what we might term 'routine practice'. These cases are embodiments of this problem. In particular, the extent to which proposed changes go 'against' the grain of systemic incentives for action or run up against existing material and routine constraints. In this issue, we have an example of what we might call 'overdetermined' alignment. By this we mean that a change suggested by an enhancement strategy may be aligned at the level of rhetorical discourse (shared national vision) but misaligned at the level of routine practices on the ground or the power of existing sectoral incentives for practice (e.g. sustaining the reputation and prestige of a research intensive university).

3　*Resource dependency and incentives*: the cases show the way in which resources are used as a lever to 'incentivize' the enhancement process. The question of 'incentives to engage' in change is an interesting one and can be interpreted as a focus on what it is that enables or 'persuades' individuals, groups and organizations to shift their practice or indeed to adhere to one practice rather than another one. The most straightforward form of incentive is of course the promise of new 'resources' if the proposed change is enacted. However, there are many other ways of interpreting the idea of incentives. For example, we might consider moral or ethical incentives to change, based on a professional imperative or a set of values about the quality of teaching that are being constrained or somehow compromised in the present circumstances. A proposed change might incentivize by providing a mechanism to express beliefs or values through new teaching methods.

4　*Low fidelity and transferability*: we also find in these cases examples of the way a policy struggles with prescription (high fidelity) and openness (low fidelity) with differing and concomitant effects on the process of change. The QEF was, at the same time, both high and low in fidelity. It was low in fidelity in that it attempted a change in perspective and emphasis on quality from assurance to enhancement, but allowed institutions to embody this shift in such a way that it expressed their own institutional culture and systems. On the other hand, it identified themes that were expected to form the main emphasis across the sector (e.g. employability) irrespective of the priorities that an individual institution might want to emphasize. We find that the lower the policy is on fidelity, the better it travels and is reconstructed or 'translated' on the ground, as we put it elsewhere in the book, and is capable of being adapted to the 'real politique' of situated change. On the other hand of course, low fidelity change means that there can be little standardization or control over the detail of the changes across a whole system. This is anathema to policymakers who tend to eschew local versions of change because they make policy look incoherent at national level.

Shared visions and alignment

We have in the case of Davidson et al. (Chapter 10) an insider account of the way in which the QEF policy was developed. They show that the idea of a shared vision was important in the genesis of the QEF in that it was based on an agreement that assurance based approaches to quality were disliked and that a more positive, integrated and enhancement-led approach would galvanize support and reflect a 'Scottish way'. However, this consensus concealed tensions. Among them were issues associated with a move too far from an assurance based approach. Such an approach might lack 'teeth' and allow poor practice to continue. Other tensions concerned what would happen to the policy on the ground in the light of assurance and enhancement proceeding hand in glove – would it produce compliant behaviour, for example, where Themes were targeted in the belief that they alone would bear the brunt of external review?

The issue here is not that we must continue to search for the 'perfect' enhancement approach: this doesn't exist. Rather the issue is to develop our understanding of what happens when certain change strategies are used. In this case, do the underlying tensions tend to destabilize consensus and produce a dysfunctional implementation process? Davidson et al. suggest that using a particular dimension of the QEF approach (the emphasis on specific themes), which we have argued is relatively high in fidelity, can be an effective enhancement mechanism, despite the tensions. He argues that by the production of interlocking communities of practice of designers and users of the artefacts or knowledge resources, the approach was able to support a coherent approach to a Theme across the sector, but via communities of practice the members of which were often in common. The argument suggested here is that shared vision of the participants in policy production can be sustained on the ground through 'layered' communities of designers and users embedded within the institutions themselves.

Beyond enclaves of interesting practice

Mason and his co-writers (Chapter 11) outline the way in which an institutional mechanism to bring the QEF alive had some interesting effects. Their case raises the interesting scenario of institutional mechanisms which aim to change engrooved, deeply embedded L&T practices, highlighting the difficulties of moving such change beyond enclaves of enthusiasts, and beyond the immediate point of contact with the funding mechanism. The mechanism, broadly, is based on the resource dependency model whereby systems of small grants were offered by the learning and teaching support unit to encourage projects or the exploitation of research findings. We will turn to the effects of the resource dependency model in the next section. Here we are interested in the way in which this strategy of categorical funding as it is known, creates 'enclaves' of interesting or excellent practice and how such instances can then be used to create positive effects in the wider context. The idea of an enclave is useful here in that it implies the way in which a teaching and learning project might stimulate interesting and exciting changes and improvements in those directly involved in the project or in receipt of resources – but how is the wider context influenced? In effect we have a weak theory of change because this connection is rarely addressed beyond exhortations to disseminate. This of course begs the question concerning how wider practices might be enhanced on the basis of an embodiment in an interesting case. It might be useful to adjust our discourse to refer directly to the relationship between the embodiment and wider practice by introducing the term 'engagement'. By this we refer to the way in which groups and individuals across and outside the institution might connect in such a way that their practice shifts to include the characteristics of the embodiment. Engagement might be understood, therefore, within the following frame – see Figure 14.1.

In Figure 14.1 we see that as we move from strategies of engagement on the left (distributing what has been called the 'cold unresponsive text') through various types of presentational practice (seminars, presentations, questions and answers, even active workshops which people attend out of their normal context) to, on the right, types of interactional practice (working alongside colleagues, working out enabling and constraining factors in context) there tends to be less engagement with the practice based implications of the embodiment.

Having said this, however, the targeted funding programme might be repositioning T&L practices at institutional levels in ways that were difficult to precisely determine or predict. It may, for example create 'ripple' effects through recognition that they are creating a shift in the way T&L

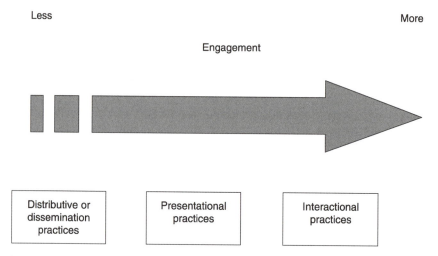

Figure 14.1 From distribution to interaction

practitioners are being rewarded, and the way resources and attention might be flowing toward T&L. The model suggests that at the outset of the programme, excellent practice was essentially taking place in pockets within institutions and it is these pockets of practice that have been rewarded with funds. The key question is how this process encourages engagement.

Because we use the metaphor of an 'enclave' to depict these pockets of interesting practice, the issue of how to encourage or sustain the process of deepening or widening effects is critical. Our cases suggest that it involves the principles, ways, means and approaches that constitute practice moving out from these pockets or enclaves of practice and influencing the wider case through a series of 'engagements.'

The case provided by Edward (Chapter 12) provides a further set of considerations in moving from the interesting case or embodiment to wider practice, that relates to the idea of (mis)alignment we have mentioned previously. To reiterate, this idea focuses on the extent to which a change idea or the embodiment of a new practice connects in some way with the dominant mode of practice or set of practices. Edward's case suggests that these practices might be shaped by quite mundane yet critical factors, such as timing of sessions, but they might also depend on the judgement of the target group of the congruence of the embodiment with their own 'learning styles' or with their own judgement of a cost/benefit balance.

Resource dependency and incentives

We mention above the way in which an enhancement is often supported by resources. Normally this categorically funded approach involves targeting funding on an approved or sought after policy goal. In this case we have identified the QEF interest in particular areas; as Mason et al. (Chapter 11) suggest 'staff were constrained by the criteria for successful bids to target their innovative ideas for teaching redesign to meet aspects of the enhancement Themes'. The case suggests that there was alignment between the value placed on these themes and on estimations of value at the ground level within a specific discipline. In this case it was based on the projects that were submitted from the medical school. Moving from enclave to wider practice is not analysed in detail, but the process of developing the projects and the congruence/alignment of the central ideas with core curricular issues has generated widespread discussion.

This targeted approach also suggested some interesting unintended effects that were created by the bidding system. It is clear that those in direct receipt of funds benefited. This is congruent with the issue of enclaves we discussed earlier. However there are other dimensions of this process of grant success, one positive and another not so. The positive dimension is that those in receipt of funds enter what might be called a positive cycle in that they are usually able to build on their initial experience and become more proficient at further bids, thus creating a strong corpus of innovative work. At the same time, the involvement of postgraduate students in the projects further deepened the effects.

The downside of this process, however, lies in the uneven development of capacity, not only in a teaching and learning area but in the process of bidding itself. As the authors of the case study suggest, 'to they that hath, more shall be given'. They outline how funded projects were restricted to a relatively small group of staff who were successful in seeking funding, and how the individuals involved in engaging with the interesting teaching and learning strategies were also restricted to the 'usual suspects' of 'extended professional' in the teaching and learning domain.

Overview: low fidelity and reconstruction

Our cases suggest that in one critical area of the QEF approach (the QEF Themes), the fact that the policy of enhancement is relatively low in fidelity allows for departments and individuals to situate their own expressions of the policy in institutional realities. While the Themes were restricted, there was not a high level of disagreement about the authenticity or legitimacy of their focus. Where criticisms did arise, they focused on the lack of prior *discussion* as to choice of Themes, but raised no substantive objection to the QEF Theme focus.

The cases demonstrate the way in which institutions and departments were able to interpret the Themes in terms of an institutional sense of what was required for specific students or as a way of enhancing existing practice or what connected effectively with new professional requirements. Fisher's case study of the way in which the QEF framework enabled the impetus for enhancement within the art, design and media domains illustrates the power of legitimacy for a shift in emphasis from assurance to enhancement.

The capacity of a new policy to be reconstructed rather than transferred at ground level depends on the relationship between fidelity and the extent to which policies can be reconstructed and translated. In general terms, low fidelity means the extent to which the vision or thrust is clear but generic enough for enactors to situate it in their own contexts of practices, circumstances and priorities. It also implies, and the QEF was adept at this, the need to build on a level of consensus and 'ownership' of the policy shift such that practitioners were confident enough to modify and adapt the policy messages to local circumstances. A more bureaucratic or centrally prescriptive approach inevitably reduces local adaptations or produces rhetorical rather than practice based change. It can also result in strategic conduct which makes sure that all the surface characteristics of a shift are present, but this overlay disguises few changes in practice. It can mean that practitioners actively subvert or undermine central prescription. If ground level adaptation of expressions of HE policy is a good thing, then we should encourage policy to be clear and strong in broad vision, grow out of consensus and eschew detailed prescription. There is an interesting dynamic at work within the cases in this theme between the sense of central license for local expressions of the enhancement approach, sectoral engagement with the design of the policy, a strong vision that has broad legitimacy across the sector and a perception from the institutions that central coordination is relatively light and non-bureacratized.

Theme 3

Developing frameworks for action

15

Theme 3 introduction

Veronica Bamber

The key premise of this book is that change, enhancement and learning happen within social systems. It will be no surprise, then, that this Theme, 'Developing frameworks for action' focuses on the interplay of the different elements in university activity systems. In these systems or architectures people, their cultures and practices are inseparable. Efforts to change parts of the system will come up against conservatism and resistance. However, if we can understand the likely effects of trying to improve the institutional frameworks within which learning and teaching take place, then perhaps we can work around the pits, instead of falling into them.

So this section of the book considers attempts to enhance the systems and structures which frame, support and shape enhancement efforts. The cases describe initiatives which do not influence learning and teaching (L&T) change directly, as in the previous chapters, but which attempt to develop frameworks within which L&T change can happen. As mentioned above, structures do not exist in isolation: they are interwoven in the cultural and human aspects of the organization, and are part of the wider social and political systems of the university. This Theme cannot simply be seen through the apparently rational lens of organizational structure.

The key area is culture. A university's culture could be seen as the core beliefs and values held by staff, which have been developed over time and are shared to varying degrees by different groups within the organization. This culture is inextricably threaded through the structures, processes and roles which provide the backbone, what Allen and Fifield (1999: 8) call the 'cultural web' of the institution. However, the idea of a web suggests all aspects of the organization being tied together in a pattern, when in fact disagreements may be more present than common assumptions (Hannan and Silver 2000: 84). Since universities have intrinsically conservative traits, any attempt to change cultures, structures or systems is likely to meet resistance. By sheer persistence and ignoring what can be ignored, powerful groups within universities can inhibit change.

Each of the cases in the Theme describes initiatives in which enhancement happens from the outside in. Institutions respond to external challenges, and universities exist *interdependently* with the external environment (Johnson 2002: 121). In some case studies (Lycke, Chapter 16), proposed change is externally driven, while in others a top–down internal management initiative is the driver (Stefani and Tynan in Chapters 18 and 19, respectively). In Watson's case (Chapter 17), change ideas are brought into institutions via the externally organized professional learning of staff.

In the first chapter, looking at national level change, Lycke (Chapter 16) discusses the introduction of compulsory teacher training for HE teachers in Norway, an initiative which aimed to improve learning and teaching through developing the teachers. In her analysis, Lycke finds that the change effort was largely successful, since the training was eventually adopted by all Norwegian universities and became part of the higher education culture. This could, perhaps, be contrasted with the UK experience, where attending lecturer development programmes became a probationary requirement for new staff in most universities following the Dearing Report (NCIHE 1997). While the UK programmes also appear to have been successfully introduced, it could be argued that they are not yet an integral, stable part of the academic culture in some types of university and in some subject disciplines. Some ten years on, this is still contested terrain.

Watson's case, at the institutional level, is about the author's experience in leading a pioneering course for mid-career professionals, an MBA in higher education management. Again, this initiative was judged to be largely successful, from the point of view of the managers who studied on the programme and who went on to promoted positions. Less clear is the notoriously difficult process of transferring their studies back into their workplaces. An important question here is how institutions can best ensure that their staff are well prepared for management responsibilities.

In Stefani's case, at the departmental level, the topic is again professional development of staff, but this time the change effort centred on restructuring as an approach to improving provision. In the case institution, there were three distinct centres involved in enhancing teaching and learning, which management wished to combine. In the face of staff resistance, the three centres were pulled together, and the case describes the difficulties of 'bringing reluctant staff to the party'. Efforts by senior management to consult and communicate may have alleviated opposition, but only in the unit whose staff felt successful were they happy to collaborate. In the end, top–down diktat prevailed over staff preferences and territorial protection. Stefani's use of the word 'battle' is not accidental.

As with Stefani, Tynan's analysis of change was fuelled by external drivers, as institutions line up to gain or maintain competitiveness in an increasingly challenging international 'market'. While universities need to adapt to their environment in order to be successful (Sporn 1999: 24), the clash of values can make adaptation an uncomfortable experience for all involved. So Tynan presents an individual level case study which was clearly harder to recount than other cases in this theme, since the writer did not feel her change efforts had been completely successful. She went into a foreign culture to lead a strategic change, with the brief of establishing a faculty with a focus on e-learning. This included setting up the technical infrastructure, undertaking detailed market analysis, developing strategic business plans and developing courses for distance delivery and professional development of staff. Some successes were achieved, but misalignment of institutional (business) values and her own (educational) values, combined with unfeasible management demands, led to her not achieving the institutional objectives.

In the chapters which follow, these four writers analyse their enhancement experiences. Their insights are based on reflection in the light of the change and enhancement theory summarized in Chapter 2 of this book, and data from a range of sources play a key role. Lycke mentions the impact of institutional and national surveys: surveys as 'nudges' for change. In her analysis, data were used not only to monitor change, but to persuade those involved to embrace change. Watson also uses key data, this time course monitoring reports (including student and graduate feedback), a questionnaire survey of graduates, and an informal survey of the teaching team. For Stefani it was vital to publicize successes as the structural change was being implemented, while in Tynan's case data had a negative effect: institutional data used to fuel change were not reliable and only served to increase the distance between corporate aims and the perceived realities of those expected to achieve those aims. While institutional self-review can be a major strategic tool in change situations (Hopkins 2002: 5), it will become clear that this occurs when the data are used dialogically, as part of the process of gaining and sharing knowledge of what works in the particular situation.

16

Strong vision, low prescription: compulsory lecturer training

Kirsten Hofgaard Lycke
University of Oslo, Norway

Introduction

Traditionally, teaching in higher education has been a private matter. The quality of teaching – often regarded as synonymous with lecturing – has been an individual responsibility for academics who primarily identify themselves as researchers (Quality of Studies 1990; Karseth and Kyvik 1999). Rising student numbers and diversification in student backgrounds in the 1960s and 1970s in Norway strengthened, but also challenged the role of mass lectures as the dominant teaching activity. It was time for a change, in individual teaching approaches/activities, in the status of teaching and in the educational culture of higher education. In the face of such broad and far-reaching aims, the question of change was directed at how to raise general awareness of issues related to teaching among academics as much as how to develop their teaching skills. The notion of compulsory teacher training for academic teachers emerged as a change that was intended to change teaching and thinking about teaching – in sum the culture of teaching in higher education (Lauvås and Handal 1978; NOU 1988; Quality of Studies 1990).

A driving force in the initiation of compulsory training for academic teachers in Norway was the University Pedagogy Committee (UPC) under the National Council for Universities.[1] The Council was an organization of and for Norwegian universities which established the committee to look into issues of teaching and learning in the sector. The UPC consisted of dedicated developers and academics who saw the need to enhance the quality of studies offered to students. The idea of compulsory educational training was, in other

---

[1] Higher education in Norway: Norway has six universities, five specialized universities and 25 state university colleges. In addition there are 29 private institutions of higher education. Each institution has considerable academic and administrative autonomy. Basic pedagogical competence was first introduced in the universities, followed later by some state university colleges.

words, not a directive from the authorities, but rather based on perceptions in the field of the need to ensure good teaching (KIUP 1985).

Strategy for change

In the UPC's promotion of compulsory training the following strategy can be traced:

- Identify the need for change.
- Suggest structures and strategies to change the situation.
- Create acceptance for the chosen change processes.
- Evaluate and review the change.

It should be noted that compulsory teacher training has not been the only measure used to improve teaching in Norwegian universities, but it has been an important focal point.

Identify the need for change

The conditions to invoke change through compulsory training were not particularly favourable. Norwegian studies of teaching in higher education have focused on teaching methods and use of time for teaching (Vibe and Aamodt 1985). There are no actual studies of the quality of teaching in Norwegian universities in the 1970s or 1980s (Karseth and Kyvik 1999), but anecdotal information points to excellence alongside questionable practices. In the late 1980s there was, however, an increasing awareness that professionalizing academic staff in universities should not only focus on research qualifications but also on pedagogical competence. Training was seen as a road to general improvement of teaching in higher education. The personal experience of leading academics as participants in existing faculty development activities underscored the idea that *all* academics should participate in such training.

The UPC did not argue that current teaching practice was unacceptable, but that as long as academic teachers had no educational training whatsoever they were poorly prepared for their everyday teaching obligations, and perhaps even less prepared to participate in improving teaching and learning in their departments (KIUP 1985). The UPC also documented that the rules for considering the pedagogical competence of applicants for academic positions at the universities were rarely followed (KIUP 1987). University study programmes, teaching in general and the educational culture would benefit by all academics having undergone some educational training.

The underlying rationale however was linked to an understanding of teaching as a cultural phenomenon, later stated by the Quality of Studies (1990: 11) commission: 'One of the basic understandings of the committee was that the curricula, the teaching and learning in higher education, are all expressions of the culture which exists in that field'. In consequence 'Any significant and lasting improvement of quality in higher education has to happen in a dialectical interaction between changes in structure and changes in culture'.

Suggest structures to change the situation

The structural change suggested by UPC was that all academic teachers should have basic educational training. Over time all academic staff should have what was termed 'Basic Pedagogical Competence'. In 1988 the National Council of Universities recommended the proposition and subsequently all Norwegian universities adopted it into their institutional rules and regulations.

Basic pedagogical competence is defined in terms of participation in a teacher training programme. Training cannot be substituted by, for instance, extensive practice of teaching in higher education. The requirement applies to all academic staff in permanent teaching posts in all the Norwegian universities. The rules are put into practice when new academic staff are recruited or evaluated for promotion. They may be summarized as follows in Figure 16.1.

Rules for basic pedagogical competence: summary

1 Applicants for academic posts must be evaluated on the basis of documented research and pedagogical qualifications.

2 New academic teachers without basic pedagogical competence must document such qualifications within two years after appointment.

3 Basic pedagogical competence is defined as participation in an educational training programme equivalent to a 3–4 weeks full time course (approx. 100 hours).

Figure 16.1 Rules for basic pedagogical competence: summary

The way to achieve basic pedagogical competence is to attend a training programme for academic teachers. The universities were encouraged to establish provision for such programmes.

Voluntary faculty development activities were introduced in Norwegian universities in the early 1960s. These activities were experienced as innovative and presenting new approaches to issues of teaching and learning. The courses were extensive and demanding, attracting academics from different disciplines. Collaboration on educational improvements across disciplinary boundaries gave a broader understanding of higher education (Lauvås 1987). The early courses provided a model for the current training programme for basic pedagogical competence, the compulsory teacher training. The programme structure at the University of Oslo[2,3] with its three main features: an introductory course, tutor groups and elective courses is mirrored in the programmes at the other universities (Lycke 1999).

Create acceptance for the chosen change process

Acceptance of the notion of basic pedagogical competence and compulsory teacher training offered for that purpose has been dependent on the perceived quality of the training programme and on continuous advocacy.

The quality of the programme and the satisfaction of participants is probably the most important aspect in creating and upholding acceptance of the change to compulsory teacher training. All courses are therefore evaluated by the participants and reviewed closely by the course leaders for continuous improvement. A systematic analysis of satisfaction ratings at the University of Oslo over a span of five courses showed that more than 60 percent of the course participants marked the course in the two most positive evaluation categories on a five point scale. Given that these courses are compulsory and not all academics are all that positive when they start the programme, these results are noteworthy (Lycke and Handal 2005).

---

[2] The University of Oslo, founded in 1813, is the oldest and largest in Norway with approximately 33,000 students and 3000 academic teachers. The university adopted the rules for basic pedagogical competence in 1989.

[3] The programme for basic pedagogical competence at the University of Oslo can be summarized as follows:

Introductory course (2 + 2 days)

Theories of teaching and learning
Course planning and educational strategies
Methods of teaching and assessment
Micro teaching sessions

Tutor groups (4–5 half-day sessions)

Four participants and a course leader meet to observe and discuss each others' regular teaching activities.

Elective courses (1–2 days each)

Students' evaluation of teaching
Improving lectures
Problem and case based learning
Research supervision
Writing as a tool for learning
Portfolio development
Quality assurance

The introduction of criteria for the educational competencies of academic teachers also provided the *students* with powerful leverage on the leadership of the universities. Norwegian students are represented on boards at all levels of higher education and their demand that the rules should be followed has been a strong force in the implementation process. Over the years the students have initiated new debates to keep the issue high on the institutional agendas.

Previous *course participants* (by now in more senior positions) have promoted the idea that all academic teachers should participate in educational training and have been active in placing it on institutional agendas.

Programme leaders of compulsory teacher training have been involved in institutional activities and steering committees on educational quality assurance and enhancement. They have had a strong voice in promoting compulsory training programmes through discussion papers and debates, but also in demonstrating the usefulness of educational perspectives in consultations on curriculum change and innovation.

Evaluate and review the change

A national survey of quality enhancement measures in higher education for the Ministry of Education (Handal and Lycke 2000) showed that by 1999 all the universities had implemented the rules for basic pedagogical competence. The universities also had units for faculty development that offered teacher training and consultations directed at more general academic development. The universities also developed administrative routines related to recruitment and promotion together with manuals for review boards/applicants on how to document/evaluate pedagogical qualifications.

Has the change made a change?

As noted in the introduction, the aims for introducing compulsory teacher education for academic teachers in Norwegian universities were directed at changing teacher thinking, changing teaching practice and changing the educational culture.

Taking the University of Oslo as an example, studies of teachers who have participated in the compulsory programme show significant changes in their thinking about educational issues. Enhanced teaching practices have also been identified as effects of participation in compulsory training activities (Lycke and Handal 2005). The effects are based on self-report, but they are consistent with the course aims over course groups and over time.

The impact of compulsory teacher training on the academic culture is more difficult to document. What we can discern is that such training is less controversial and more taken for granted. (The current elected Rector of the University of Oslo had support for compulsory teacher training as one of his campaign slogans.) University colleges nationwide are now in the process of adopting the same rules and structures introduced in the universities in 1988.

Reports indicate that the programme has contributed to an interest in developing teaching, a common 'language' for discussing educational issues, and an understanding of the need for fora for such discussions. Effects can also be detected in readiness to perceive the need for change and innovative ideas. Previous curriculum changes in the faculties of medicine, oral medicine and law have to a large extent been initiated and carried out by former course participants. These observations are underscored in the last external institutional review (Norgesnettrådet 2002). The national change to new grade structures, assessment systems and quality assurance procedures in the wake of the Bologna process can also be seen to have benefited from the resources and insight developed through compulsory training. Many of the academics actively involved in the local implementation of the 'Quality Reform' – the Norwegian variation of the Bologna processes – were former course participants.

Discussion

The structural change of requiring academic teachers to have basic pedagogical competence has changed practice in the sense that teacher training is now compulsory in Norwegian universities. There are also observed changes in teacher thinking and practice related to participation in the training activities. Whether the changes in structure and practice also have changed the culture of teaching as hypothesized is difficult to document partly because other 'winds of change' in higher education have been strong in the two decades since compulsory teacher training was introduced. Public and political interest in the higher education sector has increased dramatically. The quality of teaching has become an aspect of broad concern. Research on learning has led to a new interest in and rationale for reform pedagogy and collaborative learning.

Given the aims and long term processes to achieve the noted changes, we might well ask if they could have been achieved more effectively by other means. Technological approaches to educational change with demand for efficient reform ruled the day in attempts at educational change in schools, without notable success (Fullan 1982).

A more recent and more forceful initiative to improve education in higher education is the introduction of national audits of quality assurance systems in Norway since 2002 (Lycke 2004). The sanctions on institutions that do not have QA systems that meet required standards are sufficiently severe to ensure that all institutions developed and implemented such systems within short time limits. It appears that these top–down processes have increased teacher feedback on student work and the amount of interactive teaching at the University of Oslo (University of Oslo 2007). However, if the teachers have a restricted repertoire in dealing with formative assessment and interaction with students, classroom practices might not become all that different. Tutorials may come to resemble lectures, portfolio assessment to resemble traditional tests and exams. Furthermore, if the teachers are not attuned to the rationale of the new structures, they may create resistance and withdrawal of the engagement that is vital to good teaching. Teaching culture may be affected by the need to comply, rather than by creative innovation.

The change sought by introducing compulsory teacher training represents a more 'cultural' approach to change (Dalin 1994). Faculty development activities contribute to readiness, to insight and awareness of possible ways to enhance teaching and learning. Even if participation is compulsory the courses do not instruct teachers what to do, but encourage educational innovations that are sensitive to local cultures and norms. The approach acknowledges that no one has the *one* solution. The courses prepare for future boundary crossing in setting contexts for translating directives and perspectives and aid in developing bridges to new practices (see Chapter 2).

Well into the 1980s teaching was the responsibility of the individual teacher. University leadership played no active role in changing this one way or the other. Introducing rules for basic pedagogical competence for all academic teachers contributed to a shift in focus. Providing the resources for training and ensuring such competencies among faculty became a management responsibility and thus increased the leadership awareness of these issues. This change of practice consequently changed practice, not only in the primary target group – the academic teachers – but also in the leadership at different levels.

International studies shed some doubts on the effects of faculty development programmes (Gibbs and Coffey 2004). The faculty development courses as they are currently conducted at the University of Oslo, however, are just one part of the package. This university has a strong and long tradition of combining training courses with consultations with groups/units/departments. Examples are the development/change of programmes, new exam/assessment structures/formats, and lately the introduction of ICT based flexible learning programmes and quality assurance systems at different levels. There is a noticeable link between the contact with academics through compulsory training and demand for consultations in relation to educational revisions or changes. The role of compulsory teacher training and the impact of such training depend on how it is aligned to other quality enhancement activities and how these are situated locally (Trowler and Bamber 2005). In the case of Norway even the national context has proved to have an impact on compulsory teacher training.

Acknowledgement

I would like to thank Professor Gunnar Handal, University of Oslo, for his generous comments on this case presentation.

17

Can we teach higher education management?

David Watson
Institute of Education, University of London, England

Introduction

The particular take on enhancement in this chapter is that one important component in improving what universities do is to improve the management abilities of their staff. The chapter describes the author's experience in assuming the course leadership of a pioneering course for mid-career professionals in higher education management. Sources of information include the original validation record, regular course monitoring reports (including student and graduate feedback), a questionnaire survey of graduates carried out by Celia Whitchurch (CW) with support of the Leadership Foundation for Higher Education (LFHE) in June 2006, and an informal survey of the core teaching team. A series of challenges raised by the development is explored. Conclusions are reached about the risks accepted in the process (by the institution, the students and the staff), about the professional context (collaborative and competitive), and about the pressures for further change.

Genesis and context

In October 2002, the Institute of Education offered for the first time an MBA in higher education management. The course had been designed by a senior professor and Director of the Centre for Higher Education Studies (CHES) (Gareth Williams (GW)) and a visiting professor (Michael Shattock (MS)) recently retired from a distinguished career as Registrar of the University of Warwick. In reflecting on the original design MS identifies three key features, as follows:

> A key element was not to present it like an MA – all theory – but to include practitioners in the teaching line-up and to include practical work via syndicate work and the project thus emphasising the management side . . . Another key element was to aim the MBA at the academic

community and the support services (librarians et al.) and not just at the administrators thus recognising the special feature of management in HE institutions. A third key feature was to emphasise the holistic nature of the HE institutional management, the pulling together of the various aspects of management to create better institutional performance

(MS)

The course has recruited – from a competitive pool – between 21 and 25 students each year. Many graduates have been promoted either while on the course or subsequently; 13 of the 27 respondents to CW's survey had changed job during or after the programme. Interestingly, it has yet to produce a significant brand rival: several universities now offer MA/MSc courses in similar areas, and a small number a professional doctorate, but (at the time of writing) it is the only specific MBA (one university offers a 'higher education' route within its general MBA). While the programme is very much constructed around the experience of UK higher education, it has also attracted a small number of experienced practitioners from overseas (the team has elected to attempt to keep these to no more than one-third of each cohort): from Holland, Denmark, Germany, Greece, Ireland, Switzerland, Japan, the United Arab Emirates, Australia and the United States.

The course is taught over two years, mainly through five intensive one-week residential periods, with support from personal tutors during and in between these. There are compulsory modules on strategic management, management of teaching and research, and finance; together with options on institutional governance, internationalization, lifelong learning, human resources, marketing, physical resources and the 'third stream'. These are assessed through incourse syndicate work and written assignments. The course concludes with either a 'real-life' consultancy project (taken by the vast majority of students) or a dissertation.

Analysis

At the conclusion of my second year of full time teaching on the course (I contributed occasionally as a guest speaker in earlier years) and my first as course director, I became aware of a number of challenges, including the following.

The intellectual challenge

The argument about whether 'management' is an art or a science – whether it is better incubated in a studio/conservatoire or in a lecture room/laboratory – and whether it can be formally taught at all has long been explored, and (to their satisfaction at least) resolved by the business schools. GW has reviewed our 'content' against the recent QAA Benchmark statement for

MBA courses and concluded that we are 'safe', if a 'little bit light on some of the organizational theory and underpinning economic theory' (GW; QAA 2007).

There are, however, ongoing controversies which keep the debate alive. It is interesting, for example, how at the undergraduate level 'general' qualifications are on the decline and 'sector-specific' degrees (retail, hospitality, leisure, etc.) on the rise. At the postgraduate level, sector specificity is also growing: see, for example, Warwick's Masters of Public Administration (MPA) for the spectrum of public sector professionals. The Institute probably wisely rejected the notion that the course should be called Masters of Higher Education Management (MHEM).

There is also a growing body of concern about postgraduate (or post-experience) provision that does not require serious prior and concurrent professional experience. The key text here is Mintzberg's *Managers Not MBAs*. Mintzberg's excoriation of an approach based on abstract case studies, few of which would occur in the real world (and those that do, not simultaneously in the same week) has been taken seriously by the MBA HEM. So, too, have been his strictures about experience, of which the following are examples:

> Playing at management is not management. Management is a responsibility not a game played in a classroom . . .
> (Mintzberg 2004: 44)

> Put differently, a central purpose of management education is to encourage the development of wisdom. This requires a thoughtful atmosphere in the classroom, where individuals can probe into their own experience, primed by interesting ideas, concepts, theories
> (Mintzberg 2004: 249)

We have striven to develop course materials – and problems – that, on the one hand, are theoretically challenging and stimulating, and, on the other, arise in the real world. Reassuringly, our programme does not look much like Mintzberg's own satirically proposed (I think) Masters of University Administration (MUA) (Mintzberg 2004: 156–7).

The challenge of higher education exceptionalism

What is that 'real world', and how is it different? A colleague (PT) argues that 'some aspects of higher education management are reasonably generic public sector stuff – strategy and HR, say – and we try on the MBA to link with the NHS, local government etc.' However, he goes on:

> Other aspects are pretty much unique to HE: things to do with students, research, finance, third stream and marketing for example . . . The university also raises management issues around its unique role as a producer of public goods (T and R) – and this applies just as much to

private institutions as to publicly funded ones. It is this position, straddling the public/private divide, that creates many of the tensions that management has to deal with.

(PT)

Higher education does represent a peculiar enterprise, mode of production and organization. Universities and colleges are not just using knowledge, they are creating, testing and critically evaluating it. As a result they are professionally argumentative communities, with their performance and reputations in the hands of a wide range of groups and individuals. Until relatively recently, the notion that the institutions are 'managed' and not simply 'administered' was anathema. Understanding how and why that change came about has to be one of the elements of professional formation and development of managers.

The interprofessional challenge

The essence of higher education is a 'conversation', between more and less experienced learners. At the postgraduate level, it is also ideally a conversation between peers. In an environment like the MBA it is a reasonable expectation that your teachers will also be in some respects your peers.

Susan Lapworth – a graduate from the second cohort – reflects eloquently on the resulting dilemmas of identity:

More specifically [she states], the expertise of the MBA student in some areas was greater than that of the 'teacher' – a Professor of Accounting provided ad hoc tutorials on understanding financial ratios, a statistician proved more adept with tools for statistical analysis, and so on. Here the identities of those involved in delivering the material – academic, professional, manager – are replicated by those receiving it. The stabilisation of student identity through markers of difference in this context fails. Difference cannot be maintained and the process of exclusion of 'other' no longer functions.

This is not the only potential source of tension. The course team has acted specifically to try to construct a mixed cohort. Approximately one-third of the students are 'academics' of reasonable to significant seniority. Meanwhile the other two-thirds mix those who have specific professional identities (in finance, estates, personnel, ICT, librarianship and so on) with those who perform professional support roles that exist in a special way in universities (registry functions, quality, student services, etc.) These groups are deliberately mixed in 'syndicates' of about six members, who work together for a calendar year. Often, they say, participants are compelled to confront and respect each other's professional identities in ways which they never have to in their home institutions. CW's survey showed academics occasionally perceived by administrators as 'controlling and not good team players'; in the other direction academics occasionally bemoaned the 'lack of rigour' (see also Whitchurch 2006). There is a political dimension here, which the course provides a 'safe' place to explore.

The challenge of relevance

The international students on the MBA HEM are particularly interested in it because of the speed of change in UK HE, and they suspect that the kinds of experiments conducted on its members may soon be applied to them. In looking back on the sector's experience of the last 25 years, Rachel Bowden and I concluded that the British institutions had become the experimental 'fruit-flies' of the higher education world (Watson and Bowden 2005). The MBA HEM solution has been to try to expose students not only to real-world case material, but also to people who are facing real-world dilemmas, at a variety of levels, within institutions and across the sector. In 2006, for example, students working on strategy had the benefit of working directly with the vice-chancellors/principals of four very different UK HEIs on scoping strategic options for their particular institutions.

Meanwhile, in the words of a colleague who specializes in workplace learning:

> The sting in the tail is the extent to which students can (and are encouraged to) apply their learning – the workplace learning literature has explored this dilemma for a long time . . . and has shown that student dissatisfaction often arises out of their frustration when they return to their workplace and find their colleagues and/or line managers (a crucial role in supporting learning at work) have no interest in what they've learned or actually suppress that learning – this applies across the public and private sector.
>
> (LU)

The pedagogical challenge (including assessment)

One of Lapworth's most acute dilemmas (above) is in the area of what she calls 'the symbolic and social practices of assessment'.

These practices (as is often the case, in my experience, of innovatory courses) are highly traditional. Students write essays (in a standard social scientific 'voice' as befits the marriage of management and education), throw their very considerable energy into syndicate presentations (group assessed on a pass : fail basis), and characteristically really shine in the real-life experience of completing a consultancy project for another institution (which like their essays is graded A–D). Distinctions on the degree are awarded to those with a high proportion of A grades, and those graded D (fail) on individual modules are allowed one resubmission.

In these circumstances members of the team worry about the phenomenon of 'good enough' performance: about how to get more students operating at the level of the best. A personal observation is that the most creative – and successful – students are those who not only possess but also make use of a 'hinterland', helping them to get beyond the hangups of the course team. There is also a debate about what might constitute a 'signature pedagogy' for higher education management. This powerful concept has been developed by Lee Shulman, President of the Carnegie Foundation for the Advancement of Teaching, to examine how the professions look at the 'challenge of teaching people to understand, to act, and to be integrated into a complex way of knowing, doing and being'. Examples are the clinical ward round, the law school case conference, the engineering project, the priestly apprenticeship and so on (Shulman 2005b). The question remains open, although the 'syndicate task' is probably as close as we get to an answer.

The personal challenge

Returning to the team's individual and collective hangups, it has been a rewarding personal experience for me (as a vice-chancellor (VC) of 15 years (1990–2005)) to take over from a registrar (of 16 (1983–99) – who, I am delighted to say, still contributes fully to the course). There are (I perceive) differences in our world views, and not just because I am generally more sympathetic to VCs and the academic estate, and he to registrars and professional administration. There is a subtly different pattern of views about where responsibility really lies, about leadership and about representation, and we hope that our students benefit from both. I am also conscious of having returned to where I began my career as an academic manager: as a course leader (Watson 2007).

The challenge of renewal

Professional courses, like course directors, have shelf-lives (and in the latter case atomic half-lives). There is no sense yet that we are fading, although our detailed curriculum is constantly evolving. The MBA ticket is still attractive to good students, as is the experience we offer. We have resisted developing a related professional doctorate for two reasons: because of the availability of the Institute's highly regarded EdD programme, and because of a desire not to send confusing market signals. This is a highly appropriate course for those at the beginning of the middle of their careers, who meet the Mintzberg test mentioned above.

Conclusions

It is a truism to say that any innovation involves change, and the more substantial the change the riskier it is likely to be. In a 'new' course, risks are taken by the sponsoring institution (economic and reputational), by the staff (who put themselves on the line in conditions of intellectual and moral uncertainty), and most emphatically by the students. Especially in a professional field, 'future proofing' new qualifications is essential. The record shows that the first cohorts did take risks, the benefits of which are being enjoyed by their successors. Partly these were financial: the evidence shows that as the course continues, employers are more likely to bear a greater proportion of the fees and costs. There is also a powerful element of trust: a member of the first cohort told the course director that he would only join the course if he (MS) would agree not to retire until he finished (he did graduate – just within the maximum period – and the bargain was kept.)

As for progress, there have been some distinct hits. Most importantly the course continues to attract well qualified and motivated applicants, who have a high rate of completion for professional Masters courses, and make progress in their careers. There is also evidence that – like a number of successful innovations – the course has begun to grow its own competition in other universities' portfolios.

There have also been misses. An attempt to launch – in partnership with a number of European centres – a European version failed, as recruitment across the rest of the EU (for various reasons) failed to match the interest in the UK. The traditional pedagogy alluded to above continues to worry the team. There are also features of the professional context which the course is powerless to affect (at least quickly). CW's survey shows the frustration for administrators getting 'stuck' in a departmental silo, as well as the apparent continued block on promotions to PVC roles from 'professional' backgrounds.

In terms of the theoretical models outlined by the editors in Chapter 2, this case resonates strongly in one sense and hardly at all in another. Where we barely register is in terms of several of the conditioning statements about power, hegemony and overcentralized decision making. Once the decision 'to go with' the innovation was made, the course team has felt free in the best sense of the word to develop the initiative. The managerial context has been anything but 'tightly coupled'. This sense of 'change' was unproblematic, probably because of a clear fit with the Institute's corporate sense of its developing business. This might not have been so true had we experienced less satisfactory outcomes of quality monitoring as well as any difficulties with recruitment and financial projections.

The models that do ring true are those about learning in professional life, especially the reflections about 'boundaries', about the 'translation' of theory into practice, and the very profound, ethnographic, formulations of Michael Eraut and his collaborators (2004) of how professional learning develops. We have experienced, directly and indirectly, several of the elements outlined in the editors' discussion of 'change theory'. These include:

- Issues about the role of the course within a wider activity system – the employment life of our students is at least as important in this course as their study lives (some are in a position better to integrate the two than others).
- The consequent question of the students' own 'implementation staircases' – some have positively influenced their immediate professional contexts; others have had to move or be promoted before they can fully realize the products of their learning; a minority remain frustrated (and we may inadvertently have exacerbated such frustration).
- Issues that arise from boundaries and mutual respect (or the lack of it) – the course demonstrates for some (sometimes painfully) that some professional relationships (or 'social practice') could (and should) be different.

So we *can* claim to teach higher education management, we trust in most circumstances to good effect, and thereby bring about the effective innovation sought by the editors. However, even in less promising contexts, where the prospects for applying learning are constrained, we hope to have improved the prospects of self-reflection, confidence and ambition on the part of our colleagues across the sector.

Acknowledgements

I am especially grateful to the following colleagues on the MBA HEM core team for their comments and guidance (initials are used in the text to identify direct contributions): Michael Shattock (MS), Gareth Williams (GW), Paul Temple (PT), Ron Barnett, Lorna Unwin (LU), Celia Whitchurch (CW).

18

Changing learning architectures, shifting practices

Lorraine Stefani
University of Auckland, New Zealand

Background

This chapter discusses restructuring in a university, changing its 'learning architecture', as Dill (1999) calls it. This was a top university in a land now famously known as Middle Earth, a research-led institution wherein until recent times, teaching and learning issues struggled to find space on the institutional radar screen. External drivers such as the quality audit process and internal recognition as well as the competition for students, particularly international students, all highlighted the importance of enhancement of the student learning experience – and hence the need for a more positive attitude to professional development relating to teaching and learning among academic staff.

The Middle Earth top performing institution had for many years three distinct centres oriented to enhancing teaching and learning. First, a centre for professional development which provided development opportunities for both academic and general staff – encompassing teaching, learning, research, IT literacy skills. Second, a student learning centre providing workshops, resources and one to one consultation for students. And third a centre for flexible and distance learning whose remit was to provide a leadership role in establishing best practice for e-learning and to develop organizational knowledge and capability to implement technology mediated learning.

In an ideal world, these three centres would have much common ground, overlapping and complementary remits and ample scope for collaboration. However, in the situation being described, a collaborative model did not exist. As a result of the findings from the teaching quality audit, institutional committee meetings and the report of an external consultant, a decision was made at senior management level that the three centres should be restructured into one overarching new centre: the Centre for Academic Development (CAD). This would achieve three goals: enhanced collaboration, better fulfilment of the development needs of staff and (ultimately) an enhanced learning experience for students.

The change management process

As well as the above aims, an overarching intent was to enhance the university's international standing and performance as a leading university in teaching, learning and research. Senior management and human resources staff held open sessions for staff from the three original centres to discuss the changes and to give reassurance that this was not about downsizing or redundancies – it was about maximizing institutional resources and procedures to achieve the goals set out in the university strategic plan.

Some preliminary issues that would prove to be problematic included:

1 The senior management decision that a director for the new Centre for Academic Development would be appointed from within, i.e. it would be one of the current directors of the three individual units. This gave the *impression* of demotion for the other two directors.
2 There was significant geographical dislocation of the three existing centres.
3 A prevailing view that change/restructuring implies dissatisfaction with the current status.
4 Territorial protectionism.
5 Fundamentally different philosophies, working cultures, values and management styles existed within the original three centres.

While issues 1–4 are difficult issues, they are nevertheless manageable and not particularly unusual. The points outlined in 5 are challenging, multi-faceted and if unresolved can lead to levels of dissatisfaction which in turn can impact negatively on the core business of the centre(s). The potential for and risk of losing valued members of staff during a period of restructuring is high, and perceptions of senior management and target audiences can shift through a period of change, not necessarily in a positive direction.

When change efforts fail, it is common to blame organizational resistance. However, in general, change goes wrong for systemic reasons: poor vision, inadequate communications, insufficient planning and resources, failure to make a compelling case and inconsistent messages, with leaders not following through.

So what steps were taken to construct a new centre, to shift mindsets, to develop a culture, philosophy and ethos with which staff could feel comfortable and to align the centre with the institutional mission and goals?

In the first instance, a leader/director of the new centre was appointed through a rigorous interview process. The director chosen had previously been director of the Centre for Professional Development (CPD). CPD had already undergone significant change and turnaround and was already more closely aligned with the strategic objectives of the institution. There was less resistance to change within that group even though one facet of the restructuring was that the general staff development function was to be removed from CPD and reallocated to a new unit within human resources. The leader had put significant effort into CPD to inspire followers through clear articulation of the mission of the centre, optimism, enthusiasm, emotional appeal and through developing positive relations with senior management. CPD staff therefore already felt 'successful'. This was a major factor in managing change. CPD staff did much to smooth the path, to talk positively about the benefits of restructuring and to act as role models who didn't just work at or in the university but *for* the university.

A second positive opportunity was to delegate responsibility to the administrative staff from the three original centres to work together to 'build an administrative team' for the new centre. This move was intended as a positive signal that 'change' would not be dictated but rather, staff would have the opportunity to have a constructive role in the 'shape' of the new centre. The administrative staff worked through a continuous improvement project (CIP) model to delegate roles and responsibilities applicable to the centre, e.g. budgeting, secretarial, receptionist, leave applications, resource development, etc. This allowed for almost immediate streamlining of administrative processes carried out by a group of staff who were positively predisposed to the changes. Once the administrative team was set up, a leader was appointed from within the existing administrative staff. Apart from being a necessity, appointing an existing staff member to a leadership position gave a clear signal that there were positive career development opportunities arising from the restructuring.

Significant efforts were made to include all CAD staff in developing a vision and strategy for the centre: a transition group was set up, chaired by the DVC (Academic) with representatives of all three original centres. The role of the transition group was to provide a high level of oversight to the development of the new centre, and to assist the successful integration of the three units. This group would also address any policy or operational issues associated with the new Centre. A CAD planning group was set up for the purposes of:

- Developing a mission and vision for CAD.
- Sharing views on the overall management, administrative and leadership models for CAD.
- Drawing up action plans for collaborative projects.

The CAD planning group membership was drawn from all staff members, without consideration of status or position, giving scope for as many staff as possible to take a level of ownership of the future direction of CAD.

These initial structures and committees were intended to be developmental for staff members. The Director of CAD shared information to enable staff to see the 'bigger picture' of the institutional culture, our potential to contribute to institutional goals, the expectations and demands that would be made of CAD. It was hoped that CAD staff would connect more to the mission and vision of the institution, and of CAD itself and reflect on their own roles and performance and thus contribute to and enhance the organizational culture of CAD.

Much of this was carried out against a backdrop of hostility, reluctance, anger and fear of the future from many staff within the original centres – and a sense of loss when one of the original directors left the university. Staff who were not hostile to the change itself were often not sufficiently empowered to take or show leadership. Indeed it was easy to detect divided loyalties among some – those who were not unhappy, and in some cases delighted with the idea of change but were thwarted by management styles and swayed by more hostile, more vociferous staff.

The most difficult aspect of the restructuring was to develop a coherent structure which would break down barriers, engender collaboration and support achievement of the mission, vision and goals we were setting. This was a major battle, exacerbated perhaps by relocating one of the centres which in itself had two geographical locations. The relocation meant that CAD was now split over only two sites on the campus instead of four.

The territorialism was immense – but it wasn't just about location. It was about values, ethos and philosophy of the roles of the original centres. Two of the three centres essentially operated as 'silos' with one being almost dis-located altogether from institutional mores. In other words, the centres were often too inward looking, and highly possessive about their work and how they worked. Understandably from their point of view they did not want any scrutiny of how they worked – and they certainly didn't want to change the way they worked.

Developing an organizational and functional structure for CAD was, as mentioned above, a thorny issue. All staff within their original groupings were given opportunities to suggest a structure or to comment on structures put before them – but there was nothing that could be considered even close to securing all staff agreement. In the end a structure was imposed. This structure is shown diagrammatically in Figure 18.1. It was arrived at through interrogation of roles and responsibilities and functions carried out by the original groups.

Remarkably, there were almost no complaints. While on the one hand, the structure is not immensely hierarchical, on the other hand, it allowed for and required devolved leadership. It allowed for four staff members to be appointed to leadership roles who were not previously recognized 'leaders'; it ensured no loss of functionality but encouraged much closer collabor-ation. The devolved leadership empowers staff and allows for them to have positive input to the direction of the centre.

While all these changes were occurring, the core business of the three original centres was continuing with some changes in the style if not sub-stance. All significant successes, whether of individual staff members or collectively, were flagged up, publicized and highlighted; groups of staff from across the new 'divisions' worked together to develop the CAD website (www.cad.auckland.ac.nz) and a CAD magazine, *aCADemix*. Other mem-bers of staff are actively engaging in professional development, seeing new opportunities for themselves within the new structure. For the first time, there is transparency of all administrative procedures including the allocation of conference and travel funding.

Centre for Academic Development (CAD)

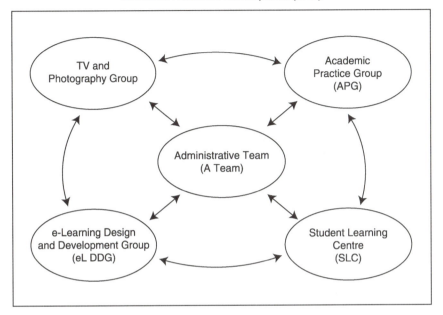

Centre of Academic Development encompassing functional groupings
all of which have a group leader reporting to the Director of CAD.

Figure 18.1 The Centre for Academic Development (CAD)

From the first mention of restructuring to finally agreeing an organizational and functional structure took almost 18 months.

Conclusions

Is it all fabulous? Are we achieving our goals? Have we made significant progress across the centre?

Nothing is perfect and settling down after significant change takes time. There are still some tensions – but too much change is now anchored and embedded for any pulling back. One area has been extremely reluctant to change in any way, but more engagement with the Director of CAD is shifting mindsets and empowering the staff. There is no turning back. There is vibrancy within the centre and a sense of success.

For the author of this case study, it is the most strenuous task she has ever taken on but at the same time, it has been a hugely developmental period. While 'development' of the individual is a somewhat intangible concept, not easily amenable to measurement or evaluation, my observations indicate that for many staff within the centre the restructuring has been a positive developmental process. Using the potential to develop the staff during restructuring stands out as the most positive and significant factor in bringing reluctant staff to the party.

Taking a holistic view of the restructuring, there are two key issues which have led to a high degree of success. First, even with staff providing central services, Becher and Trowler's (2001) stance on the 'culture of disciplines' comes into play. An important issue was recognizing that there are different cultures in operation, in this case between professional staff whose roles spread across student learning development, academic staff development and e-learning and all that is encompassed within embedding technology in teaching and learning. A second issue is the development of a community of practice (Wenger 1998) within the Centre for Academic Development and the structuring of teams with a clear identification of roles and responsibilities. There is scope for blurring of boundaries between the teams, and yet at the same time a strong sense of identity for team members.

19

Bringing new learning to old cultures

Belinda Tynan
University of New England, Australia

Introduction

The manager in this case, myself, was enticed to what could best be described as a 'clean page' in an Asian institution. My brief was to establish a faculty with a focus on e-learning. This included setting up the technical infrastructure, undertaking detailed market analysis, developing strategic business plans and developing courses for distance delivery and professional development of staff. This presented an extraordinary opportunity that crossed arts education (my discipline base) and the use of new technologies (a passion). It was critical to initiate processes that were in alignment with the organizational vision. It was an exciting time but not one that I was completely prepared for: in experience, in my ability to negotiate a different cultural context or in the management processes of the institution itself. There is much that is not explained in this case, and the reader can draw inferences about any gaps. The case study is an attempt to analyse the challenge of introducing change to a 'clean page', and the personal impact of this process.

A new context

Over the past 40 years, this part of Asia has become a regional leader through its investment-led economic strategy, where previously there was a reliance on the manufacturing and service industries. A new strategic agenda emerged with an increased focus on the health, education and creative industries. These strategies aim to increase the area's involvement and participation in the burgeoning globalization of knowledge, which is driving change and transforming world economies at an extraordinary rate. Economies like this one are increasingly active in the information technology and communications industries, and e-learning has risen up the HE agenda.

The institution

The institution strategically aimed to become the preferred regional provider of arts education. Government funded, but privately owned, the not-for-profit institution competes for students with a range of other universities, polytechnics and private providers of arts education across the South East Asian region. With my background in arts education combined with distance education I was optimistic about what might be possible.

The vision

The vision of the institution was closely aligned with the new national economic strategic agenda. Swift change prior to my arrival had seen a restructuring of the operational structure and recruitment of a considerable number of new management level personnel in response to becoming more outwardly focused and competitive. An ambitious new organizational vision underpinned by values such as quality, internationalization and cultural leadership had also emerged, and reflected the external global and national directions.

The institution's strategy for achieving its vision was multifarious and required all stakeholders to share new understandings of the vision in action (Senge et al. 1994; Tichy and Sherman 1994; Collins and Porras 1996). The institution was embarking on a combined planning and entrepreneurial approach to management processes (Mintzberg et al. 1998). However, a change process was not embedded and anxiety was present at a number of levels.

Management processes within the institution

The organizational culture was strategically controlled, so formal planning included the detailing of objectives, so that processes could be made explicit. Capital budgeting was embedded within the planning process and as a section manager I often provided bottom–up strategic plans that were assessed on a cost–benefit basis. My section would then accept responsibility for the performance of these plans. Performance was measured through strategic control, which was broadly understood. For example, the difference between planned and actual outcomes enabled questioning of the strategy itself. While planned strategies can and should be measured, there was scope to include emergent ideas. The institution needed to be flexible and able to respond to market shifts quickly, which it did on a number of occasions by accepting opportunities.

However, I was aware that strategic planning had a number of fallacies. Mintzberg et al. (1998) state that planning in this way assumes that an organization is 'able to predict the course of its environment, to control it, or simply to assume its stability. Otherwise, it makes no sense to set the inflexible course of action that constitutes a strategic plan' (pp. 66–7). I was aware that I could not abstract myself nor my executive managers from the daily detail and could not entirely rely on hard data in formalized institutional memoranda such as reports, accounting statements and business plans. Relying on hard data could impede my own and the executive's ability to formulate responsive strategies. There was a danger in relying on neat and tidy numerical quantitative assessments of performance, especially from isolated, discrete business units and initiatives (such as the section I managed), as this could discourage strategic thinking and disempower executive managers in viewing the broader institutional picture (Mintzberg 1994). However, communicating outside of a capital costing model was at odds with overall institutional strategies, especially with regards to technological infrastructure where benefits could be shared and costs centralized.

Mintzberg et al. (1998: 71–2) state that 'effective strategy-making connects acting to thinking which in turn connects implementation to formulation. We try things, and the ones that work gradually converge into patterns that become strategies'. They suggest that systems can become control tools rather than facilitating tools for thinking and learning organization. For me and ultimately the institution itself to be truly creative, it required a manager who was ready to explore and create new perspectives and acquire a broader understanding of the value of both planned and unexpected initiatives that might result in better outcomes. It was something I attempted to do and on some levels achieved. However, institution level enhancement was at odds with the major focus on distance learning students, rather than the whole institutional cohort. Realistic figures foretold disaster and predicting student numbers was farcical, since the faculty of e-learning was to be accountable for student numbers that did not exist in the market. A spreadsheet can be adjusted easily to show a surplus to get the initiative across the line. However, there was no substantiation in the market assessment, which was reported as poor. This was very challenging, given the millions of dollars at risk should student numbers not be achieved. If the strategy had been a combined strategy to enhance the current offerings, market advantage might have been obtained.

Challenges for e-learning

In the area of e-learning this was certainly true. The current strategic model would present some very pragmatic difficulties in meeting both the educational and business imperatives of the institution. This is a reality for many in the higher education sector. While the financial surplus attached to increased student numbers may be attractive, the intangible benefits of organizational efficiencies, enhanced reputation and knowledge capital and how this might contribute to the knowledge economy of arts education were also worth consideration. The few examples of how these costs and benefits are attributed highlight the high level of uncertainty in expanding e-learning (Oslington 2004). The challenge to find sustainable e-solutions is full of risk. This knowledge was of no comfort when the bottom line had to balance substantial risk against student numbers. Oslington states that many costs are sunk costs such as hardware and software which have little resale value. He states that 'expenditures on setting up systems for delivering online courses and expenditures on marketing courses are specific to the institution and hence have no outside market value if a project is abandoned' (pp. 233–4).

Costing e-development is essential but extremely difficult. Careful assessment of how e-learning might impact on other aspects of the institution's infrastructures and external perceptions also needed to be considered. An assessment of benefits against risk did lead me to more realistic judgements about the potential of e-learning. However, I had difficulty in persuading senior managers about the risk, and it was decided to move forward regardless. This decision forced me to reconsider whether I could lead the e-learning strategy – when data indicated what I considered an extremely negative end scenario.

Learning organizations

Theories of change which informed my experience and thinking related to the concept of the learning organization to inform my work (such as Quinn 1980; Nelson and Winter 1982). I believed Laurillard's (2002) thesis that learning organizations need to be adaptive in the increasingly messy and altering landscape of higher education. I was convinced an organization could learn from experience and adapt to its environment. For the institution, I thought that understanding these concepts and applying them could result in an e-learning policy, implementation strategy and consequent change management processes. I wanted to draw upon the idea that we could adapt to our environment through understanding and acting within the context (Mintzberg et al. 1998). The focus on mirroring organizational infrastructure similarly to how individuals learn was attractive, given the organization and cultural context. Laurillard (2002: 215) states that 'organizational knowledge creation is seen as a continual dynamic process of conversion between the different levels of the individual, the group and the organization'. In a learning organization routines are challenged by new emergent situations, which leads to conflict, change and strategic learning.

If according to Laurillard (2002: 215) a learning organization attempts to conduct internal learning conversations that help it learn from experience and adapt to its environment then institutional conversations are critical for ensuring the effective implementation of e-learning. For the institution, the conversations were to be linked to all levels, from student to chief executive officer. This was in part achieved. De Freitas and Oliver (2005: 86) also argue that 'by negotiating practices and their meaning, forms of work are legitimated or de-legitimated and lessons are learnt'. Strategic learning in this way would offer the institution an opportunity to inform actions in an ongoing, responsive and cyclical manner (Schön 1983). However, I had not considered the hierarchical nature of the institution carefully enough, as conversation and agreement were perceived as poor leadership from both above and below me.

Flexible learning and technology

Pedagogy and technology-led development are often mismatched with the economic imperatives of being part of a global economic influence in the sector, despite a proliferation of research focused investigations of web based learning development (Beetham 2005). For the institution, everyone else seemed to be 'getting into' e-based solutions, but the costs were substantial and the benefits not always clearly identifiable. The imperative to ensure cost effectiveness and the potential of the technology to transform educational transactions was at odds with the market driven vision of the Institution.

Conclusions

The challenge for me as a middle manager was in reconciling the high level of uncertainty in costs and benefits with desirable educational values. This meant identifying and assessing opportunities that could both meet the vision and aims, and at the same time meet economic pressures and technological advances. I was unable to persuade the institution to follow my approach. There were projections, budgets, risks identified and finally not enough of the thoughtful discussion or consideration which appear to be essential for change. I negotiated, ran tenders, got budgets approved and generally remained positive and open to what was possible. In the end it was not enough. One positive note was that I did achieve what others had not, in bringing in multinational partners and creating connections that could ultimately benefit the Institution. Many of these business connections have remained within my network.

Eventually, after extensive and stressful processes, I decided the task was not achievable. I had been through an intense tendering process, I was harassed by companies, funding was withdrawn, new funding had to be applied for, appointments were on and off again, a programme for distance delivery was franchised and validation of new programmes had been achieved. I had intense pressure from my line manager to behave in a way that was 'more Asian' (I am still unclear what this means, but perhaps 'more respectful'), but I was unable to achieve the balance of respect required. In my new position it was noted that I had behaviours consistent with hierarchical practices, so I was able to discuss what was learned with my current manager, who had also worked in Asia.

When I resigned, much had been achieved: I had set up an English language centre in order to improve poor student recruitment practices, and within a month of my resignation funding came through and a preferred supplier eventually signed up to deliver the e-learning infrastructure. Although this was an intense learning experience, the institutional culture was so at odds with what I had experienced elsewhere that I lost confidence in my ability to lead and manage within the context of chaos, uncertainty and ever-changing expectations.

I take full responsibility for my decision to accept the position and then to eventually leave, but I still ask myself an uncomfortable set of nagging questions: *Why didn't I ask more questions in the interview stage? Did I listen carefully enough to what they wanted me to do before accepting the position? What if I had stayed? Could I have done it? Did I give up too soon?* There was also much that was positive, not least the friends and the achievements, despite the stress of it all. I have not focused on these here, as it is the challenges of the position in which I found myself that may provide lessons to others. The main lessons are that managers of change in a new culture should:

- Not be naïve about promises made on being recruited.
- Work out how to deal with culture shock.
- Strive to achieve reconciliation between what is true and possible, and what is wishful.
- Seek help in solving communication difficulties with line managers.
- Be assertive about what they believe.
- Decide how to tackle the gap between top–down mandate and personal conviction.
- Seek mentoring and support to help with this.
- Not blame (only) yourself if cultures and structures don't allow you to do the job which needs to be done.

20

Theme 3 commentary

Veronica Bamber

The case studies in this Theme have highlighted four significant issues in enhancement efforts:

1 *Uniqueness*: universities have unique characteristics, and enhancement activities need to take these into account.
2 *Cultural characteristics*: enhancement initiatives take place within social systems, and so cultural factors need close attention.
3 *Context*: respect for the enhancement context is vital.
4 *Contextually sensitive actions*: change is effortful, and there is no magic bullet. However, some contextually sensitive approaches can help. These are:

   a have a theory of change, and keep adapting it;
   b be aware of the nature of learning in universities;
   c involve staff;
   d do the required groundwork for change, build commitment; and
   e even when effort is made to implement successful change, there is likely to be an implementation gap between what was planned and eventual outcomes.

In the remainder of this chapter, we will consider how each of these ideas has emerged from the case studies.

Uniqueness: universities have unique characteristics, and enhancement activities need to take these into account

As indicated in Chapter 1, universities are still largely loosely coupled institutions (Weick 1976), unlike, for example, most commercial organizations. Institutional and national higher educational politics are characterized by heterogeneous goals and expectations of autonomy. However, the truth in modern HE systems is that managerialism is on the rise (Henkel 2002;

Deem 2004; Deem and Brehony 2005), and a mix of the different cultural forms which McNay (1995) described as collegial, bureaucratic, enterprising and corporate is found in each institution. 'Shifting balances' (Silver 2003: 164) mean that corporate cultures are existing alongside collegial, academic cultures and departments are asked to show that their activities support institutional policies (Newton 2003: 433). Tensions between these conflicting cultures and values are not easy to resolve, as illustrated in Tynan's case (Chapter 19), where the major disjunction is between the value systems of entrepreneurial corporate forces and staff imbued with educational values. The tensions are increased as uncertainty and worry about an increasingly competitive 'market' prevail, and processes to combine academic and corporate values are required (Sporn 1999). This is not to say that proactive responses to environmental conditions are bad, simply that some creativity is needed in gaining acceptance and evolving overarching beliefs for a more entrepreneurial culture (Clark 1998). For example, using the processes of collegial governance, such as committees and working groups, was found to be helpful in the change activities described by Stefani (Chapter 18) and Lycke (Chapter 16) – although this type of activity may founder if staff perceive it to be managerialism masked by consultation. Since entrepreneurial and market demands are likely to increase, rather than disappear, a key task for change agents and universities themselves is to find ways to accommodate both managerial and academic values.

From Tynan's point of view, it was difficult to see how this fusion could occur, especially from her position as novice manager within a foreign culture. Economic pressures were at odds with educational ones, with the institutional imperative to build distance learning provision blinding senior managers to market and institutional realities. The managerialist culture emphasized strategic control and formal planning, without 'thoughtful discussion' of how to achieve institutional goals. The end result was stress for all those involved.

Cultural characteristics: enhancement takes place within social systems, and so cultural factors need close attention

Even in change situations which are apparently about adapting structures, as in Stefani's institution, cultural considerations dominate. Where senior management concentrate on 're-structure-ing' rather than on working with the values, aspirations and attitudes of the different subgroups (Bloor and Dawson 1994), the change effort can easily founder.

'Culture' has many meanings. One of these is 'the framework we use to give meaning to our day-to-day lives' (Knight and Saunders 1999: 145). This framework allows us to share and construct meanings within our social contexts, and renegotiate these meanings during change processes. Since we are in the terrain of values, assumptions, norms and tacit understandings, there are many opportunities for misinterpretation. Where meanings and cultural phenomena are ignored and the change activity is seen through one lens to the exclusion of others, as in Tynan's case study, then the likelihood of conflict and misunderstanding increases. This can also happen when culture is acknowledged, but seen as something static rather than an emerging and developing net which the change agent has to constantly reappraise. For Tynan, she was struggling to accommodate both Culture and culture: the norms and values of a different country, and the culture clash of managerialism versus educational values.

This is even more problematic when change is happening – as is usually the case – under pressure, often because those involved are carrying out their 'day job' at the same time as leading change. So when Stefani notes that change can fail for systemic reasons ('poor vision, inadequate communications, insufficient planning and resources, failure to make a compelling case and inconsistent messages, with leaders not following through') these important considerations are already a significant burden to take forward. Add to this her further requirements of needing to 'shift mindsets, to develop a culture, philosophy and ethos with which staff could feel comfortable and to align the centre with the institutional mission and goals in general' and we begin to appreciate the enormity of the task. The task of working with what Stefani tells us are 'fundamentally different philosophies, working cultures, values and management styles . . . within the original three centres' is perhaps a long term initiative which had to be condensed, in this case, into 18 months. The outcome is that staff in different parts of the organization do not want to change the way they work, the way they relate to each other and the institution, or even where they work: battle over each of these issues ensues.

Lycke also advocates a cultural approach to change, with sensitivity to local cultures and norms. Somehow, changes in structure and changes in culture need to interact in a complex dance, to achieve improvement in a complex and changing environment. This requires management skills and sensitivities far in excess of the ability to plan, set targets and implement. Brookfield (1995: 133) tells us that university senior managers need to be self-critical and reflective. We would add that they need the difficult quality of being able to maintain credibility while simultaneously 'bending in the wind' as a result of that reflection.

Context: respect for the change context is vital

We noted in Chapter 1 that much of the complexity in enhancement situations arises from the pluralistic nature of university departments, interest groups and universities themselves. Any change which hopes to succeed in this environment has to be made relevant for these different contexts. Lycke points out that lecturer training has to be aligned with other quality enhancement activities and how these are situated locally. In other words, if trainee lecturers feel that what is provided is appropriate for their teaching context, they are more likely to accept the training.

For Watson, the success of the MBA programme depends on it being contextually relevant, since it needs to be situated within the frame of HE institutional management. Although HE organizations have many functions which are similar to business functions (such as human resource management), a generic MBA would not be culturally appropriate to the 'professionally argumentative communities, with their performance and reputations in the hands of a wide range of groups and individuals' of university life.

Contextually sensitive actions: change is effortful

Change is effortful, and there is no magic bullet. However, some contextually sensitive approaches can help. These are as follows.

Have a theory of change and keep adapting it

A theory of change sets out what the intended change is, along with how and why it works (Weiss 1995); in other words explicit articulation of the enhancement activity. This is often neglected, since innovators do not always have a well articulated theory. If they do have one, they may not wish to share it, fearing that this will alienate those who will be the objects of change. Change agents have the vain hope that 'change by subterfuge' will go unnoticed. However, opening a dialogue about the theory of change can turn objects into subjects, and commitment can be grown.

Stefani's theory of change was rooted in the notion of communities of practice, and respect for disciplinary affiliations. This was a useful theory to some extent, but only within the frame of the different power, needs and attitudes, not only of the different groups involved but also of the different individuals.

Tynan expresses the most explicit theory of change, since she endorses the notion of the learning organization (Senge 1990; Laurillard 2002), drawing upon the idea that the institution could adapt to its environment through understanding and acting within the context. However, her theory of change was not shared by senior management, whose hierarchical approach was not consistent with Tynan's perspective. The lesson here is that, perhaps, a personal theory is only as good as one's ability to use that theory within the specific situation, and that the theory of change must also bend in the wind.

Be aware of the nature of learning in universities

Enhancement involves learning. Change does not simply occur through deliberate planning, but through informal learning about what is needed, as the change process is occurring. Watson found that professional learning in universities is different from elsewhere, and Sporn (1999: 31) states that traditional management theories do not apply. For Watson's programme (Chapter 17), this presents the challenge that learning about HE management should have its own 'signature pedagogy' (Shulman 2005a, b). This corroborates what we have said previously, that change should be context sensitive and adaptive. We have also mentioned the difficulty of transferring either learning or change from one situation to another, and Watson highlights the sting in the tail of learning to be an HE manager: course participants meet resistance to their ideas when they try to move them across the boundary between the learning situation and their institutional context. As outlined in Chapter 2, learning from formal learning situations cannot simply be transferred from one situation to another. Eraut et al. (2004) confirm that non-formal professional learning is also very important, and this, again, is shaped by many contextual factors.

Involve staff

Given what we have said about the nature of universities as organizations, and the importance of staff feeling involved in change, then enhancement efforts are helped by staff feeling they have ownership of changes: this is no simple matter, when many change initiatives are top–down. However, even change emanating from outside of the work or organizational unit still has to be implemented locally: change can be introduced from outside, but it is executed internally. Elton (2002: 5) describes the 'difficult pas de deux' of combining top–down push for change with bottom–up facilitation of the change. So external policies set broad parameters, but the real 'action' takes place at the institutional level, not outside (Slowey 1995: 26). Local staff influence outcomes, and in each of the case examples in this Theme we see the importance of gaining acceptance from the staff involved. This seems so clearly beneficial, since staff will accept their own recommendations, and may also contribute to improved decision making, that it may seem hard to understand why enhancement initiatives do not always start from this perspective. However, the conservative and contested terrain of universities, especially in the academic heartland of learning and teaching, and existing political contours, may deter senior staff from taking this route. Knight and Trowler (2001: 23) tell us that

> Achieving consensus on any important change is impossible in most university departments: waiting for it will stop change in its tracks. But at the same time imposing change in the face of opposition will bring resistance, delay, non-compliance and innovation responses with unintended consequences.

So, involving staff may be difficult, time consuming and will certainly lead to enhancements turning out differently from what was planned – but *not* involving them will also lead to these outcomes, and may bring further negative repercussions. Those involved all need to perceive some benefits in the proposed changes, and these benefits must be significant enough to overcome their own parochial interests and natural conservatism. In order to achieve this, those leading change require knowledge and sensitivity not only to the institutional culture, but also to the cultures of the sub-groups involved. Bourdieu (1977) tells us that 'the map and the mapped' need to be reconnected, and that means taking account of the situated demands of staff involved. If not, the best outcome from staff might be cynical obeisance, rather than commitment and involvement.

In Lycke's case study, it was important, therefore, that change to training of lecturers in Norwegian universities came from the universities themselves, in the form of a national body. It was not simply a top–down, government initiative, which would have produced more teacher resistance. In contrast, Stefani describes a senior management initiative. Although meetings and consultations were held, these were led by senior managers and human resources staff; this may have toughened territorial resolve, rather than dissipating it. One successful action was to give administrative staff a constructive role in shaping the new centre, by asking them to lead in building an administrative team. These staff were able to decide what would work, and then organize themselves around their own decision making.

Staff in Tynan's institution were also working with an imposed vision which was underpinned by managerial values and financially oriented aims. Although it was hoped that staff would share this understanding of the vision, the management processes, entrepreneurial approach and lack of dialogue with staff led to anxiety and a lack of common purpose. Strategic vision was not reflected in staff commitment, and aims were not sensitive to the local culture or needs. Change agents need to work hard not only to lead change, but to take those affected along with them.

Do the required groundwork for change: build commitment

Building commitment is a slow, complex process. It might otherwise be entitled 'consensus building', but this term gives the false impression that consensus can be built and that it needs to be unanimous. Change may not be consensual. There is little likelihood of building consensus among the multiple sub-groups with varied value systems who will be affected by change. However, collaboration can be built, as staff consider the range of options, and gradually move towards an agreed position (Martin 1999: 104). Unfortunately, what is seen as collegial consultation may not be perceived as collaboration, as colleagues see consultation as a sham which leads inevitably to whatever the change leaders were planning to do in the first place (Martin 1999: 97). Instead, change leaders need to put in place processes and incentives which will encourage staff to work more or less in the intended direction (Trowler et al. 2002: 5).

In Lycke's lecturer training case study, for example, the groundwork for teaching enhancement was laid because earlier versions of lecturer training had been tried, and staff had been able to see that the approach was acceptable. Nationally, the change was nudged along by the circulation of survey data. In Lycke's own university, there was also a strong and long tradition of consultations with groups and departments, so staff did not perceive the dialogue as a sham.

However, there is normally no rosy picture of staff gradually being persuaded by sensible management reasoning: the scenario is more likely to be one of 'creative conflict' (Pascale 1990) with strong debate and compromise. Brushing dissent under the carpet can lead to compliance and an atmosphere of resentment, but not commitment. In Stefani's restructuring case study, staff were consulted, but it is possible that the clear senior management conviction about the shape of the new unit, and the management discourse used in discussing it, inhibited staff involvement in planning the new centre. Staff were having to align with the institution, without the institution aligning with them and their concerns. Returning to an earlier point, management being open to self-critical analysis and reflection (Barnett 1994: 121) in the company of their staff could be helpful.

In the different culture of Tynan's Asian institution, her proposal to build staff commitment was seen as inappropriate in the highly hierarchical environment, where 'conversation and agreement were perceived as poor leadership from both above and below me' – another reminder of the need to make change effort situationally appropriate. Even when effort is made to implement successful change, there is likely to be an implementation gap between what was planned and eventual outcomes.

As discussed in Chapter 2, enhancement efforts happen in systems which are both resistant to change and also affected by the change. This results in these efforts looking different in execution than they did in planning. The metaphor of the implementation staircase depicts staff as being positioned on different stairs, changing the direction and force of the implementation 'ball' as it moves up and down the staircase. The difference between planned and enacted outcomes is the implementation gap between plans and reality.

In Tynan's institution, the implementation gap is a wide one: managers' strategic plans do not reflect market realities, and the plans cannot be accomplished. Staff standing on the staircase can be left feeling frustrated and stressed by trying to achieve the unachievable. For Watson, his course participants may experience similar frustrations, as they discover that their professional learning on the MBA programme is not easily converted into action back in their institutions. This may result in some of the staff who are involved in developing their ideas through formal or non-formal learning moving institutions in order to use what they have learned.

Not only is there a gap between intended outcomes and unintended outcomes, but unforeseen consequences can also emanate from enhancement initiatives. For Tynan, the change activity did not result in the benefits which were desired by senior managers, but some unplanned benefits did accrue, such as the development of an international network. Lycke also experienced this phenomenon: the lecturer training programme helped to encourage interest in developing teaching, provided a common language for discussing learning and teaching issues, and an understanding of the need for such discussions. According to activity systems theory, explained in Chapter 2, unintended consequences are more likely to occur when different elements of the activity system are out of alignment; for example, if a focus on a particular object (such as recruiting distance learning students) is not aligned with institutional effort in other parts of the system.

What we have seen in this Theme of 'Developing frameworks for action' is attempts in a number of contexts and in very different environments to create the structures and processes required for learning and teaching to be enhanced. In all of the cases it is clear that there is no 'magic bullet' for achieving enhancement. As discussed in Chapter 2, it is better 'for innovation to be based on understandings of how the probabilities of desired outcomes materialize than on the romanticism of policies that underestimate the sheer difficulty of making a difference'. As the case study writers have found, this is no mean task.

Theme 4

Challenging practices in learning, teaching, assessment and curriculum

21

Theme 4 introduction

Paul Trowler

Theme 4 is entitled 'Challenging practices in learning and teaching, assessment and curriculum'. There is, of course, a double meaning to this, and those two meanings are closely related. The enhancement efforts in this Theme go beyond incremental adjustments to current practices: a definition of 'enhancement' which implies tweaking what is already there. The changes discussed here are big enough to challenge those practices, and the attitudes and values underpinning them, and to envisage their replacement by totally new ways of doing things as well as new understandings. Enhancement in this sense questions old ways of doing things: there is contestation rather than simply incrementalism. And so of course these new practices, at least as proposed, are themselves challenging: our second sense of the title. They challenge academics and students to relearn what they do, to address old assumptions, to behave differently using new skills, perhaps overturning what has gone before.

Allen and Layer (1995) distinguish between 'big bang' and incrementalist models of change. Both approaches have their advantages and problems. The big bang approach is revolutionary, involving an attempt to make a number of simultaneous radical changes on a broad front. The hope is that the force of change will sweep across old assumptions and practices and that the suite of new ways of doing things will have its own momentum and internal logic, giving it sustainability. The incrementalist approach, by contrast, is slower and more evolutionary. It attempts to garner understanding, support and ownership of change among staff. The hope is to persuade, to provide a sense of ownership and to permit local adaptation according to needs and circumstances while broadly sticking to the trajectory of change. However, this can lead to resistance from staff, ghettoization and stagnation, or a 'snapping back' to old ways of doing things under the pressure of other priorities. On the other hand the big bang approach requires the rapid introduction of 'highly centralised and sophisticated management and administrative functions, well supported through mainstream funding . . . bringing together registry, management information, and guidance functions' (Allen and Layer 1995: 47). This is not easy to do, particularly at a time of resource constraint.

We have argued in the first chapters of this book that when change is introduced it is always inserted into a particular context, never into a white space. And the characteristics of context are significant in shaping, modifying the nature of the innovation so that it becomes 'domesticated' in some ways. Marx made a similar point, quoted earlier: 'Men make their own history, but they do not make it just as they please; they do not make it under circumstances chosen by themselves, but under circumstances directly found, given and transmitted from the past' (Marx [1852] 1869: 1). This casts doubt on the big bang approach: even radical change introduced on a number of fronts simultaneously will encounter the force of conventional ways of doing things. More positively though, a key point in our argument is that policy-makers and change agents would do well to think carefully about the context of enhancement as well as the enhancement itself (the normal focus of their attention). We argue that it is important to carefully consider three things: the proposed enhancement, its context and the interrelationship between them. This is a helpful first step in identifying potential obstacles and facilitating factors, and in predicting the possible path of implementation, including ways in which the innovation might become refracted, domesticated. A second step is to consider ways in which the planned enhancement might be changed to achieve a better fit, and likewise aspects of the context might be adapted to better suit the innovation.

This way of thinking makes one sceptical about the big claims that are often made for the latest innovation. Too often we hear heralded *the* new approach which will lead to revolutionary change in education. Currently this is information technology in general and, more recently, mobile technologies in particular. In the past such claims have covered nearly every imaginable type of innovation: 'Television was going to be different, said reformers. In the 1950s, when the Ford Foundation entered the arena of electronic teaching with its subsidies and publicity, the campaign for instructional television gained momentum. Soon an airplane was circling over the Mid-West, beaming down programmes to six states' (Tyack and Cuban 1995: 123). Tyack and Cuban note how teachers in different schools used these television programmes in different ways: some quite creatively; some ritualistically, not really impacting on the curriculum generally, and some using 'TV time' as an excuse for a coffee and a smoke. When the funding stopped, the reform died. Farrell (2000) (in reviewing and discussing Tyack and Cuban's account and others) reports that on a recent visit to affected schools he could find not one television. Farrell's point is that the rate of change is usually very slow and that the 'grammar of schooling' as he calls it (the basic familiar structures and practices of formal education) acts as a brake on change. Farrell says this:

> Schools *do and can* change, but usually *very* slowly, and seldom in ways which fundamentally alter the basic and familiar structures or

'grammar' of schooling as we know it. Moreover, when such change occurs it is seldom if ever the direct result of the fashionable, funded, and heavily promoted educational reform movements or waves with which we are so familiar, and which have been passing, with little observable effect, across the North American educational scene for at least a century

(2000: 87)

In an imaginary world, policymakers, institutional leaders and change agents have time to think carefully about innovation, context and process. They are able to shape proposals for change free of other factors, and free of the necessity for conflict and bargaining. They are able to persuade rational actors of the need for change and are able to offer rewards and to impose sanctions which work. They think clearly about what they want, and use evidence and research to understand both it and the current situation better. They have a well defined and agreed notion of what it is and how to get it, and they have a good implementation plan which is likely to involve and engage relevant people. In that world brave new worlds are quick to appear, where new technologies transform learning and teaching so that education becomes a more efficient, effective and enjoyable experience.

In another world, the one we usually inhabit, things are a little different. Pressure comes from above, or from the environment, for change *now*. Sometimes the alternative to changing is ruin: the university that must generate considerable income quickly or perish; the science department which suddenly finds its recruitment of students has dried up. There is resistance from entrenched interests, there are union organizations seeking to defend hard won agreements about practices (as was the case in Canada, resisting changes to lecturers' tenure arrangements; Horn 1999). Others in the policy-making arena have different agendas around a single initiative. There is confusion and fuzziness. Sometimes changes just have to be imposed, whether they ride roughshod over existing practices and conventions or not, whether or not they offend the 'grammar of higher education' (to paraphrase Farrell). Or sometimes policymakers decide that things are so bad that changes *will* be imposed, come what may.

The case studies in this Theme describe a variety of situations in which proposed enhancements are challenging in one way or another. In some the changes are imposed, in others they come from below. Some are driven by urgency, others less so. Some are closer to the big bang model, others more incremental. Rob Moore's case study (Chapter 22) concerns the attempt to shift the South African higher education system rapidly from a 'Mode I' curriculum (focused on disciplines) to a cross-disciplinary 'Mode II' approach (Gibbons et al. 1994; Nowotny et al. 2001). Here was a country struggling to overthrow its apartheid past and to regenerate its economy in a postsanctions world. The view among higher education policymakers was that the sector needed to concentrate on the demands and needs of the economy, of technologies and on solving the immediate problems that faced the country and region. A discipline based approach would not do that and so a curriculum focused on *issues* and *challenges* would need to replace it. Quickly. Moore discusses what happened.

At the institutional level, Simon Barrie discusses the attempt to introduce a 'generic graduate attributes' programme in an Australian university (Chapter 23). Here policy development and the implementation plan *was* research-led and theory based. The implementation plan was well thought through and was followed with care. This is a very unusual example of a situation close to the imaginary world described above. This case shows the ways in which the 'change sandwich', as Fullan (1999) calls it, can work well: an appropriate mixture of top–down guidance and support and bottom–up energy, enthusiasm, ownership and local adaptation to circumstances and needs. The outcomes were not perfect, as Barrie shows, but they were certainly satisfactory and the whole process of change seems to have been undertaken smoothly and efficiently. Needless to say, this does not mean that Barrie's approach can be mirrored in other institutions with their own identities and agendas.

The personal development planning (PDP) initiative discussed by Marilyn Higgins (Chapter 25) also challenged conventions significantly, though less radically than in Moore's case study. This was taking higher education into the realm of the personal and the affective: a process which deeply concerned Foucault (1975), who saw the increasing surveillance of the state manifested in such developments. This case study is also written from a very personal perspective and argues that one person's commitment and passion for change can ripple out across an institution, and perhaps further, affecting others. However, when values are not shared there are, as Higgins suggests, blockages to this ripple effect. Another issue is the question of sustainability. This is not addressed but is a significant issue. Could the PDP initiative flare up but then die away precisely because it is the product of one person's passion, becoming just another initiative which passes 'with little observable effect' over the higher education scene?

If Higgins' case study argues for change coming from the efforts of one person dedicated to an initiative, the one from Molesworth and Nixon (Chapter 24) comes to a very different conclusion. This case study concerns an attempt to break deliberately an aspect of the 'grammar of higher education': the power relations between lecturers and students so that students become the producers of knowledge rather than its consumers. The mechanism was an online learning space deliberately set up to achieve this effect. Molesworth and Nixon's analysis shows the resilience of traditional roles and, while they suggest that these roles can be challenged and altered, this is likely to be neither easy nor quick.

22

Contesting discourses in higher education curricula

Rob Moore
Wits University, South Africa

Introduction

Two competing discourses about the nature and structure of higher education are found in the South African context. One, the disciplinary discourse, refers to 'the traditional currency of courses and qualifications, based on longstanding academic propositions about the need for sequential learning within defined disciplines' (Ensor 2004: 342). The other is the credit exchange discourse, based on modular programmes and the accumulation of credits, with students able to choose modules and construct their own programmes of study in a flexible way, ostensibly allowing for a more seamless interface between work and study.

The credit exchange discourse is found in many South African policy documents. In particular its National Qualifications Framework is based on this discourse, recommending the organization of higher education by programmes rather than departments. It is propagated by senior figures in the higher education system there who draw on the work of Scott (1995) and Gibbons et al. (1994) to provide a rationale for this model of higher education. Those writers were invited to South Africa to discuss their ideas and helped to provide the model adopted there.

Implementing Mode II

The argument underpinning the credit exchange discourse is that globalization and the needs of developing and developed economies require a more 'up-to-date' structure of higher education, commonly referred to as 'Mode II', to distinguish it from the earlier discipline based approach which was 'Mode I'. How strong that argument is need not detain us here: the point is that the credit exchange discourse and its curricular model were being promoted in South Africa as a preferred model which should replace the earlier disciplinary model and the discourse associated with it.

The credit exchange model became enshrined in the South African National Qualifications Framework (NQF), which aimed to reshape and rationalize the qualifications system in the country. Another policy initiative, the National Commission on Higher Education (NCHE), then proposed that qualifications be based on 'programmes' that are 'responsive' to social and economic imperatives and that are typically inter- or multidisciplinary. A programme would be designed according to a set of 'responsive' end-of-qualification outcomes, and disciplinary content would be subordinate to the instrumental purposes of these programme outcomes. Although the programmatization reform may have found its initial logic in the credit exchange discourse, the notion of 'programmes' modified the discourse somewhat in laying the responsibility for determining curriculum design with the programme outcomes (and thus the team of academics designing the programme), rather than with the student who, in the classic credit exchange model, could pick and choose from a smorgasbord of discipline based units. One academic summed up a common understanding of what the programmes policy suggested:

> [It required] actually getting consensus on what a programme entailed. I think the central theme, really, was the outcome. There's a little person that you have to produce at the end of the day . . . to produce someone who would be able to go out there and do a specific job. We looked for a niche out there where we think we would be able to place people . . . and then you said, okay, if this is the field in which there is an opening, then what do you require to be able to be trained for that purpose?
>
> (Moore 2003a: 133)

A change process was put in place to implement the framework. The main elements of this change involved a move towards programmatic forms of curriculum and the reshaping of universities to become closer to a Mode II formation (Gibbons et al. 1994): one which addressed problems rather than disciplinary issues; which was flexible; which involved both universities and industry; and which was essentially temporary so that as problems were solved organizational structures dissolved. The intention was that the dominant, Mode I, formations (like subject departments) would wither away.

The problem for the influential academics and policymakers who were promoting the programmes model and discourse was that most faculties of science and humanities in South Africa were, and continued to be, orientated around the disciplinary discourse. The curricular implications of the latter were to organize modules or courses into coherent pathways, linear in nature, with the aim of inducting students into a discipline in a kind of apprenticeship. The attempt to impose the programmes model and its discourse within institutions was accompanied by different levels of anxiety and turmoil (Moore 2002). Where attempts were made to re-organize the undergraduate curriculum wholesale along programme lines there was often great antagonism from academics. Battle lines were drawn and conflict broke out between those determined to hang on to the disciplinary discourse and the ideology underpinning it on the one hand, and those determined to implement a programme based curriculum and a different discourse and ideology on the other. Once it seemed clear that the programme based reform was inevitable, and that survival of individuals within institutions might depend on their successful integration within programme structures, the battle shifted to contestations between academics as they sought to establish their individual identities and intellectual frames of reference within the multidisciplinary constructs of individual programmes. The details of these battles are spelled out in Ensor (2001, 2004) and Moore (2002, 2003a, b, c, d).

Moore (2003a) offers two case studies of this conflict, reflecting instances where programmes in development studies were initiated in two strong research universities in South Africa (here called UniA and UniB). It would be easy to assume that the field of development studies would provide promising grounds for the emergence of a coherent cross-disciplinary programme, given that there exists a field of practice (or perhaps fields of practices) that could be referenced for the outcomes of the programme, and that other exemplars of development studies programmes exist worldwide. Indeed, in both cases the efforts to establish these programmes were led by enthusiasts committed to their respective visions of the domain. In both cases, however, the results fall short of the ambitions projected in the policy discourses.

While in both institutions the attempted reform prompts tensions and conflict between academics and management, and between academics themselves, it is notable that these stresses are more marked at UniB than UniA. In a more comprehensive analysis of the programmes reform at the two institutions (Moore 2003d), it is suggested that the less conflictual experience at UniA was due to an approach to programmatization that saw the building blocks of programmes as disciplines and whole courses, while the approach at UniB was to dispense with traditional academic units of construction in an effort to achieve a more radical integration of knowledge in the curriculum. The latter approach was doubtless more profoundly unsettling for UniB academics as they sought to place themselves as individuals within the new curriculum constructs.

But even in the less disruptive context of UniA, the ideals of programmatization ran aground on quite practical matters: limitations in resourcing, and the need for disciplinary courses to serve the needs of several programmes at once so as to maintain optimal levels of enrolment. This set limits on the possibilities of customizing content according to programme outcomes. One academic commented:

> People might say, 'Okay we should do this or that in terms of a specific module', and we would say, 'Well, you can't really do that because you already are in a programme elsewhere, for which your particular module was found to be coherent with the outcome of *that* programme. You can't just unilaterally change that now, because then you are disrupting the fabric of that programme' . . . I think the moment you narrow the

focus down to specifics, then you get a problem with coherence in specific programme packages. It is a lot easier to keep things rather broad,
rather vague, and then it seems coherent.

(Moore 2003a: 133)

In this way, the economics of curriculum within the institution worked
against the intentions of the reform. Similarly, efforts to introduce innovative pedagogic approaches, like problem based learning, in some modules
limited the acceptability of these modules in some more traditionally oriented
programme contexts. However, the fact that existing discipline based modules could largely be used to construct the programme at UniA meant that a
negotiated accommodation between competing interests could be achieved,
and a reasonably stable programme construct was the result.

At UniB, the effort to achieve interdisciplinarity (rather than simply multi-
disciplinarity) across four participating disciplines faltered in the face of
the determination by academics to preserve the distinctiveness of their
theoretical bases:

Okay, so instead of having a [single] carefully constructed notion of
Development Theory, [the] course called Cities of the South . . . has a
whole lot of human geography theory about where cities come from and
so on. [Politics] has got a course in Development Management which
has its own set of theories. Anthropology has got another one. Sociology
has got something called Introduction to Development Theory . . . and
then there was a very interesting argument about a discipline which
said 'In other disciplines we don't treat theory in the same kind of
way as you do' . . . We have to accept the notion that we treat theory in
different kinds of ways . . . We had a situation where people were saying
'We're not going to offer anything new, we're just going to take the
existing courses and shove them in' . . . and [they] will pretend that they
fit together, but they didn't. There was no way that they were designed
together. In fact, we had quite a strong argument from people here who
were saying 'We don't have time to make them fit together. We refuse
to have meetings, or even to circulate course outlines to each other to
see what each other is doing'. There was that level of recalcitrance and
disillusionment.

(Moore 2003a: 136)

While in both contexts we have seen academics respond negatively to the
policy, resentful at their loss of autonomy, at the challenge to well established roles and identities, and at the escalation of their administrative loads,
these were features of the UniA context mostly at the start of the programmatization process, and by early 2000, these resentments seemed to be
replaced by a general acceptance, even some enthusiasm, in some quarters
for the new arrangements. At UniB, by contrast, protests, challenges and
conflict were much more persistent, and some of the programme constructs
have been much more unstable as a consequence (Moore 2003a: 135).

Commentary

This vignette illustrates two competing discourses. One stresses the continuing significance of disciplines as necessary for the development of systematic knowledge, while the other makes the case for curriculum restructuring as a means of responsiveness to changing social conditions. Underpinning this narrative is an ideological dispute between traditionalism and its defence of the integrity of disciplines on the one hand, and the ideology of 'responsiveness', and its preoccupation with the use value of knowledge on the other hand. Each position projects a different vision of the ways in which higher education and science systems work to benefit society.

Importantly, the case studies force the question of how, in cross-disciplinary contexts, a sufficiently authoritative basis can be established to resolve questions of curriculum content and design, especially when the logic of integration has not arisen organically among the participants. In conventional disciplinary or professional settings, epistemic order is usually founded either on disciplinary theory (which may suggest various options for ordering content), or on application (which orders content for problem solving purposes). In a cross-disciplinary curriculum setting which is mandated by an external policy injunction, rather than by a logic arising internally within the curriculum context, the case studies suggest that a stable new epistemic order may be elusive. It is evident that academics from different disciplines were reluctant to concede their respective theoretical bases, or failed to agree on what constituted an appropriate focus of application. Official policy texts alone could not provide a sufficient base for epistemic authority. What, then, are the limits of the policy field in shaping the intellectual practices of the academy (Muller 2003)? These case studies suggest that the internal dispositions of institutions and their constituent disciplines, and the identity commitments of academics, are powerful conditioning factors on the outcomes of policy. This in turn has implications for the kinds of conditions (including the rooted disciplinary foundations, the secure intellectual networks, and the necessary resourcing arrangements) that need to be in place to sustain cross-disciplinary curricula that are, in properly considered ways, 'responsive' to economic and social priorities.

23

Academic development as changing social practice: the generic attributes project

Simon Barrie
The University of Sydney, Australia

Genesis and context

This chapter explores a strategy for achieving institutional learning and teaching enhancement which is characterized as being both research-led and firmly situated in the ideas of practice theory discussed in the opening chapters of this book. The process of change itself has as its central tenet the notion that it is necessary to effectively re-engage academics as citizens of the university (Macfarlane 2006) who participate in collegial decision making to achieve the sort of institutional teaching and learning change which was the goal of this initiative.

The teaching change project which forms the basis for this chapter centred on the revision and effective implementation of the university's policy specifying the institution's 'generic attributes of graduates'.

The original generic attributes of graduates policy in Australia dated from the early 1990s, when the Australian government made publication of such a statement of generic university outcomes a condition of public university funding. The policy describes the generic skills that the university community agrees all graduates of the university will develop as a result of successfully completing their undergraduate studies. These generic attributes are to be developed regardless of the field of study. While the initial government requirement was that institutions articulate such outcomes, subsequent government quality assurance activities have increasingly focused on institutions demonstrating that they achieve these espoused outcomes. This increasing focus on outcomes based quality assurance strategies in the Australian higher education sector has prompted many universities to review these statements and the teaching and learning experiences they provide to help students develop such outcomes. This undertaking provides opportunities for examination of existing teaching and learning arrangements and has the potential to promote significant curriculum renewal and reform. However, this potential for change has rarely been realized in similar reviews and development undertakings in other institutions, both in Australia and overseas.

The relatively few, system-wide reviews of the impact of a decade or more of generic skills agendas has found that despite pockets of excellence there is little evidence of systemic change (Drummond et al. 1998; Baird 2007).

The institution on which this chapter's discussion is based is an Australian comprehensive university, offering undergraduate degrees in professional disciplines such as law and medicine, as well as generalist and specialist degrees in both the sciences and the humanities. The university is a large research intensive institution with approximately 50,000 students and 5000 staff and was (at the time) organized as 17 faculties along traditional disciplinary lines.

The challenges faced in the change process were many and varied in this context. First, there was a need to engage a research focused institution meaningfully in the process of reviewing a teaching policy, and instigating changes to curricula and teaching to implement the new policy. There was also the organizational challenge of implementing such a policy across a large university which operated with a highly decentralized model, in which the majority of decision making about teaching and curricula resides deep within the 17 highly autonomous faculty groups, separated on discipline lines, and, in terms of the development of students' generic attributes, often at the level of individual teachers within these faculties. A third challenge was the scale of the undertaking, with the possibility of the project encompassing anything from localized curricular reform to wholesale curriculum revolution. Added to which the project would unfold against a background of competing teaching and learning change agendas and limited resources to enable such change in an era which has been characterized by many as top–down bureaucratic, management driven change in higher education (McNay 2006).

A process of change

There were some key features which were explicitly built into the change process. First, the project was 'research-led', in that it drew upon relevant educational research into the theoretical and conceptual basis for the teaching and learning of generic attributes, and used the insights offered by this research to drive both policy development, curriculum development and teaching development. This research basis was considered important in an institutional culture which prioritized and respected research. Moreover, the research 'spoke' particularly closely to the university community, in that it was research conducted initially at the university itself and subsequently extended, with the participation of other respected international research universities, to other contexts. The use of a research based argument to frame a teaching policy was a strategy the university had already successfully employed in developing its teaching quality assurance policy. In both cases the research evidence provided a convincing and useful argument to support change. This support was in part through the provision of evidence underlining the need for change; in part to explain the barriers to change; and in part to provide a direction for change. The research revealed the need for a 'two-tiered' policy of generic attributes/outcomes organized around two different levels of these outcomes. The teaching and learning processes identified by the research as being associated with developing these different sorts of outcomes provided the direction for subsequent teaching and curriculum development work in implementing the policy.

The second feature was a deliberately collegial strategy to engage members of the academic disciplinary communities. The initiative established a core group of individuals from the 17 university faculties, and key organizations such as the library and careers centre, to work on the project. The dean of each faculty was invited to nominate a member of her or his faculty to represent the dean on the working group. In forming the group, the first task was to negotiate the roles and responsibilities of these deans' nominees. In doing so the participants collectively agreed to work in their faculties as leaders of change on the project. As will be discussed later, the extent to which this commitment was upheld by subsequent representatives, over the five years of the project, varied, with perhaps predictable results. However, the strategy sought to enable the participants to 'own' the processes of collegial decision making in relation to the specification of generic attributes and teaching and curriculum strategies enacted in their own discipline areas. Such decision making power has been considerably curtailed in recent years with increasingly centralized management of teaching and learning, especially as a result of increasing national quality assurance activities (Marginson and Considine 2000).

Stage one: local engagement

The first stage in establishing the group as a community of practice around the research derived concepts of generic attributes (Barrie 2006, 2007) which informed the initiative was to develop a shared understanding of the research on which the project was based. This was achieved by providing seminars, articles and discussion papers as education. This shared knowledge provided the basis for subsequent capacity building within the organization, around a new practice community. The second stage of this development of a shared discourse and set of practices was facilitated through the enrolment of the participants as collaborative developers of the institutional policy, through their leadership of the disciplinary statements of generic attributes that formed the second tier of the policy of 'generic' outcomes (Barrie 2004). Each faculty shared a commitment to developing three overarching attributes of scholarship, lifelong learning and global citizenship which would be achieved primarily through embedding the development of five clusters of disciplinary attributes in their curricula. However, the five clusters of attributes were shown by the research not to be generic but to be differentiated by the nature of the discipline knowledge they related to. Each faculty agreed to develop attributes relating to the same five clusters:

- Research and inquiry.
- Communication.
- Ethical social professional understanding.
- Personal intellectual autonomy.
- Information literacy.

While the disciplinary statements of attributes were firmly anchored in the disciplinary communities of practice, the shared architecture of the policy provided a commonality that allowed institution-wide conversations between the disciplinary communities.

The discipline representatives assumed the responsibility for leading the development of their own disciplinary definitions of these attributes. As such, there are different definitions of what constitutes the attributes of communication or research and inquiry, depending on whether you are from the conservatorium of music or the faculty of engineering. This variation was a consequence of the structure of the policy, which was determined by the research finding that this level of attributes was not 'generic' but differentiated by discipline.

The process of developing these faculty statements of attributes was led by the faculty representative who was responsible for negotiating an agreed statement of attributes, by facilitating discussion among the faculty's academic community, consultation with the relevant professional bodies and with accrediting agencies, graduates and students. As the project moved from policy development to policy implementation, these individuals also led the development activities to support their colleagues in enacting the policy in their teaching (discussed below). As part of a university-wide community, the members of the group supported each other in these undertakings in various ways. For example, by sharing consultation strategies at group meetings, collaboratively planning development strategies and cooperating on tasks across faculties, such as teaming up to run seminars on the new attributes in each others' faculties. These early faculty based consultative activities were designed to initiate the spread of the original working group community of practice to embrace discipline based communities of 'related' practice. To support the growth of the community and hence the embedding of the faculty based attributes into teaching and curricula, a range of second stage strategies was initiated.

Stage two: aligning institutional frameworks

As the project entered the implementation phase, the strategies focused on encouraging and supporting implementation of the policy by moving the community of practice from a shared discussion and vision to shared engagement with curriculum development. This is a far more significant challenge and one that has met with varied success in different faculties. In supporting this process, one of the core strategies was to embed the incorporation of generic attributes in teaching into the other policies and institutional frameworks that shape teaching and learning practice and culture. Chief among these are the ways teaching is measured/monitored/recognized in the institution, and the way it is rewarded on the basis of these measures. These are complex processes, which are typically articulated in central management policies, and the pressures they exert are varied in a devolved implementation model. To provide this institutional framework, the extent to which a student's studies fostered the development of the generic attributes was built into the central quality assurance systems as a key element of the student experience data collected in relation to graduates' and current students' perceptions of their degree, and current students' perceptions of the quality of the subjects taught in each degree. This quality assurance data is used for various purposes, including:

- Institutional funding through the new national Learning and Teaching Performance Fund.
- Faculty funding through the university's internal Teaching Performance Dividend allocation.
- Institutional and faculty decision making about applications for teaching awards.
- Institutional and faculty decision making in relation to the individual academic's promotion, probation and performance management.

As generic attribute development is a part of this teaching quality assurance data, various individual and institutional drivers for embedding come into play. However, these still require academics to 'engage' in order to have any effect. The implementation of many aspects of these quality assurance mechanisms is devolved to the level of the faculty. Faculties are fairly autonomous in how they decide to respond and act upon centrally generated quality assurance data. While there are institutional drivers for responding (largely in the form of performance based funding allocations) the processes that implement the university quality assurance policies are under the control of faculties. As a result there is considerable variation in how effective these are and hence in how effective these quality assurance drivers are in supporting curriculum change in relation to graduate attributes in those faculties.

The inclusion of generic attributes as an element of other key learning and teaching policies was also intended to support engagement by academics in embedding generic attributes in their teaching. For instance, the policy on course outlines requires that generic attributes are explicitly integrated with the subject learning outcomes specified for a course, and the assessment policy explicitly requires that the subject assessment be aligned with these outcomes. As a result of the strategy of aligning the generic graduate attributes policy with several other policies, the support required by the representatives leading this work in the faculties became quite diverse – for example, extending to support in running staff development on 'alternative assessment methods' and 'writing learning outcomes' (see stage three below).

In addition to aligning these other institutional frameworks through coherent policies, new ways of rewarding effective practice were established. These included supporting those leading the initiative in their faculty in successfully collaborating and applying for institutional and external funds to support their scholarship and development work related to the project. Another strategy involved the development of a new series of teaching awards based explicitly on best practice in developing curricula to foster the development of the new attributes – for instance, an award recognizing excellence in teaching 'research and inquiry' and one on excellence in teaching 'professional ethics'.

These sorts of quality assurance and enhancement drivers exert a significant influence in shaping practice and represent the second stage of creating communities of practice, in addition to the dialogues, debate and discussion around shared values and ideas about the intended outcomes in stage one.

Stage three: capacity building to enable change

The third stage of the enhancement strategy involved capacity building in terms of curricular resources and skills. This was facilitated by collecting and disseminating examples of shared practice and instigating a range of teaching development initiatives in the faculties. This process is still ongoing and is again under the local leadership of the group of faculty representatives, with central coordination. These initiatives are based on a shared focus agreed by the 17 faculty representatives at an annual meeting each year. For example, one year the focus was on developing skills and resources to support the development of generic attributes in first year transition to university; another year the focus was on developing the capacity of colleagues to write learning outcomes that integrated generic attributes development with discipline content acquisition; or the development of assessment strategies that addressed the new generic attributes. These capacity building activities were supported centrally but developed and run by the faculty representatives in cooperation with each other. This phase of the project is still ongoing and different faculties are progressing at different rates for various reasons discussed later in this chapter.

Stage four: moving from the classroom to the university experience

The next stage of the change project is intended to target the top level of overarching attributes identified in the policy. These attributes are high level dispositional stances that are developed by more than explicit curriculum activities. The research indicated that these sorts of attributes are developed through a student's participation in the broader university community. Primarily, this suggests the need for new ways of bringing students into the academic community of the university through different academic inter-actions with other students in different disciplines and with staff. This prompts serious questions as to the sort of community we offer students the opportunity to engage in. It requires a reconceptualization of how students engage with our research and service as much as with our teaching. This provides the opportunity for a new way of approaching efforts to link teach-ing and research and is a significantly longer term undertaking than the sorts of curriculum development that we have undertaken thus far, and will require new strategies and approaches to achieving change.

Let us now turn to a reflection on the variations that have been observed in how successful this change process has been in different contexts within the university.

Analysis of effectiveness of change strategies

The first point to note is that this was a long term and highly ambitious project. Renewal of undergraduate curricula to achieve generic attribute outcomes across such a large comprehensive and highly devolved university is not an easy task. The project has been running for five years and maintain-ing momentum is difficult as participants change and competing agendas arise. This is rendered more so as the curriculum renewal impacts on all aspects of teaching, from mechanistic activities such as writing learning out-comes to complex practices such as assessment, and in the future, funda-mental issues about the nature of academic practice and the sorts of learning communities we offer students the opportunities to engage in by attending university. Leaving aside the future aspirations of the project, viewed across the institution, there has been significant change, for instance significant improvements in some faculties' scores on student experience survey items reporting on the development of generic attributes since the beginning of the project. However, this change to date has been variable in the different faculties and the factors influencing this variable engagement are worth considering.

Disciplinary contextualization

The project has managed to engage all faculties of the university in develop-ing their own policy statements of generic attributes and all faculties have used these statements to some extent in their curriculum review and develop-ment activities. The level of engagement has been highest in faculties where there was a culture of considering the outcomes of education as a key factor in designing teaching and learning, notably the professional disciplines where accreditation drivers have much in common with the aims of the generic attributes project. However, the nature of the accreditation process was a significant factor influencing the extent of engagement. In some disciplines accreditation is still based primarily on inputs, for instance students must have X hours of lectures on a particular topic, or X hours of practical experience. This 'input' model of accreditation is one that has been abandoned by many professions who have recognized that the need of employers is for graduates who have been educated to be capable, not graduates who have only been trained to be competent (see Stephenson and Yorke (1998) for a discussion of this distinction). In the generalist faculties where accreditation drivers were not present, the focus on education rather than vocational entry requirements is perhaps stronger and exerts a different positive influence, in that the tradition of cultivating a habit of mind finds many echoes with generic graduate attributes outcomes. While this was recognized in the enrolment of discipline leaders, taking greater account of these different epistemological and accreditation drivers would have assisted in planning how to facilitate the ways discipline communities have engaged with the shift from content input to capability output as the way to frame the curriculum. However, the strategy did recognize that different disciplinary conceptions of knowledge do raise particular challenges for discipline communities engaging with the concept of generic attributes. For this reason the local leadership of somebody inside the discipline was considered essential. Fostering disciplinary engagement recognizes the variation in the ways different discipline knowledges interact with and shape generic attributes at the first level of the policy (Barrie 2006). This will become even more important in the next phase of the project, as it is this explicit disciplinary relationship that provides the bridge between the explicit curriculum strategies and the implicit academic community strategies which are needed to foster the development of the sorts of dispositional stances described by the next level of the new policy.

Local leadership

Leaving aside these epistemological considerations, a key practical factor that appears to have influenced the level of engagement with the graduate attributes curriculum renewal project was the nature of the leadership at the faculty level. In some faculties deans championed the project and local influential teaching and learning leaders were nominated to lead the initiative in their faculty. In these cases it became a priority for discussion and a focus for teaching development work in the faculty. In other faculties where it was not seen as a strategic priority, or was possibly not seen as congruent with the vision for teaching and learning, there was no strong local leader delegated by the dean and the initiative has not engaged the academic community in the same way. For instance, some faculties were notable for their limited attendance at project meetings and change in these contexts has been less apparent. This highlights a key issue for such change initiatives. Unless the leadership of the faculty is convinced of the need for change and the benefits of change, there is unlikely to be any change. This challenge might be recast as the challenge of creating the necessary conditions of dissent. The right people, those with the capacity and mandate to lead the academic community, must be convinced of the need for change before change can be expected to occur. The project leadership rarely engaged directly with deans except for an annual report and request for a nomination of the deans' delegate to the project. Instead, the expectation was that deans' nominees would establish regular communication with key leaders and decision making groups in their faculty and indeed this was the case in many faculties. Some faculty representatives arranged regular briefings with the dean or associate dean teaching, in others a report on the project became a standing item at faculty teaching and learning committees. However, in other faculties such communication was absent. In these faculties, the pressure on deans and associate deans of many competing priorities for teaching development may well have meant that some remained largely unaware of the work taking place in their faculties. While the project focused on engaging the local teaching communities of the faculties, it perhaps did not pay sufficient attention to engaging the real faculty leaders.

The initial education stage of the project was intended to achieve this engagement with the deans' nominated representatives. However, in targeting deans' nominees rather than deans themselves to attend this meeting, the project relied on these nominees being able to return to the faculty and actually lead change. While in many cases this was true, in retrospect it was clearly not true in all cases. In some cases the faculty nominee was too junior, or too busy as a result of the role not being recognized in their workload allocation. In other cases it was a lack of access to internal communication strategies to embed their activities in the strategic priorities and planning of the faculty. Regardless of the reason, in all such cases where leadership capacity was limited, progress has been slow. The reliance and need for a local leader capable of integrating the initiative into local priorities and systems cannot be underestimated.

Variability in the devolved institutional drivers

A key driver for change in this project was the institutional quality assurance strategies. As noted, the extent to which these are effectively implemented in faculties varies and to date there has been little central interference in this. As a consequence these drivers were effective in some cases and not in others. It is no coincidence that the faculties with the most effective implementation of internal quality assurance processes are also the faculties in which the engagement in curriculum renewal related to generic attributes has also been greatest. Recent moves at the university to

make faculties more accountable for responding to quality assurance data
are likely to have a significant effect on the way these drivers influence
teaching change, though obviously only on aspects embedded in the performance measures.

Academic engagement through the establishment of a community of practice

The establishment of the working group brought together some of the key
people in the faculties to engage in debates and discussion to develop a
shared, though not homogenous, understanding of some of the complexities underlying the graduate attributes initiative. Such an activity bears many
of the hallmarks of a 'community of practice' (Wenger et al. 2002). These
individuals were then equipped with the knowledge and resources to engage
in similar debates and discussions in their faculties. The common framework
of the policy and conceptual understandings allowed these leaders to come
back together to support each other's work and allowed an ongoing dialogue
across the institution in relation to the initiative. One of the vulnerable points
of this community became apparent as the membership of the core group
changed. In retrospect, more effort needed to be made in supporting new
faculty representatives in developing the shared knowledge that character-
izes a community of practice, when they first joined the project. Over time,
much of the shared understanding in such communities is tacit and while
embodied in practice is not easily picked up in the space of a single meeting.
As such, many of the newer members of the group did not necessarily share
the same insights as those who had been part of the initial capacity building
and education phase.

Research-led change in a research intensive university

Another feature of the project that has contributed to its success is the
research-led nature of the initiative. Not only was a research basis necessary
to engage and convince the members of a research intensive academic
community of the proposed teaching change, the project has fostered an
ongoing research community around the topic. As much research does, the
research has grown beyond its original local context and has informed and
been taken up by other researchers and investigations elsewhere. In the
process it has been enriched by the insights gleaned from further investigations and applications in different contexts, and these insights and developments have been fed back into the project. As the research has an applied
as well as conceptual focus, it has formed the basis for conversations not
only with the research community but more broadly with the community of
employers and government. Perhaps most significantly in terms of the members of the university involved in the project, the applied research focus has

allowed the community of practice which has grown up around this teaching initiative to develop on the research front, as well as the teaching dimension of academic practice. With the relevance of the work to the community through employers and government, the initiative has the potential to allow the multiple faces of academic practice to be expressed within the community of practice.

Central support and leadership

While issues of local context, be they variations in disciplinary epistemologies or local leadership, are important, the other key feature (and vulnerability) of this change strategy is the ongoing provision of central support, leadership and vision. The faculty nominees who participated in the project noted on several occasions the importance of these factors. Such support is only possible as long as the initiative remains a priority of the central management and leadership of the university. From an institutional change perspective, it is hard to envisage how such a large scale and long term curriculum renewal undertaking could be sustained without central support to ensure congruence with other institutional initiatives, support and capacity building for local leaders and the coordination and brokering of collaboration between the diverse local initiatives.

Conclusions

Some features of the project have made it particularly effective. Chief among these was the recognition of the need for local contextualization of the policy and implementation in the discipline through engaging the members of these diverse academic communities. This was achieved in the form of the disciplinary statements and in the location of teaching development workshops and activities at the faculty level, but more importantly by distributing leadership and allowing these individuals responsibility and agency in the undertaking. The distributed leadership retains coherence through central coordination and vision, and the alignment of the surrounding policies and institutional frameworks. The 17 local statements, while unique, share a common architecture of five clusters of attributes and the three common statements of overarching dispositional attributes. As a result, a coherent institutional identity is preserved and there is the capacity to align local activities with institutional missions. This distributed approach only worked where local leadership was present and was only possible because it had well resourced central support and strong central leadership. The central organization of the project facilitated a number of activities:

• Cooperation between individuals working in the different faculties.
• The sharing of resources.

- The provision of central capacity building and leadership development for the local leaders.
- Most importantly, the alignment of local implementation with other central policies and systems.

This hybrid model of locally led, faculty based implementation, with central support and coordination of the change process, appears particularly well suited to diverse devolved organizations such as this particular university.

24

Frustrated aspirations: discovering the limits of a virtual learning environment

Mike Molesworth and Lizzie Nixon
CEMP CETL, England

Introduction: the script

For tutors and students, lectures are the focus of HE, despite suspicions that perhaps not much learning happens in these ritualized performances (e.g. see Ramsden 1992). In this chapter we consider the seemingly taken for granted roles of tutor and student. We note how they may be in the process of being transformed by the market, and reflect on the implications of this as we report on our online space that was designed to invite new educational performances where the focus is on the student as the producer of knowledge. To do this we draw from Goffman's (1959) ideas. We aim to show that there is a tendency to replicate familiar, passive and now consumer-like performances in the online spaces provided by HEIs, despite the fact that other online spaces readily produce new roles that might be more closely aligned with the competencies we desire for our students. We are of course advocating resistance to the use of virtual learning environments (VLEs) as tools for the 'efficient delivery of HE commodities' and instead that we tap into a growing participatory online culture.

Goffman (1959) uses a theatre analogy to account for the regularity of social behaviour. Interactions between people are based on their understanding of the frames around them: 'I'm in a restaurant'; 'I'm in a doctor's surgery'; 'I'm in a lecture room'; etc. When we understand our role within a performative space, we 'act it out' as if we are 'front of stage'. Performative spaces therefore have clear spatial and temporal settings, in our case the lecture theatre, the seminar room, or teaching lab, and 'incorrect' framing may lead to failed performances. Should you start lecturing in a pub, others probably won't reciprocate the 'correct' role of 'student'. For 'dramatic realization' there is also a need to make a performance visual. As the most visual spectacle of education, lectures are given a special status such that when we think of higher education, we tend to think of the lecture as where learning takes place. But in addition to this front of stage, there tend to be backstage regions where the preparation for the performance takes place, *and* where 'out of character' discussions thrive. The 'unguarded' aspects of backstage produce a secondary performance that is more 'truthful' in that it may knowingly contradict the front stage performance. So discussions in the backstage bars and cafés inhabited by staff and students include routine complaints (that students are too passive, or that lectures are too boring) that seldom take place in the lecture theatre itself. This leaves a third space, 'outside' the stage, where individuals cannot access a specific performance because they can see no role for themselves.

We tend to establish and refine our accepted roles and over time develop not just regular performance, but mapped out life plans (see Cohen and Taylor 1992). For example, for students doing a degree, it may be experienced as little more than a temporary continuation of the 'pupil role'; a reluctant and inauthentic 'hurdle to jump', tolerated only as a way to gain access to the performances, and ultimately the life plan (job, career, money, material goods) that they really desire. In such a situation, the focus may be on getting this script 'right' rather than questioning the value of the roles and performances required along the way. So even when we become aware of the degree to which we are 'merely' acting in a particular situation, we go along with it anyway to protect our 'grand plan'. Backstage reflection on our performance then serves a conservative role. Distanced cynicism becomes no more than a strategy for dealing with the recognition that our lives are scripted and by telling ourselves that 'this isn't really me', we can continue to perform successfully. Rather than confront or change a performance, we go along with it safe in the knowledge that the now distrusted script is not really 'what we are about'. Hence front stage performances may become 'cynical'. Lecturers are cynical about the lecture, but continue because otherwise the 'performance' of education would be ruined and their script undermined, allowing students to accept a passive, docile role and the authority of the tutor. The backstage complaints (that lectures are boring and that theory is pointless) are simply another aspect of the overall script of being a student: the cynical distancing of themselves from the role they have just played. Depressing isn't it? But we continue to let it happen and there may be worse to come. One of Goffman's own examples of a cynical performance is of the shoe salesman telling the female customer the size they want to hear, rather than the one that fits best. Perhaps it is significant for us that this example is from a service profession because it suggests that if education is also performed as a service, tutors may be tempted into similar cynical roles, supplying the bullet-pointed information students appear to want, or even giving the customer the assignment mark they desire. As the framing of HE changes into a commercial space of financial transactions, tutors and students may accept this new frame and the accompanying roles of service provider and customer as the reality of higher education, with tutors subsequently suppressing critical comment on a student's work in favour of the flattery of a shoe salesman. Such a shift may even reinforce the 'value' of the lecture in exchange for a fee. Students pay and the tutor 'gives them' their knowledge in a fair transaction. The script for students/consumers who pay for someone else to dispense predigested information is to ask, 'What am I getting for my money?' rather than, 'What am I learning?' or even, 'How am I learning?'

So education is performed and, using Goffman, we understand that staff and students accept lectures as the reality of education. To be a tutor, or to be a student, is to manage the appropriate presentation of the self in these performative spaces. Even when the backstage roles of students and staff might suggest that a good part of the performance is cynical, there appears little attempt to change things. Currently, HE may be transforming into something like a marketplace, but this is far from the transformation that many academics want. Rather than the passive yet demanding performances of student–consumers, and the value-for-money and flattery focused performance of tutor–service staff, we might consider other aims for higher education. Calls remain for universities to provide challenging and effective learning environments for their learners. If we want students to be autonomous, creative and critical thinking practitioners, the onus is on us to design education such that these performances are agreed upon and taken up over their time with us.

As a disruptive technology we might expect the Internet to impact significantly on education. But in our experience when VLEs are introduced they tend to create spaces that replicate the familiar frames and therefore performances of education: the lecture and the seminar, the tutor as authority and the students as passive, or paying, 'rank'. VLEs are password protected, controlled and monitored by staff, divided into courses, and available only to students and staff for the duration of the course. The web as a place for free expression and experimentation (for example see Turkle 1995) seems largely irrelevant in this context. Yet the performances encouraged by other online spaces (YouTube, Facebook, Wikipedia or Secondlife) seem much more fluid, and online communities, wikis and user-generated content sites contain considerable material that might be relevant to the subjects that we teach. Projects like Wikipedia demonstrate the ability of collaborative groups to construct knowledge *and* highlights its contested nature, and YouTube invites participation and peer review, for example. Participation in these online spaces is not part of a course, or for financial exchange. They remain outside the formal performance of education, despite the fact that they may be examples of thriving communities of practice (as suggested, for example, by Wenger 1998) containing just the sorts of learning that some educators view as ideal because they are participative, egalitarian and involve mutual learning. Arguably this is the sort of convivial education that Illich, Freire and others envisaged but with digital knobs on.

Creating an online space: high ambitions

With these apparent contradictions in mind we set out to create an open, informal online learning space. 'CEMP communities' were an attempt to encourage students to develop as creative, critical thinkers and knowledge producers and sharers via an online space that is more like those that students inhabit for pleasure and social networking. We created a series of subject based sites that contain group blogs, forums and wikis and an invitation for anyone interested in the subject area (not just our staff and students) to join in, share ideas and otherwise collaborate in constructing knowledge. The communities are not based on any one course, but rather on broad subject areas: broadcast media, interactive media, journalism and marketing. They contain no university or course 'branding' and are therefore a 'neutral' space to discuss specific topics, not unlike many of the other forums found on the web and quite different from our VLE. To reinforce the open nature of the site, open source software was used (Mediawiki, Textpattern and Phpbb). So the site was designed to be outside the normal spaces in which education is performed, and the invitation to participate as a member of a community of learners was open. For example, we envisioned that marketing and interactive media students, tutors and practitioners might debate aspects of online behaviour to gain new insights and understanding. We hoped that in discussing such things on an equal footing (or rank) that the tutor would be removed from the centre of focus and that students would have the confidence to express their views and experiment with ideas. We further hoped that with growing confidence and experience students would begin to take on the role of knowledgeable scholar, or practitioner; a role which they might carry seamlessly beyond their course.

Ambitions frustrated: 'snapping back' to traditional performances

But this 'ideal' has not happened so far, after one full year of use. Instead, participation has been rejected by most that we invited to take part (staff, students and practitioners). So, for example, although we invited over 30 staff at this and other universities to take part, and expected others to 'spontaneously' join, there are at best only six or seven active staff users, all from our institution. And although all 1500 students in our department have been invited to join, most of the 90 or so student participants are from one unit. And of these 100 or so users, only 22 have made more than one post a week on the forum or blog. Worse still, far from creating new performances, most users, including the tutors, have been dragged back to their familiar scripts. So, for example, despite the open invitation to join the blog, only staff have posted to it and very few students ever add comments. The blog has come to resemble something suspiciously like a lecture: tutors produce content for student consumption. In the forum we find again that very few students start discussions and most topics are consistent with the sorts of issues that might occupy seminars or tutorials such as assessment issues or topics from the course curriculum. Almost 20 percent of the 2177 posts relate directly to assessment and many student posts are addressed directly to tutors. Staff make 25 percent of the posts to the forum, yet make up about 7 percent of the user population. In terms of views, staff threads dominate even more and passive consumption is confirmed by our log files: 30,000 views for the blog and 175,000 for the forum. Lurking is prevalent: far more view than participate.

Students have not generally strayed from their rank, despite invitation. For example, we offered users the chance to use the wiki to create the 'ideal interactive media course', but they let the opportunity pass; designing courses does not fit their script of a 'student'. When we asked students about this they even confirmed a consumer role: 'but we pay you to teach us', they told us, 'and now you ask that we teach each other'. And most staff seem to accept that they too are only 'paid to teach'. Despite numerous invitations and announcements about the site, so far most staff see no point in participating. In short, users have coopted the space to allow for a continuation of their existing educational performances, or simply ignored it, unable to grasp a possible role within the community. Even worse, it seems that as the site was coopted to continue the existing 'traditional' performances of education in our school, other potential users were left feeling like 'outsiders' to the performance. There are no practitioners active either, again despite invitations to many.

We could of course also explain our students' behaviour in terms of the common discourse in pedagogical literature that maintains that many students hold fixed, absolutist notions of knowledge and therefore expect to be 'given' packets of predigested information from experts. Such students aim to get the 'right' answer for an assignment and therefore elevate staff posts to the most valuable content in the assumption that they contain the 'correct' knowledge (see Lucas and Leng Tan 2006). Alternatively, our failure may be explained by a lack of familiarity with the 'new' technology. We acknowledge that our online space is still young. Maybe we just need more time? Or perhaps we failed because there was too little inducement to adopt the new roles. Rust (2002) and Webb et al. (2004), for example, suggest that assessment is the answer to online participation. But to ensure participation in the communities by assessing their online activity only reinforces the passive role of students who merely follow what tutors tell them to do. The desire for students to begin to see themselves as able to co-construct knowledge and learn independently is replaced by the instrumental script, 'I have to do this to pass my degree'. And when outside the educational setting and playing a different role, young people easily learn to use online spaces, such as social networking sites to share their ideas with their peers. Apparent notions of truth, incompetence and motivation don't seem to extend beyond the situated experiences of education. Simply explaining our analysis as premature is not congruent with significant changes in online media (for example the rapid rise of social networking and participation media) that *have* happened over a very short timescale. We would contrast the limited student contribution here with the amount of time these students may have spent on other online spaces such as Myspace or Facebook. So we tend to think that a better explanation is a separation of the HE performance from these more authentic experiences, ones which *involve* learning though that may not be their manifest purpose. For example, when asked about his failure to participate one student commented, 'I think people participate online when they are interested in the topic'. He continued 'you know, football, or music and stuff'. Then finally seems to realize what he had just said: 'well obviously I am interested in my degree subject too, but . . .' Of course, ours is not the only online community with few contributors and many passive readers, so we might be tempted to dismiss our experience as simply 'normal' for online groups. But again, our hope was that students would use the site to express their ideas; we did not want to create just one more community of a few producers and many more consumers.

Formal education has given students educational roles that are often 'cynical', but changing them is not easy. Our initial experiences of the online space suggested that the existing performances of higher education are sufficiently 'fixed' that both staff and students worked to reproduce them online by turning the blog into a 'lecture space' and the forum into a tutor-led 'seminar'. But there was some 'success'. For example, the forum produced 2200 posts, compared to 800 on the department's VLE the previous year. And some students did 'spontaneously' start sharing ideas by responding to each other's questions and by starting threads on issues that interested them. For example one student protested that student creativity was undermined by the tutor's insistence on the use of theory. This thread produced 101 posts, 5000 views and over 17,000 words. It involved a complex and at times passionate discussion about what both students and staff wanted from a piece of work. Without the forum it is perhaps unlikely that there would have been space for such a discussion. So this is evidence that some students rejected their more usual passive role and some staff found new ways to interact with students. But there were very few threads like this.

Conclusion: scripts for the future

Perhaps projects to break students out of comfortable, established, accepted behaviour need to be actualized on a broader scale. Perhaps we must also consider physical learning spaces, faculty cultures and organizational value systems too, as suggested by Somekh (1998). And as Van Note Chism and Bickford (2002: 93) also identify, one of the key barriers to the creation of effective learning spaces is the 'body of persistent, often tacit, assumptions that hamper our thinking and action'. We must do more to address these. To exploit online spaces that are free from the constraints of the curriculum and assessment, we need to first provide students with a capacity for an HE learning performance that is free, at least for a time, from framing by a 'formal' educational setting. But in fact we persistently and perhaps increasingly reinforce the very behaviours we find frustrating by responding to students'/consumers' desire for content, structure and especially assessment.

The fact that lectures and seminars continued alongside the online community served to legitimize the existing performance of HE and position
other spaces as unnecessary, yet demanding, add-ons. As we are positioned to
perform as service staff we might be tempted to further emphasize these
things, demonstrating how much 'valuable knowledge' we are 'selling' in
exchange for fees, or focusing on work skills and graduate recruitment as a
way to tap into students' consumer life scripts. In such circumstances perhaps our online efforts are doomed to rejection. In our initial 'experiment'
we made only a small invitation to 'act differently'. Yet for staff, radical
departure from accepted behaviour – especially when this directly challenges
student behaviour – may be rejected by students and frowned upon by faculties that keep a sharp eye on 'customer satisfaction'. Again, in order to transform roles we need an institutional culture that supports this ambition rather
than a culture that acts to undermine changes through existing structures
such as timetabling, course design and especially marketing efforts.

What might we do in the future then? Anthropologist Victor Turner
(1982) suggests another way to 'manage' change in scripts: the liminal or
border-crossing ritual that separates people from one performance, symbol-
ically provides them with a new one, and then re-introduces them to society
in their new roles. Taking this approach we would need to engineer activities
that first separated students from their previous educational roles, and then
re-introduced them to a different conception of learning. We might suggest
that such activity needs to take place at the start of their university studies,
creating activities that deliberately and self-consciously allow students to recognize that they have changed and in doing so have taken on a new role
which they may subsequently perfect. In this way, new scripts can be provided where critical, creative and autonomous abilities are given space to
develop. We'll leave it to further research to imagine what such liminal rituals
may actually be like, but we suspect their focus would not be on delivering
curriculum content via lectures. Until we are able to attempt such a transformation our online learning space remains problematic, but perhaps
not pointless. At least we better understand the tendency to revert to more
familiar performances (and the insidious creep of market roles) and we can
continue to challenge these in small ways. We cannot help but notice the
sharp contrast between the failure of CEMP communities and the flourish-
ing of websites such as Myspace, Facebook, YouTube and others; robust sites
whose usage has mushroomed rapidly without any 'assessment needs' or user
training at all. This might mean that we can achieve more by making our site
closer to existing online communities in terms of content and tone or even
taking our content to these other spaces.

If we consider education as performance we can reflect on the fact that
both students and tutors accept and perform reasonably 'fixed', yet often
'cynical' roles. These performances are strongly related to the spaces we
choose for them to take place, but although digital technologies provide us
with considerable scope to devise new stages, the urge to recreate existing
performance is likely to be strong. We have seen this with our attempt at

building an online community of learners. Perhaps what is required then, is some more substantial effort to break down the routine of educational performance; something to separate both staff and students from the familiar roles they have adopted and accepted as reality. Adding urgency to this call is the further 'threat' that unless we can provide students (and staff) with new and satisfying roles, the role students may increasingly adopt is that of the consumer, with tutors as 'service personnel'; roles that fit too comfortably with the passive consumption of paid-for content.

25

Freedom to innovate, freedom to resist

Marilyn Higgins
Heriot-Watt University, Scotland

Context

This is a personal story, necessarily so, because it discusses change promoted at the level of the individual. The reflection is based on the example of how I embedded personal development planning (PDP) into the curriculum of a postgraduate town planning course and developed supportive processes and creative outputs over the last eight years.

In the late 1990s, the 'Dearing Report' (NCIHE 1997) spawned a national Quality Assurance Agency (QAA) recommendation to offer PDP within every higher education course in the UK. This has been variably applied by institutions, courses and individuals. Reflecting back to why I wholeheartedly embraced this practice (while many academic staff did not) caused me to do my own PDP: what was it about me and my values that compelled me to follow this path? My 18 years in town planning practice and active involvement in the Royal Town Planning Institute (RTPI) helped me articulate the skills, knowledge and qualities important for professional work. The RTPI requires applicants to submit a PDP to become members and to keep it up-to-date to guide their continuing professional development. Much of my past research has been about the interface between education and practice: creative thinking, work based learning, change management and skills development. I also got in touch with my deepest values about what education is really about, summarized in the quotation: 'Change is learning and learning is change' (Mink et al. 1993: 207). This was conditioned by my American liberal arts education, where I was active in education reform and my biggest heroes were Carl Rogers (*Freedom to Learn*, 1969) and Neil Postman and Charles Weingartner (*Teaching as a Subversive Activity*, 1969).

The new PDP practices were 'challenging practices' in a number of ways. There was no tradition of anything like PDP within the institution and it was a very different form of assessment than students were used to. Innovation is context driven – what might be generally accepted in one institution or discipline is very new to another. In this example, PDP is introduced at induction, where students begin reflecting about their reasons for doing the course and their aspirations for their education and career. Later, it is the assessment for a management and professional development module near the end of the course. We stress holistic and personal reflection of oneself as an individual, which makes it a bit different from other PDPs. The other lecturer involved and I share our own PDPs to model both the process and the product. In recognition of different learning styles and to encourage creative reflection, students are shown various ways to produce a PDP, including a skills matrix, mind map, collage, Sigmoid curve (a tool for managing change, as developed by Handy (1995)) and medicine wheel (a tool for creative thinking; see Filmore and Thomond (2003)). A week before they are due, students assess each other's PDP, to gain from peer feedback and the chance to see another person's approach.

This work was pioneering and preceded institutional and departmental policies on PDP. There has been continued opposition from some academic staff, who see it as a 'mickey mouse' exercise, resent yet another new demand, or do not see the place for the 'personal' in higher education. There might also be a fear or lack of confidence in being able to deal with what PDPs might throw up.

Support from key players helped me over time and, in turn, the changes I have introduced have influenced them. Most importantly, positive feedback from students has fuelled my will to continually develop the practice because I had considerable evidence of the benefits they experienced. The Head of Careers helped me develop the initial skills matrix. He used our PDP as a pilot for the whole university and our positive results fuelled his own enthusiasm for the practice and influenced subsequent institutional policy. The modules where PDP has been used for assessment were taught in part by two other senior academics (including one of two deans of the university), who have been 'inspired' and 'humbled' by student efforts, saying it is their 'favourite marking of the year'. I have also been supported by our HEA subject centre, the Centre for Education in the Built Environment (CEBE). I have written a CEBE case study and staff briefing guides and have given presentations at national and local workshops; in my experience, every time one is engaged in such activities, new insights develop.

Analysis

An imposed national requirement (for PDP) provided the framework and gave the opportunity to unleash the latent potential of an individual academic to promote useful change. A positive aspect of both national and institutional PDP policies is that they can be adapted to local circumstances, giving freedom for creative implementation. Even though academics often complain about the weight of bureaucracy and new requirements, course leaders and lecturers have considerable freedom when it comes to actual delivery, as long as they don't stray too far from overall course structures and frameworks such as learning outcomes and assessment criteria. This example shows that L&T delivery is influenced by our personal values, beliefs and experience, which are in turn conditioned by factors such as professional requirements. Constraints to this freedom are usually self-imposed, often blamed on someone or something else. But this is precisely what makes wholesale change difficult to achieve across departments and institutions. Everyone is conditioned by *different* experiences and values. Personal conviction led to the changes discussed in this chapter, but leads others to resist. This example also shows how important it is to convince people of the need to change at the beginning of the process. At the end of the day, just as it is impossible to *make* students learn, it is also impossible to *make* academics change, without draconian sanctions.

This PDP initiative started in isolation, due to the enthusiasm of the lecturer. It is an example of how one person can make a difference and how the ripples can spread outwards. I was supported by others and the experience in turn has influenced them. The Head of Careers confirms that the enthusiasm of one teacher was a 'tonic' and increased his conviction that PDPs could work. I and one of our students gave presentations at institutional workshops to disseminate the value of PDPs more widely. In a research-led university, it was obvious that this was a feature that not many staff were familiar with. Both the Professor I work with on the module assessing PDP and the Careers Advisor confirm that they now think of PDP more creatively and positively than before, less mechanistically. The Professor says that it has encouraged him to reflect on his own career and tell students about his own PDP. It chimes with his own views about education as developing students' potential, not stuffing them full of facts that can be examined. It challenges teachers to be reflective, even though this is problematic, as Brookfield (1995) suggests, but it is also a threat to embedded cultures of how we have always taught students in the past.

Innovation to the PDPs has kept happening over time, in light of feedback from students, other educationalists and my own research. Supportive senior managers encouraged the policy and practice at key points of its implementation. The addition of more creative forms of PDP as an alternative to the skills matrix came about through someone from another more visual discipline describing our first matrix as 'icky' at a subject centre seminar. The practice thus unfolded from my own thinking, comments from lecturers in my own and other institutions, careers advisors and student evaluations. Involvement with the HEA has cemented my views and supported me, while I in turn have been able to disseminate our activities to a wider audience. It is difficult for me to evaluate what effect my work has had more widely, although a seminar I gave at the HEA recently was very well received and a participant commented, 'Thank you for reminding me why I went into higher education in the first place'.

My attempts to influence change continue to develop. On a year's sabbatical to the University of Auckland, to head the planning courses and be the Deputy Head of School, we are already discussing how PDPs might be a useful unifying practice to introduce into their curricula. The previous head of the PDP group in Scottish institutions has also gone to work at the University of Auckland and I am expecting her to be a strong ally. What started as a ripple in Scotland is being felt, albeit in a small way, on the other side of the world.

Many students have commented that when the PDP assessment was introduced, they were sceptical, but afterwards admitted they had learned a lot and appreciated its value. Inevitably, the students who put the most into their PDPs get the most out, and there have been some moving success stories. Student feedback confirms that PDP helps with job applications and promotions, professional requirements, confidence and creativity. However, last year we had our first two fails, out of a total of several hundred students over the last eight years.

But the ripples become diffused by hitting rocks along the way. Within my own school, even armed with very positive student evaluations, not all lecturers are prepared to actively integrate PDPs into their own modules. It does not square with their own ideas of what higher education is about or their own priorities for precious time. In RAE[1] driven higher education, the emphasis on 'the person' is not always seen as a goal of teachers, or education. Even with the institutional PDP policy, implementation has been patchy, depending on the will of individual staff. The ripple has certainly not turned into a tide.

Conclusions

It is possible to make linkages between this case study and the theories of change discussed elsewhere in this book. This example illustrates how change was sparked by a national recommendation that chimed with an individual's personal convictions. The national policy allowed for a wide variety of implementation methods; this is an example of the 'loose linkages' mentioned in Chapter 1, that allow for local adaptation, which I believe are more likely to ensure a positive outcome than slavishly following a template. The real driver of the change was an individual's strong belief in the relationship between PDPs and education. Underpinning this practice, for both staff and students, must lie an openness to change. Teachers can have a more powerful influence in modelling behaviour and attitudes than in what they overtly set out to teach. For me, moving between countries and professional institutions, and from practice into academia, chimed with the notion that crossing boundaries led to wider self-development, including the confidence and maturity to do what seemed right, breaking the mould. PDP is a bridging tool between academia and practice. It can in itself help us to move between boundaries.

It was quite an emotional moment for me to realize that, in reflecting on

---

[1] The RAE is the UK's national Research Assessment Exercise.

why I so passionately believe in PDP, I suddenly saw my own personal development in a new light. I came to the happy and profound conclusion that the moments I feel 'self-actualized' are when 'teaching' and 'learning' become indistinguishable. It is hard to describe, but I know when it is happening. These values led me to seek out like-minded people among my colleagues in the school, the university and the HEA. I was influenced by the wider community of practice and in turn was able to influence them – or at least some of them. This includes students – or at least most of them. This positive feedback is what keeps the practice alive because it is the ultimate goal, it is what learning is surely about.

But just as some students respond more enthusiastically than others, I have also come to realize that my values about PDP and education are not shared values across all staff. Just as the higher education system allows me freedom to innovate, it gives others the freedom to resist. It is a threat to embedded cultures, particularly hierarchical and exam based learning and teaching styles. Change is best promoted when people can feel the need to change and see its value.

It only takes one person to make a difference. In education, as in PDPs, we create our own reality. The ripples do spread.

26

Theme 4 commentary

Paul Trowler

The four cases illustrate in different ways a considerable range of issues about enhancement processes when there is an ambitious project at stake. Three key issues arise:

1 *Inertia*: the tendency of change processes to 'snap back' to something approximating previous practices.
2 *Context*: respect for the context of enhancement is vital.
3 *Theory*: the value of good theory in understanding change.

Inertia: the tendency of change processes to 'snap back' to something approximating previous practices

The most ambitious of the four change projects must surely be the South African case related by Rob Moore (Chapter 22), involving a system-wide change in the curricula and approach of higher education and, underpinning that, aspirations to change in fundamental ways the purposes and direction of universities in that country. Here indeed was a serious challenge to established social practices and conventions, and a challenging project. In terms of 'lessons for change' there is a lot to learn from his study, but perhaps the most clear lesson here is the power of established ways of doing things – the 'grammar of higher education' we discussed earlier in this book. It is easy to imagine that changes can be quickly introduced given sufficient determination, juicy enough carrots and big enough sticks. Yet an array of factors leads to inertia (what Elton (2003) refers to as 'dumb insolence'), resistance, mere rhetorical compliance or reconstruction of initiatives that undermine or reconfigure their intended effects. Social practices become engrooved, as we discussed in Chapter 2, and when they do they are very difficult to shift unless circumstances are right and implementation strategies are appropriate and sensitively engaged.

The case from Molesworth and Nixon (Chapter 24) highlights the same issue. They refer to the phenomenon of 'snapping back' to traditional social practices (though the language of 'roles' is used), and this can happen all too easily. Moore also mentions the resistance to the switch to Mode II curricular structures and arrangements from many academics in South African universities, where a variety of factors were at play. In a number of senses the discourse of this initiative offended them: it offended their identities as affiliates to a particular discipline, it offended their notion of what they were about as academics, their fundamental purposes, and for some it simply didn't make sense. The Mode II 'solution' was based on a misdiagnosis of the problem and certainly was the wrong prescription, from this point of view. In short there was a fundamental incompatibility between the initiative and extant social practices. Of course in any 'challenging' initiative this will be the case. But part of the route to success involves not directly challenging current practices but leaving space for negotiation, compromise and domestication into a shape that works. This 'low-res' approach (Chapter 2) may result in something less than the policymakers want, but would at least be attainable and sustainable. In these South African universities this was not done.

Another way of minimizing resistance and reconstruction, of achieving greater sustainability for change and thereby avoiding the snap-back phenomenon, would have been to, first, think carefully about the initiative and the context of its application and then, second, to develop and put into action a careful implementation plan which foresaw and forestalled possible deleterious responses. Again, in these South African universities this was not done.

Context: respect for the context of enhancement is vital

Case 2 by Simon Barrie (Chapter 23) shows how beneficial having a carefully considered implementation plan can be, particularly when it shows respect for the details of context. As Barrie shows, fundamental to success was reflection on the particular characteristics of the university in question: a research-led elite institution which, at least in parts, might be resistant to an initiative, seeking to change in quite fundamental ways some of the purposes and aims of undergraduate education. Finding areas of congruence, and positioning the initiative discursively so as to emphasize compatibility with current practices, was really important. Then, based on that, careful planning and a staged implementation plan which takes into account as many factors as thoughtful consideration of the issues can identify was very effective in this case.

Barrie sets out four carefully integrated stages to this implementation process:

- Stage one: local engagement.
- Stage two: aligning institutional frameworks.

- Stage three: capacity building to enable change.
- Stage four: moving from the classroom to the university experience.

As Barrie shows, each stage took into account the particulars of the context, though the level of analysis of that context shifts as one moves through the stages. This is replicated in the account of another experience of change by Shrives and Hall (2006) which is summarized in Figure 26.1.

One key difference between the account summarized in Figure 26.1 and Barrie's account is summed up in words like 'anxiety', 'fuss and argument' in that figure. The introduction of graduate attributes appears to have been done remarkably smoothly, and this is very much the exception rather than the rule. An apparently smooth ride can indicate superficiality and lack of sustainability. *Sturm und Drang* is often just a part of the change process that has to happen, both in the sense of 'storm and stress' and in the literal sense of 'storm and impulse'.

Theory: the value of good theory in understanding change

If Barrie's account of the graduate attributes initiative fills us with optimism, Molesworth and Nixon's (Chapter 24) story is likely to cast us into the pit of despond, or would do were it not for their careful analysis of reasons why their online space failed to achieve some of its ambitious aims. They use the theory of social roles to understand and explain the inertia and the 'snapping back' to conventional practices and assumptions that happened in their project. There are some similarities between the tradition in social theory that sees social life as dramaturgical and the more recent social practice theory that we outlined in Chapter 2. For example, both see behaviour as partly, even quite strongly, conditioned by the social context in which the individual is situated. The idea of 'role' has us acting out prescribed behaviours and words that are considered 'right' in a particular situation. Likewise the notion of recurrent practices suggests that we behave in unconsidered ways repetitively, just taking for granted that those are the ways things are done. In both cases practices are 'hardened' and difficult to shift. But both role theory and social practice theory see some space for agency too, for the individual to use free will to shift and reshape, to reflect on and critique the conventions.

There are, however, some fundamental differences in the two approaches which are important for our thinking about change. One is the way in which the individual identity is conceptualized. For role theory there is a clear split between the 'shell' and the inner person. The inner person is constantly there and stable. Reflective and analytical, it is the source of agency, it is the actor beneath the act. The shell is the 'part' the actor plays, speaking the lines written by society more widely. It is literally an act, false in a way. Social practice theory conceptualizes identity quite differently, and in fact

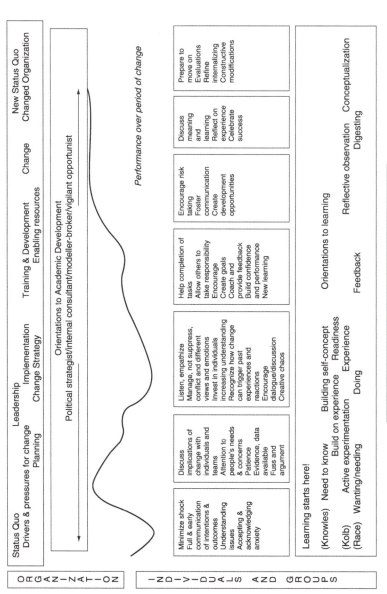

Figure 26.1 Interventions through the change process

Source: Hall and Shrives 2006

sometimes avoids that word because it is singular and has connotations of stability and permanence. In this theoretical strand identity or, better, subjectivity, is inseparable from social context. Individuals are 'positioned' in particular ways by the context they are in, by the interactions going on around them. The notion of subjectivity means that people change in fundamental ways in the different contexts they operate in, sometimes in quite contradictory ways (though they themselves do not recognize this because people compartmentalize those different contexts). Contexts 'hammer' new subjectivities into shape through the moment-by-moment as well as long term cut and thrust of social interaction, contest and power, negotiation and consensus building.

What does this mean for enhancement? Fundamentally it means that a 'role' metaphor is a more pessimistic one for shifting practices than the 'hammering' one. The actor inside is not particularly malleable while the roles he or she plays are prewritten and hard to change, as Molesworth and Nixon argue and demonstrate in their case. Given a social practice understanding of the social world, change becomes something that is happening virtually every moment. Subjectivities change with context, and context changes as the individuals involved change and environmental factors shift. For role theory the social world is a static place. For social practice theory it is in constant flux. And for the change agent the implications of this are quite striking and the tasks presented are very different: rewrite the scripts or attempt to engage with the complexities of context in ways that move things in a desired direction. The first sounds simple but is hard to do. The second sounds complex, and it is.

The final case study illustrates nicely an attempt to shift the nature of contexts, to realign values in subtle ways. The story is an optimistic one and illustrates again the point about the different theoretical understandings and their separate implications for change. Higgins (Chapter 25) is influenced by Carl Rogers, among others, and Rogers' understanding of the individual in their social world is very close to that of social practice theory. For Rogers, individuals act in a very dynamic 'phenomenal field'. The context of the social world is the world of experience. It shapes them and is shaped by them as they perceive it and act in it. Sets of values and the idea of the 'self' are shaped by the interaction with the social:

> the organized consistent conceptual gestalt composed of perceptions of the characteristics of 'I' or 'me' and the perceptions of the relationships of the 'I' or 'me' to others and to various aspects of life, together with the values attached to these perceptions. It is a gestalt which is available to awareness though not necessarily in awareness. It is a fluid and changing gestalt, a process, but at any given moment it is a specific entity.
>
> (Rogers 1959: 200)

And we see this understanding in Higgins's account of, and optimism for, the PDP initiative in her university.

What all of the cases in this theme of challenging practices offer is an insight into what has worked more or less well in the change initiatives described. Change is often driven forward either on the basis of a tacit theory of change (Trowler and Bamber 2005), or with no explicit theory in place. In some cases, the writers had articulated a theory of change before embarking on the project. In Barrie's institution, for example, a clear and shared theory of change seemed to be present. Even if the initiative does not turn out as expected, as in the Molesworth and Nixon case, it is helpful if change agents have crystallized what they hope to achieve before starting the change effort. Then, the theory of change can be re-examined within the context of that change, and light can be shed on why the intended enhancements were not obtained. The next iteration of the change process can then be discussed, to decide whether the theory of change was right in the first place, or whether different approaches need to be used. The important question of 'why' the change does or does not work (Weiss 1995) can then inform future change projects.

27

Making practical sense of enhancing learning, teaching, assessment and curriculum

Murray Saunders, Veronica Bamber and Paul Trowler

Introduction

We stated in Chapter 1 that we intend this book to be 'useful', within an expansive notion of 'use'. We interpret the idea of use in two ways. One refers to style, attempting to write accessibly. The other has to do with usability to the reader. We want you to be able to use the ideas and approaches contained within the book, and with the approach that sees enhancement as involving change practices. We offer the reader: 'a glimpse of what is possible, the basis on which it might be possible, the theories and concepts that enable us to understand what is possible and which help us to see the present differently, embodiments of examples of what is possible, and finally who can make it possible' (Chapter 1).

The cases in the four Themes above demonstrate the complexities of working with the idea of enhancement as change. We set enhancement within a particular type of change dynamic which focuses our attention on sociocultural approaches, and an emphasis, specifically, on social practices. Social practice thinking highlights the way 'practice' itself yields knowledge and learning. Having drawn on the case examples and our own theoretical framework, in this final chapter we turn firmly towards the reader. We ask you to imagine or rehearse the enhancement process(es) in which you may be involved and capture the 'framework for action' we offer. We ask you to relate the ideas to your own enhancement practices. The frameworks for action are low in fidelity. In other words, they are not very highly specified, have high adaptive capacity and are designed for use. They are intended to bridge between the ideas in our text and new actions in situ, in an actual teaching and learning environment with real colleagues in real time. As we said in our Introduction to the book, we don't offer tips and tricks, but we do advocate action on the basis of ideas, conceptual tools and reflexive questions for those involved in change efforts at national, institutional, departmental and individual levels.

This concluding chapter reminds us that higher education is a particularly complex site for enhancement initiatives, so that change agents need especially well developed approaches and techniques for implementation, along with a good conceptual understanding of the enhancement initiative being undertaken, of the change context, and of the probable interactions between them. The chapter offers conceptual tools for change implementers, emphasizing 'reflexivity', in three sections. It first suggests that the way the enhancement process is understood by those engaged within it is a useful place to start, so categories of implicit change theory are considered. Second, it examines how those engaged in change understand their own enhancement identities. Third, it summarizes key questions in the process of achieving enhancement through change, our 'framework for action': questions to interrogate our own change approaches, based on the lessons which have emerged from our analysis of the four levels of change efforts across the HE sector in the chapters above.

While the book takes a multifaceted look at enhancement implementation, it is clear that our readers will be a range of stakeholders at each level, and that different parts of the book are likely to resonate with each group. A reader with a national remit will have read the cases, and the ensuing conclusions, with a different frame of reference from a reader who has a departmental or institutional role. Nonetheless, the Theme introductions and Theme commentaries for each Theme have drawn together accounts and analyses which have relevance for each group of stakeholders. No matter what your role, you will now be aware that change is achieved due to a complex combination of factors, and that a common sense approach to leading change is inadequate. The analyses and frameworks for action are applicable at all levels.

We mentioned the idea of reconstruction and translation in Chapter 2 in the context of the bridging tools that might be required to cross boundaries in a change process. Of course this is shorthand for the complex processes typified in our cases. However, all the cases show how practices at individual, departmental or project levels *and* at the systemic levels of whole sectors are emerging as translations of learning and experience from one environment to another. But we are using the idea of a 'bridging tool' here to emphasize the way in which the cases and the distillation of experiences might be used as a resource for others engaged in their own enhancement processes.

However, we need to explore how these bridging tools might be used. We have said that ideas, practices and processes that emerge in one context or situation may not be reconstructed in a simple way in another. Indeed, some theorists (as Fuller et al. 2005 suggest) have overemphasized how singly effective *contextualized* learning might be. While acknowledging the need to be aware of the situated nature of learning through practice, we also believe that some 'decontextualized' resources in the form of new classifications of practice, theories of change or how people see themselves as 'change agents' can evoke personal and systemic comparisons, aid understanding of situated processes and act as a resource for planning ongoing actions. In other words, we can provide the frameworks for action so important for 'bridging' from one situation to another. These categories are tentative and designed to be evocative to stimulate refinement and self-reflection. They are grounded in narratives and depictions of change by those engaged in it. We now summarize our frameworks for action, as depicted in Figure 27.1.

Framework 1: change agents' implicit change theories

We suggest that it is important to understand on what basis enhancement practices might be initiated and sustained. This understanding can be built from a combination of components which are external to ourselves (change theory awareness, examples from other enhancement encounters) and internal to ourselves: contextual alertness, and an awareness of how we conceptualize change and our role in it. The case studies have shown that some change agents are aware of both theoretical constructs, and of their own internal reckoning, such as their implicit change theory. We present our analysis of these implicit theories here as a form of diagnostic tool for reflection, since personal knowledge of the implicit assumptions underlying enhancement activity will enable more 'knowing' judgements as to alternative strategies.

We argue that the cases presented in the themes suggest different ways of seeing or understanding the enhancement process, and different conceptions of that process. The key players have acted on the basis of implicit change theories that both guide their understanding of change and indicate fruitful actions. The categories which follow depict theories of enhancement in typological form to capture for heuristic purposes the way *agency* and

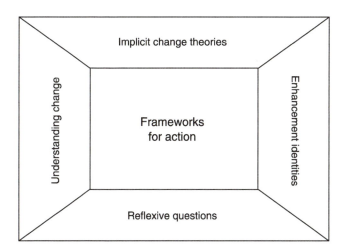

Figure 27.1 Frameworks for action

individual predilection interacts with the policy, organizational and departmental environment within HE. They build on work already undertaken on change within higher education environments across Europe (see Saunders et al. 2005).

Practice based exemplars

There were cases in which enhancement was predicated on using exemplars of actions, artefacts or curricular practice to promote teaching and learning enhancement in a particular environment. The theory of enhancement in these instances was that 'practical' examples of useful, interesting or innovative teaching will produce changes in individuals who are interested in adapting their practice or who feel change is inevitable or are experiencing other pressures to change. The idea of 'contagion' or the metaphor of epidemiology is interesting and apt here. The theory of change embedded in this conception is relatively weak: it was not clear how and under what conditions an interesting exemplar would create changes within a wider system. This epidemiological model of change is based on the idea that a 'beacon' or enclave of interesting practice becomes more widely adopted by osmosis. On what basis colleagues might take up the challenge of enacting the interesting embodiments displayed in enhanced practice is left unstated. Another perspective on this process may be that having a practice based exemplar is a necessary condition for change but is often not sufficient. Resources, political will and other chronic and conjunctural features of the environment might also have to be in place in order for change on a wider front to take place. The great challenge if these other factors are not in place is how to move from interesting but marginal enclave to influential bridgehead.

Resource driven/dependent

This category understands enhancement in terms of the resourcing incentive. Change will occur when there is a financial or resource incentive, in other words resources are offered in exchange for specified changes. In addition, enhancement will not occur or at least is dependent on resources being made available to enable change to occur. This is an interesting example of categorically driven funding change. Usually (and this is apparent in the examples we have in our cases) this theory identifies the way the centre of a university forms a policy of development. It establishes criteria against which it invites bids for developmental funding. Only those bids which display the desired profile of characteristics receive funds. This means that there is a considerable amount of steering, which might be effective or not in producing the desired outcomes. Resourcing enhancement implies an exchange with the environment to acquire resources, which might, in turn create dependencies (Sporn 1999). This model does imply relatively tight coupling between university departments and the university centre. In many cases, centrally driven change requires resourcing at the level of the department, but this model of enhancement is also seen operating at the level of institutions and at the level of national policy on enhancement.

Rhetorical support

This category has a theory of enhancement which rests on rhetorical legitimation, usually provided at the institutional level. It may involve resource allocations as we identify above but, at its minimum, it provides legitimation for the changes which are sanctioned by institutional policy. That is to say change occurs when there is institutional power behind it. In most of the cases, institutional rhetorical support is not sufficient to produce changes, which demonstrates the inadequacy of this theory of enhancement when considered alone. However, in many cases, institutional or national rhetorical support was present at the same time that practice based exemplars were being developed to embody desired changes. The process of change is interesting here in that many bottom–up exemplars run ahead of institutional or national rhetorical support. At some point though, institutional or national rhetorical support is required in order to promote wider adoption.

Professional imperative (enriching student experience)

This enhancement theory is based on the idea of professionalism in teaching. Because a 'good' teacher will be interested in providing up-to-date, interesting, well supported material and processes which aid and deepen intellectual development, often collaboratively, he or she will be interested in developing and experimenting with courses which take advantage of possibilities offered by information and communication technologies (ICTs) or any other kind of opportunity. Essentially, this is a theory of enhancement which is based on the professional values associated with core visions of what teaching should be about, and it tends to be bottom–up.

Whereas resource dependency relies on the assumption of tight coupling between central resource allocators and those who will implement enhancements 'on the ground' and is based upon the premise of the efficacy of sequential, hierarchical processes of 'top–down' change, this enhancement theory stresses the greater effectiveness of bottom–up approaches to the implementation of change. According to critics of top–down change strategies (see for example Hjern and Hull 1982; Yanow 1987), top–down approaches rely too heavily on the assumption of power and control exercised by those at the top of systems (such as central government policymakers) or within organizations (such as university vice-chancellors and senior management teams). In contrast, advocates of a bottom–up approach to

188 Making practical sense

enhancement argue that it is vital to take into account the characteristics of loosely coupled systems, such as we described in our introductory Chapter 1. The case studies analysed in this book illustrate a number of instances of the power of individuals to act in ways which were consistent with their own professional values and practices.

Technological determinism

This category of enhancement understands change in terms of the imperative embedded in 'moving forward' using information and communication technologies (ICTs). There are three variations in this category. First, the technology itself requires students, teachers and managers to change practices and teaching arrangements because of the nature of the technologies. Second, the institutions, agencies or departments have an imperative to have ICTs at the core of their enhancement activities to gain commercial advantage, to gain access to the global 'learning market' and to deliver curricula and learning opportunities more effectively. Third, there are changes in the expectations of the students in terms of learning support and ICT infrastructure, and this has produced or will produce changes in the institutions as they attempt to match these expectations through enhanced teaching and learning practice. This imperative becomes more acute in the 'continuing education' environment. The theory here is that educational institutions are learner sensitive, particularly in a global market.

Having looked at the implicit change theories which change agents carry into enhancement situations, we now turn to the types of identity which these individuals (or groups) take on. Our cases show that those involved in change can be analysed in terms of what we term the 'enhancement identities' they assume during the change process. There is synergy between their implicit change theories, the personal change strategies they adopt within the cases and the sense of 'who they are' as teachers within the change process. In this, second, section of the chapter, we consider these identities.

Framework 2: enhancement identities

We present these enhancement identities as a way of confronting how powerful the dimension of *personal styles and dispositions* are in explaining how enhancement might take place. Our argument is that enhancement processes and practices involve a mix of identities on the part of the key 'actors' in the process and some characteristics of these identities are more or less effective at different moments, different social or institutional or even national contexts and under different types of policy environment within the enhancement process. We note in Chapter 2 that the use of the term 'identity' refers to the mindsets, visions of the world and the sense of self in relation to bringing about change held by those engaged in change. What follows here are some identity types in relation to the enhancement process. We suggest that how individuals situate their identity in the enhancement process is important in explaining their orientation toward one approach to enhancement rather than another.

Awareness of this predilection is useful when we try to understand the processes of change at the heart of enhancement. Having an understanding of one's own (and others') enhancement identity will increase sensitivity to a wider range of strategies, even though they may be outside personal comfort zones. It will also help to assess the way a range of different types of identity can contribute to bringing about positive changes.

We offer these enhancement identities as examples of an approach. They are not intended to be exhaustive, but demonstrate the way considerations of identity, in the sense in which we are using it, can be part of a planned approach to enhancement. The descriptors associated with each identity are caricatures and intended to stimulate debate rather than be used as a classification. We all know, for example, prophets who are good collaborators but we argue that often, they tend to collaborate with those who think within the world view prescribed by them.

The prophet

We found examples in the cases where key individuals within the enhancement process had a strong vision, and self-image as a visionary interested in achieving enhanced practice according to *their own vision* of good practice. This identity type may not be susceptible to a strong awareness of the change process or have an idea of change theory beyond the 'exemplar' model. They tend not to be good collaborators but have the advantage of a charismatic approach that could sway opinion and be used to powerful strategic effect. Prophets can be inspirational but slow to adapt to new circumstances.

The expert

There were several examples of identity types within the cases that were built upon a strong sense of their own expertise in an area of pedagogy, such as the use of ICTs, collaborative learning or key skills. Again, this identity type may not be susceptible to a strong awareness of the change process, or have an idea of change theory beyond the 'exemplar' model. These colleagues can be rather reductive in their approach to enhancement in that they tend to see pedagogic solutions in a one-dimensional way. For example, they may emphasize the technical fix or one-stop answer to enhancement, such as a particular web based collaborative learning environment. In our perspective, they tend to emphasize the bridging tools or artefacts within an activity system and underemphasize the social, political and cultural dynamics that might be at work. Failure to take up the opportunity to use a technology is understood as resistance or lack of understanding of what 'it can do'.

The democratic collaborator

This identity type is found within our cases in circumstances in which the professional imperative for enhancement is emphasized. There is a strong sense of working in a collegial environment and a wish to work with colleagues for cooperatively derived goals. Initially, there may not be clear vision or embodiment of enhanced practice (unlike the 'prophet') but there is a sense in which enhancement is produced through the process of collaborative change which will throw up examples of good practice in an organic way. Such identity types tend to emphasize the way change originates locally and grows out from these innovative embodiments to a wider set of users. We see examples where such identities are sensitive to the social practices of the situated enhancement context and work with colleagues within that environment.

The political entrepreneur

This identity type uses a continuous sense of strategic positioning in order to drive change. Such entrepreneurs are institutionally adept and continually look for resources and opportunities, but might not work closely with colleagues or consult them. In fact, their drive is produced precisely through the colonization of means and opportunities, and exclusive command of the ways and means. They are low on personal vision, but may support the visions of others. They do not necessarily have an intrinsic interest in enhancement but understand the way the flow of resources in a particular moment is connected to particular visions of good practice. They are motivated professionally by being the provider of opportunity for others. They are adept at perceiving opportunities and smoothing the way for initiatives to develop via relevant committees. They treasure networks that may be of developmental value at some time in the future.

The practitioner experimenter

This identity type is interested in the promotion of low key, small scale enhancements in order to satisfy professional curiosity, enrich student learning or to create exemplars of change. Such colleagues may not always be known as experts or as proponents of good practice. They tend to be undeveloped in terms of institutional tactics but they may work closely with like-minded colleagues. They enjoy playing with new ideas. They are driven by the integration of the professional values associated with providing creative and interesting learning opportunities for their students, and by the excitement of pushing the boundaries of what is possible in terms of new ways of supporting and generating learning excitement on the part of their students.

The architect

This identity type emphasizes structures, systems and environments. There is a preoccupation with building or creating environments for change. They focus their energies on new programmes which can provide a more sympathetic environment for enhanced teaching and learning or new networks that can provide support for change. They have a vision of the kind of enhanced teaching and learning practice they want to bring about and recognize that present practices are inadequate or actively militate against the kind of practice they wish to see. They look for opportunities to change the way courses or programmes might be validated, or the way programmes might be integrated, or the way cross-institutional or sector-wide collaborations might be brought about. They are institutionally adept and well networked. They differ from the political broker in that they have a strong vision of 'good' teaching and learning practice. This identity is also adept at bringing together external support for systemic changes where experts are used strategically to provide legitimacy to the direction of change.

Framework 3: meta cultural concepts for enhancement – understand the theory

By now, you will be familiar with many of the concepts which underpin the thinking behind this book: the importance of sociocultural awareness and of social practices; activity systems; communities of practice within those systems; the implementation staircase; and the importance of non-formal learning and knowledge production. What might have seemed like abstract constructs at the beginning of the book will now, we hope, make practical sense in the light of the case studies. Keep these theories in mind when thinking about your own enhancement situation.

Using our frameworks for action

This concluding chapter offers three overarching frameworks: models of the implicit change theories which our case authors seem to be expressing; the enhancement identities which those involved in change have appeared to adopt; and a reminder of the change theories which can help inform our enhancement efforts. However, where complex change confronts deeply held norms and values, change implementers at whatever level are having to constantly look up and down the implementation staircase to the other levels, to see how responses elsewhere will affect our part of the enhancement process. We argue that having reflexive knowledge of the enhancement process will help bridge change. The remainder of this chapter offers a schematic example of how meta theories can act as a *bridging tool* for change embodied in enhancement. They offer a *way of seeing*, a lens through which the factors that encase enhancement might be viewed and understood. The framing reflexivity tool below suggests the integrative nature of the frameworks we have used and provides an ideal typical case of how they can be reconstructed to orientate a change process.

The last remaining principle we wish to offer is that your actions, enhancement theories and enhancement identities need alignment. While collaboration, good communication, buy-in and participation in developing enhancement change seem axiomatic, the devil can be in the detail. The key step in all of this thinking focuses on you, therefore, and the realities of your own contexts for change. To help contextualize frameworks in use, we offer a set of reflexive questions which suggest the way the meta theories can be integrated to inform an approach to your own specific enhancement activity (see Table 27.1).

While the questions are directed at you as an individual, many enhancements will be led by 'us' rather than 'me', and so we suggest a need to engage in practical dialogue with those involved in enhancement. Omitting these debates from the change process means that the opportunity to surface conflicts and work through them with 'more dynamic agendas' (Sparrow 1998: 8) can be lost; people then disengage further from the change initiative, or scupper the boat in any way they can. Confronting ambiguity and fuzziness is vital, and 'discomforting data' cannot be simply ignored (Sparrow 1998: 9). However, making sense of sometimes tacit and sometimes understage meanings requires sophisticated management skills (Sparrow 1998: 10), including 'the need to work with perceptions' (Sparrow 1998: 11), and an ability to live with uncertainty – a hard challenge when you may be under severe pressure to 'deliver' targets quickly, as is often the case in the ubiquitously changing and increasingly pressurised university sector.

The key to good dialogue is that it is composed of *questions*, a key activity in making sense of complex situations (Weick 1995: 4). Revans (1980) emphasized the need for asking fresh questions if we are going to genuinely interrogate our own practice. While recommendations might lead to a defensive position, questions can lead us into an inquiry-led approach, as opposed to advocacy and opposition. It is unlikely that the honest, reflective self-review required for deep change (Hopkins 2002: 5) will be achieved unless a change approach which embodies that inquiring philosophy is present. This approach also has the advantage of endorsing the collegial model which universities and their staff still value. Good questions are, therefore, a valuable analytical tool for planning what should happen in an enhancement activity, and for then checking progress along the way, ideally in conjunction with those involved in the change. The checking must be iterative and carried out in consultation with stakeholders, before, during and after implementing the change. The sights of change implementers must constantly scan the developing situation, if they are to avoid the 'contextual occlusion' (Trowler and Knight 2002: 207) which blinds them to what is really happening outside of their micro planning 'box'.

So what might the reflexive questions which constitute the last part of our framework for action be? We have developed questions which stem from the three frameworks mentioned above (see Table 27.1)

Table 27.1 Framing reflexivity for enhancement

Reflexive questions		*What does this imply for my enhancement approach?*

Questions emanating from our analysis of the cases in this book:

What is my implicit theory of change? Is it based on . . .	Following practice based exemplars? Incentivizing change with resources? Giving rhetorical support? Pushing the values of professionalism? Driving change with technology? Other theories of change?
Which enhancement identity do I tend to adopt? Do I act like . . .	A prophet, led by my own strong vision? An expert, based on my own pedagogical expertise? A democratic collaborator, keen to explore ideas with colleagues? A political entrepreneur, using strategic positioning to lever change? A practitioner experimenter, enjoying playing with new L&T methods? An architect, trying to build the right structures and environments for enhancement? Another enhancement identity?

Questions stemming from the book's theoretical underpinning:

What is the cultural/ social *context* within which I want the enhancement to take place? Which factors do I need to take into account?	E.g. is my institution managerial or is there loose coupling between departments and centre?

(*Continued overleaf*)

Table 27.1 continued

Reflexive questions	What does this imply for my enhancement approach?
What *practices* do I need to work with?	E.g. if staff work face to face with students, what is needed to help them in a new initiative to work online?
Which parts of our *activity system* do I need to work with (subject, objects, tools, rules, division of labour, community of practice)?	E.g. if the institution decides to restructure its 'academic portfolio', can I map the possible effects on the different parts of the system?
How can I engage the various *communities* or work groups in this enhancement agenda?	E.g. if we decide to centralize computing support, how will this affect the people in the work groups and how they work together?
Can I predict how the enhancement 'ball' might bounce up and down the *implementation staircase*?	E.g. when a national enhancement initiative is announced, who might affect its implementation? At which stage, and how? And how can these people be engaged in the process?
How can I tap the benefits of *non-formal learning* as enhancement mechanisms?	E.g. how can we promote environments in which people are encouraged to explore new ideas and practices?

We make no claim that these frameworks for action are unique. Fullan (1993) and others have produced their versions of such checklists, guidelines and inventories. What they have not done, however, is locate them in the specific frame of reference of change in universities. This book has conveyed a university relevant approach to enhancement, and related it to empirical data, to shed fresh light on a previously under-researched topic, and to produce specific tools for change implementers to use. Given the contextual reflexivity recommended in this approach, these resources can be applied in many higher education enhancement situations. As we engage in enhancement, we need to use flexible tools in order to understand dynamic environments and respect the 'network of interactions' and dispersed distribution of power which characterize HE (Trowler and Knight 2002: 228). This developmental reflexivity does now seem to have been acknowledged by national policymaking organizations: HEFCE (HEFCE, UUK and SCOP 2003: 3) has indicated that the enhancement of learning and teaching needs to be 'an inclusive agenda which runs with the grain of the collaborative ethos in higher education', recognizing a wide range of approaches and starting points, and taking a sophisticated approach to change.

Change in HE is 'a huge challenge', 'still about changing a culture' (MacLeod 2004: 22). We have, in these pages, provided cases of real people with distinctive identities struggling in real time to enhance teaching and learning within higher education. We have argued that a persuasive and authentic way of understanding how enhancement takes place is to see it as social practice using personal and systemic theories of change within institutional and organizational settings. With these examples, along with recommendations for practice in the form of distilled frameworks, we offer bridging tools to stimulate thought, to be placed in an armoury of resources for action, and to encourage a positive stance on the impulse we all have to improve and develop our capacity to generate interesting, creative and sustainable learning opportunities for our students.

References

Adams, C. (2006) Powerpoint, habits of mind and classroom culture, *Journal of Curriculum Studies*, 38, 4: 389–411.

Allan, C. (2000) Statement from the LTSN programme director, *Learning and Teaching Support Network Subject Centre Handbook*, Section 2. York, UK: LTSN.

Allen, D.K. and Fifield, N. (1999) Re-engineering change in higher education, *Information Research*, 4, 3.

Allen, R. and Layer, G. (1995) *Credit-based Systems as Vehicles for Change in Universities and Colleges*. London: Kogan Page.

Baerheim, A. and Alraek, T.J. (2005) Utilizing theatrical tools in consultation training. A way to facilitate students' reflection on action, *Med Teacher*, pp. 1–3.

Baird, J. (2007) Australian universities' approaches to embedding graduate attributes: an overview from quality audits, 29th Annual EAIR Forum Innsbruck, 26–29 August.

Barnett, R. (1994) *The Limits of Competence: Knowledge, Higher Education and Society*. Buckingham: SRHE/Open University Press.

Barrie, S.C. (2004) A research-based approach to generic graduate attributes policy, *Higher Education Research and Development*, 23, 3: 261–75.

Barrie, S.C. (2006) Understanding what we mean by generic attributes of graduates, *Higher Education*, 51, 2: 215–41.

Barrie, S.C. (2007) A conceptual framework for the teaching and learning of graduate attributes, *Studies in Higher Education*, 32, 4: 439–58.

Beach, K. (2003) Consequential transitions: a developmental view of knowledge propagation through social organisation, in T. Tuomi-Grohn and Y. Engeström (eds), *Between School and Work*. London: Pergamon.

Becher, T. (1999) *Professional Practices: Commitment and Capability in a Changing Environment*. New Brunswick: Transaction Publishers.

Becher, T. and Trowler, P.R. (2001) *Academic Tribes and Territories*, 2nd edn. Buckingham: SRHE/Open University Press.

Beetham, H. (2005) E-learning research: emerging issues? *ALT-J Research in Learning Technology*, 13, 1: 81–9

Bereiter, C. and Scardamalia, M. (1993) *Surpassing Ourselves: An Inquiry into the Nature and Implications of Expertise*. Chicago: Open Court.

Bernstein, B. (1971) On the classification and framing of educational knowledge, in

M.F.D. Young (ed.), *Knowledge and Control New Directions for the Sociology of Education*. London: Collier Macmillan.

Biglan, A. (1973) The characteristics of subject matter in different academic areas, *Journal of Applied Psychology*, 57, 3: 195–203.

Blackler, F. (1995) Knowledge, knowledge work and organizations: an overview and interpretation, *Organization Studies*, 16, 6: 1021–46.

Bloor, G. and Dawson, P. (1994) Understanding professional culture in organisational context, *Organization Studies*, 15, 2.

Bourdieu, P. (1977) *Outline of a Theory of Practice*. Cambridge, MA: Cambridge University Press.

Brookfield, S. (1995) Changing the culture of scholarship to the culture of teaching: an American perspective, in T. Schuller (ed.), *The Changing University?* Buckingham: SRHE/Open University Press.

Castells, M. (2001) Identity and change in the network society, *Manuel Castells Interview: Conversations with History, Institute of International Studies, UC Berkeley*. http://globetrotter.berkeley.edu/people/Castells/castells-con4.html (accessed 26 Aug. 2003).

Checkland, P. (1981) *Systems Thinking, Systems Practice*. Chichester: John Wiley.

Clark, B.R. (ed.) (1998) *Creating Entrepreneurial Universities: Organizational Pathways of Transformation*. London: Pergamon.

Cohen, S. and Taylor, L. (1992), *Escape Attempts: The Theory and Practice of Resistance to Everyday Life*, 2nd edn. Routledge: London.

Collins, J.C. and Porras, J.I. (1996) *Built to Last*. London: Century Business.

Dalin, P. (1994) *Skoleutvikling. Teorier for forandring*. Oslo: Universitetsforlaget.

Davis, D. and Wilcock, E. (2008) Teaching materials using case studies. http://www.materials.ac.uk/guides/casestudies.asp. (accessed 14 Apr. 2008).

Deem, R. (2004) The knowledge worker, the manager-academic and the contemporary UK university: new and old forms of public management? *Financial Accountability and Management*, 20, 2: 107–28.

Deem, R. and Brehony, K. (2005) Management as ideology: the case of 'new managerialism' in higher education, *Oxford Review of Education*, 31, 2: 217–35.

De Freitas, S. and Oliver, M. (2005) Does e-Learning policy drive change in higher education? A case study relating models of organisational change to e-learning implementation, *Journal of Higher Education Policy and Management*, 27, 1: 81–95.

Dewhurst, D., McLeod, H. and Ellaway, R. (2004) Evaluating a virtual learning environment in the context of its community of practice, *Alt-J*, June, 12, 2: 125–45.

Dill, D. (1999) Academic accountability and university adaptation: the architecture of an academic learning organization, *Higher Education*, 38, 2: 127–54.

Drummond, I., Nixon, I. and Wiltshire, J. (1998) Personal transferable skills in higher education: the problems of implementing good practice, *Quality Assurance in Education*, 6, 1: 19–27.

Duke, C. (2001) Networks and managerialism: field testing competing paradigms *Journal of Higher Education Policy and Management*, 23, 1.

Edward, N. (2002) Misconceptions as a cause of undergraduate difficulties and the development of a diagnostic instrument. Paper presented at Professional Engineering Scenarios: the 2nd international symposium on engineering education, IEE, London, 3–4 Jan.

Ekman, P. (2004a) Micro-expression training tool. www.emotionsrevealed.com (accessed 28 Nov. 2007).

Ekman, P. (2004b) Emotions revealed: recognising facial expression, *BMJ Careers*, pp. 75–6.

Elton, L. (1987) *Teaching in Higher Education: Appraisal and Training*. London: Kogan Page.

Elton, L. (2002) *Dissemination: A Change Theory Approach*. York: LTSN Generic Centre Report.

Elton, L. (2003) Dissemination of innovations in higher education: a change theory approach, *Tertiary Education and Management*, 9: 199–214.

Engeström, Y. (1987) *Learning by Expanding: An Activity Theoretical Approach to Developmental Research*. Helsinki: Orienta-Konsultit.

Ensor, P. (2001) Academic programme planning in South African higher education: three institutional case studies, in M. Breier (ed.), *Curriculum Restructuring in Higher Education in Post-apartheid South Africa*. Pretoria: CSD, pp. 85–114.

Ensor, P. (2004) Contesting discourses in higher education curriculum restructuring in South Africa, *Higher Education*, 48: 339–59.

Eraut, M. (2000) Non-formal learning and tacit knowledge in professional work, *British Journal of Educational Psychology*, 70, 1: 113–36.

Eraut, M., Furner, J., Maillardet, F. et al. (2004) Learning in the professional workplace: relationships between learning factors and contextual factors. Paper presented to the American Educational Research Association annual conference, San Diego, 12 Apr.

Farrell, J.P. (2000) Why is educational reform so difficult? *Curriculum Inquiry*, 30, 1: 83–103.

Filmore, P. and Thomond, P. (2003) The medicine wheel, in C. Baillie (ed.), *The Travelling Case: How to Foster Creative Thinking in Higher Education*, Liverpool: UK Centre for Materials Education/LTSN Generic Centre, pp. 19–27.

Foucault, M. (1975) *Discipline and Punish*. Harmondsworth: Penguin.

Fullan, M. (1982) *The Meaning of Educational Change*. New York: Teachers College Press, Columbia University.

Fullan, M. (1993) *Change Forces*. London: Falmer.

Fullan, M. (1999) *Change Forces: The Sequel*. London: Falmer.

Fullan, M. (2001) *The New Meaning of Educational Change*, 3rd edition. New York: Teachers' College Press.

Fuller, A., Hodkinson, H., Hodkinson, P. and Unwin, L. (2005) Learning as peripheral participation in communities of practice: a reappraisal of key concepts in workplace learning, *British Educational Research Journal*, 31, 1: 49–68.

Garrison, D.R., and Anderson, T. (2003) *E-learning in the 21ˢᵗ Century: A Framework for Research and Practice*. London and New York: Routledge Falmer.

Gewirtz, S., Ball, S. and Bowe, R. (1995) *Markets, Choice and Equity in Education*. Buckingham: Open University Press.

Gibbons, M., Limoges, C., Newotny, H. et al. (1994) *The New Production of Knowledge: The Dynamics of Science and Research in Contemporary Societies*. London: Sage Publications.

Gibbs, G. and Coffey, M. (2004) The impact of training of university teachers on their teaching skills, their approach to teaching and the approach to learning of their students, *Active Learning in Higher Education*, 5, 1: 87–100.

Giddens, A. (1976) *New Rules of Sociological Method*. London: Hutchinson.

Goffman, E. (1959) *The Presentation of Self in Everyday Life*. London: Penguin.

Goodlad, J. (1984) *A Place Called School: Prospects for the Future*. New York: McGraw-Hill.

Graven, M. (2004) Investigating mathematics teacher learning within an in-service community of practice: the centrality of confidence, *Educational Studies in Mathematics*, 57, 2: 177–211.

Hall, J. and Shrives, L. (2006) Leading the jazz band: conducting the orchestra or wild improvisation? New perspectives on enabling cross-institutional change. Paper presented at ICED conference, Sheffield Hallam University, 11–14 June.

Handal, G. and Lycke, K.H. (2000) Sammendrag av rapport fra undersøkelsen 'Studiekvalitet i praksis' (Résumé of the report 'Quality of studies in practice'), *Frihet med ansvar [Freedom with Responsibility]*, no. 14. Oslo: NOU, pp. 635–42.

Handy, C. (1995) *The Empty Raincoat: Making Sense of the Future*. New York: Random House.

Hannan, A. and Silver, H. (2000) *Innovating in Higher Education: Teaching, Learning and Institutional Cultures*. Buckingham: SRHE/Open University Press.

Hartman, H.J. (1990) Factors affecting the tutoring process, *Journal of Educational Development*, 14, 2: 2–6.

Harvey, L., Drew, S. and Smith, M. (2006) *The First Year Experience: A Review of Literature for the Higher Education Academy*. York: HEA. http://www.heacademy.ac.uk/assets/York/documents/ourwork/research/literature_reviews/first_year_experience_full_report.pdf (accessed 11 Feb. 2008).

Hassall, T., Lewis, S. and Broadbent, M. (1998) Teaching and learning using case studies: a teaching note, *Accounting Education*, 7, 4: 325–34.

HEFCE (Higher Education Funding Council for England), UUK (Universities) and SCOP (Standing Conference of Principals) (2003) *Final Report of the TQEC (Teaching Quality Enhancement Committee) on the Future Needs and Support for Quality Enhancement of Learning and Teaching in Higher Education*. London: HEFCE. http://www.hefce.ac.uk

Henkel, M. (2000) *Academic Identities and Policy Change in Higher Education*. London: Jessica Kingsley Publishers.

Henkel, M. (2002) Academic identity in transformation? The case of the United Kingdom, *Higher Education Management and Policy*, 14, 3: 137–47.

Hilsdon, J. (2004) Learning development in higher education network (LDHEN): an emerging community of practice? *Educational Developments*, 5, 3: 12–15.

Hjern, B. and Hull, C. (1982) Implementation research as empirical constitutionalism, *European Journal of Political Research*, 10, 2: 105–15.

Hopkins, D. (2002) *The Evolution of Strategies for Educational Change: Implications for Higher Education*. York: LTSN Generic Centre Report.

Horn, M. (1999) *Academic Freedom in Canada: A History*. Toronto: University of Toronto Press.

Huberman, M. (1993) *The Lives of Teachers*. London: Cassell.

Hulsman, R. et al. (2004) Assessment of medical communication skills by computer: assessment method and student experiences, *Med Edu*, 38: 813–24.

Humphris, G.M. and Kaney, S. (2000) The objective structured video exam for assessment of communication skills. *Med Edu*, 34: 939–45.

Johnson, R. (2002) Resources in the management of change in higher education, in P. Trowler (ed.), *Higher Education Policy and Institutional Change: Intentions and Outcomes in Turbulent Environments*. Buckingham: SRHE/Open University Press.

Kalkowski, P. (1995) *Peer and Cross-Age Tutoring*. School Improvement Research Series. http://www.nwrel.org/scpd/sirs/9/c018.html (accessed 9 Jan. 2008).

Karseth, B. and Kyvik, S. (1999) Undervisningsvirksomheten ved de statlige høgskolene, *Delrapport no. 1 Evaluering av høgskolereformen*. Oslo: Norges forskningsråd.

Kerr, C. (1980) Three thousand futures: the next twenty years for higher education, in Carnegie Council on Policy Studies in Higher Education, *Three Thousand Futures: The Next Twenty Years for Higher Education*. San Francisco: Jossey-Bass.

KIUP (University Pedagogy Committee) (1985) *Handlingsprogram for utvikling av universitetspedagogisk arbeid ved universiteter og høgskoler I Norge*. Oslo: KIUP.

KIUP (University Pedagogy Committee) (1987) En studie av praksis ved vurdering av pedagogiske kvalifikasjoner ved tilsetting i vitenskapelige stillinger med undervisningsplikt, *UNIPED*, 1, 87: 16–21.

Klein, G.A. (1989) Recognition-primed decisions, in W.B. Rouse (ed.), *Advances in Man-Machine Systems Research*. Greenwich, CT: JAI Press, pp. 47–92.

Knight, P. and Saunders, M. (1999) Understanding teachers' professional cultures through interview: a constructivist approach, *Evaluation and Research in Education*, 13, 3: 144–56.

Knight, P. and Trowler, P. (2001) *Departmental Leadership in Higher Education*. Buckingham: SRHE/Open University Press.

Lapworth, S. (2007) A crisis in identity: the view of a student of higher education management, in R. Di Napoli and R. Barnett (eds), *Changing Identities in Higher Education*. London: Routledge.

Larkin, J.H., McDermott, J., Simon, D.P. and Simon, H.A. (1980) Models of competence in solving physics problems, *Cognitive Science*, 4: 317–45.

Latour, B. (2000) When things strike back: a possible contribution of 'science studies' to the social sciences, *British Journal of Sociology*, 51, 1: 107–23.

Lattuca, L.R. and Stark, J.S. (1994) Will disciplinary perspectives impede curicular reform? *Journal of Higher Education*, 65, 4.

Laurillard, D. (1993) *Rethinking University Teaching*. London: Routledge.

Laurillard, D. (2002) *Rethinking University Teaching: A Framework for the Effective Use of Educational Technology*, 2nd edn. Buckingham: Open University Press.

Lauvås, P. (1987) Perspectives and experiences of in-service training for university teachers in Norway. Paper to the 4th International Conference on Higher Education, Lancaster.

Lauvås, P. and Handal, G. (1978): Nødvendige og tilstrekkelige betingelser for pedagogisk trening av universitetslærere (Necessary and sufficient conditions for educational training for university teachers), *UNIPED*, 1: 3–7.

Lave, J. and Wenger, E. (1991) *Situated Learning: Legitimate Peripheral Participation*. Cambridge: Cambridge University Press.

Lewin, K. (1951) *Field Theory in Social Science: Selected Theoretical Papers* (ed. D. Cartwright). New York: Harper and Row.

LTSN (Learning and Teaching Support Network) (2002) *Final Evaluation Report*. York: LTSN.

Lucas, U. and Leng Tan, P. (2006) Developing a reflective capacity: the role of personal epistemologies within undergraduate education. Paper presented at the 14th Improving Student Learning *Symposium*, University of Bath, 4–6 Sep.

Lycke, K.H. (1999): Faculty development: experiences and issues in a Norwegian perspective, *The International Journal for Academic Development*, 4, 2: 124–33.

Lycke, K.H. (2004) Perspectives on quality assurance in higher education in Norway, *Quality in Higher Education*, 10, 3, 219–30.

Lycke, K.H. and Handal, G. (2005) Faculty development programs in Norway: status, design and evaluation, in S. Brendel, K. Kaiser and K. Macke (eds), *Hochschuldidaktische Qualifizierung. Arbeidsgemeinschaft für Hochschuldidaktik*. Bielefeld, Bertelsmann Verlag.

Macfarlane, B. (2006) *The Academic Citizen: The Virtue of Service in University Life.* London: Routledge.

MacLeod, D. (2004) How to lecture, *Education Guardian*, 26 Oct., p. 22.

McGuinness, C. (1997) What constitutes good learning and teaching in higher education? Views from staff development handbooks, *Psychology Teaching Review*, 6, 1: 14–22. http://www.bps.org.uk/downloadfile.cfm?file_uuid=60EA263D-1143-DFD0-7E83-D558CA34E390&ext=pdf (accessed 22 May 2008).

McNay, I. (1995) From the collegial academy to corporate entreprise: the changing cultures of universities, in T. Schuller (ed.), *The Changing University?* Buckingham: SRHE/Open University Press.

McNay, I. (2006) Managing institutions in a mass higher education system, in I. McNay (ed.), *Beyond Mass Higher Education: Building on Experience*. Maidenhead: SRHE/Open University Press, pp. 161–71.

Marginson, S. and Considine, M. (2000) *The Enterprise University: Governance, Strategy, Reinvention*. Melbourne: Cambridge University Press.

Martin, E. (1999) *Changing Academic Work: Developing the Learning University*. Buckingham: SRHE/Open University Press.

Marx, K. (1852) *The 18th Brumaire of Louis Napoloeon, die Revolution* (trans. S.K. Padover). New York. www2.cddc.vt.edu/marxists/cd/cd1/Library/archive/marx/works/1852/18th-brumaire/index.htm (accessed 16 Feb. 2006).

Mink, O.G., Esterhuysen, P.W., Mink, B.P. and Owen, K.Q. (1993) *Change at Work*. San Francisco: Jossey-Bass.

Mintzberg, H. (1994) *The Rise and Fall of Strategic Planning*. New York: Free Press.

Mintzberg, H. (2004) *Managers Not MBAs: A Hard Look at the Soft Practice of Managing and Management Development*. Harlow: Pearson Education.

Mintzberg, H., Ahlstrand, B., and Lampel, J. (1998) *Strategy Safari*. Edinburgh: Prentice Hall.

Moore, R. (2002) Between covenant and contract: negotiating academic pedagogic identities. Paper presented at the 2nd international Basil Bernstein symposium: knowledges, pedagogy and society, Cape Town.

Moore, R. (2003a) Policy-driven curriculum restructuring: academic identities in transition? In P. Trowler and C. Prichard (eds), *Realizing Qualitative Research into Higher Education*. Aldershot: Ashgate Publishers, pp. 121–42.

Moore, R. (2003b) Curriculum restructuring in South African higher education: academic identities and policy implementation, *Studies in Higher Education*, 28, 3: 303–19.

Moore, R. (2003c) Between covenant and contract: the negotiation of academic pedagogic identities, *Journal of Education*, 30: 81–100.

Moore, R. (2003d) Adaptive responses to curriculum restructuring policy in two South African Universities: an enquiry into the identity projections of academics disposed towards change. Unpublished doctoral thesis, University of Cape Town.

Muller, J. (2003) Knowledge and the limits to institutional restructuring: the case of South African higher education, *Journal of Education*, 30: 101–26.

NCIHE (National Committee of Inquiry into Higher Education) (1997) *Higher Education in the Learning Society* (Committee chaired by Sir Ron Dearing). www.leeds.ac.uk/educol/ncihe (accessed 31 Jul. 2006).

Nelson, R.R., and Winter, S.G. (1982) *An Evolutionary Theory of Economic Change*. Boston: Harvard University Press.

Newton, J. (2003) Implementing an institution-wide learning and teaching strategy: lessons in managing change, *Studies in Higher Education*, 28, 4: 427–41.

Norgesnettrådet (2002) Institutional evaluation of the University of Oslo: the external panel's report 02/2002. Oslo: Norgesnettrådet.

NOU (1988) *Med viten og vilje.* Oslo: Kultur-og vitenskapsdepartementet.

Nowotny, H., Scott, P. and Gibbons, M. (2001) *Rethinking Science. Knowledge and the Public in an Age of Uncertainty.* Cambridge: Polity Press.

Oslington, P. (2004) The impact of uncertainty and irreversibility on investments in online learning, *Distance Education,* 25, 2: 233–42.

Owen, E. and Sweller, J. (1989) Should problem solving be used as a learning device in mathematics? *JRME,* 20, 3: 322–8.

Pascale, R. (1990) *Managing on the Edge.* New York: Simon and Schuster.

Postman, N. and Weingartner, C. (1969) *Teaching as a Subversive Activity.* New York: Dell.

Prichard, C. (2000) *Making Managers in Universities and Colleges.* Buckingham: SRHE/Open University Press.

QAA (Quality Assurance Agency) (2005) *Responding to Student Needs.* Gloucester: QAA. www.enhancementthemes.ac.uk/documents/studentneeds/student_needs_A5_booklet.pdf (accessed 11 Feb. 2008).

QAA (Quality Assurance Agency) (2007) *Masters Degrees in Business and Management.* Gloucester: QAA.

Quality of Studies (1990) *Short Version of the Recommendations of the Committee for Quality in Higher Education.* Oslo: Ministry of Education and Research.

Quinn, J.B. (1980) *Strategies for Change: Logical Incrementalism.* Homewood, IL: Irwin.

Ramsden, P. (1992) *Learning to Teach in Higher Education.* London: Routledge.

Reckwitz, A. (2002) Toward a theory of social practices: a development in culturalist theorising, *European Journal of Social Theory,* 5, 2: 243–63.

Revans, R. (1980) *Action Learning. New Techniques for Action Learning.* London: Blond and Briggs.

Reynolds, J. and Saunders, M. (1987) Teacher responses to curriculum policy: beyond the 'delivery' metaphor, in J. Calderhead (ed.), *Exploring Teachers' Thinking.* London: Cassell Education.

Rogers, C. (1969) *Freedom to Learn.* Boston: Houghton Mifflin.

Rogers, C. (1959) A theory of therapy, personality and interpersonal relationships as developed in the client-centered framework, in S. Koch (ed.), *Psychology: A Study of a Science, Vol. 3: Formulations of the Person and the Social Context.* New York: McGraw Hill.

Rust, C. (2002) The impact of assessment on student learning, *Active Learning in Higher Education,* 3, 2: 145–58.

Saunders, M. et al. (2002) Evaluating the learning and teaching support network: from awareness to adaptation, *Deliverable D10, Final Report to the LTSN Executive (HEA).* London: HEA.

Saunders M., Charlier, B. and Bonamy, J. (2005) Using evaluation to create 'provisional stabilities': bridging innovation in higher education change processes, *Evaluation: The International Journal of Theory, Research and Practice,* 11, 1.

Saunders, M., Trowler, P., Machell, J. et al. (2006) *Enhancing the Quality of Teaching and Learning in Scottish Universities: The Final Report of the First Evaluation of the Quality Enhancement Framework to the Scottish Funding Council's Quality Enhancement Framework Evaluation Steering Committee.* Edinburgh: SFC. www.sfc.ac.uk/information/info_learning.htm (accessed 5 Jul. 2008).

Saunders, M., Trowler, P., Machell, J. et al. (2007) SFC Circular 11/07, *Evaluation of the Higher Education Quality Enhancement Framework: Final Report.* SFC: Edinburgh.

www.sfc.ac.uk/information/info_circulars/sfc/2007/sfc1107/sfc1107.html (accessed 31 Mar. 2008).

Schein, E. (2002) The anxiety of learning, *Harvard Business Review*, March, 80, 3.

Schön, D. (1983) *The Reflective Practitioner: How Professionals Think in Action.* New York: Basic Books Inc.

Schön, D.M. (1991) *The Reflective Turn: Case Studies in and on Educational Practice.* New York: Teachers College Press.

Scott, P. (1995) *The Meanings of Mass Higher Education.* Buckingham: SRHE/Open University Press.

Scottish Quality Enhancement Themes. www.enhancementthemes.ac.uk/ (accessed 31 Mar. 2008).

Senge, P.M. (1990) *The Fifth Discipline: The Art and Practice of the Learning Organization.* London: Random House.

Senge, P., Kleiner, A., Roberts, C., Ross, R. and Smith, B. (1994) *The Fifth Discipline Fieldbook: Strategies and Tools for Building a Learning Organization.* New York: Doubleday/Currency.

SFC (Scottish Funding Council) (2007) *Final Report of the Joint Quality Review Group.* Edinburgh: SFC. www.sfc.ac.uk/about/new_about_council_papers/about_papers_17aug07/SFC_07_113.pdf

SHEFC (Scottish Higher Education Funding Council) (2001) Circular HE/55/01. Update on quality issues. Edinburgh: SHEFC.

SHEFC (Scottish Higher Education Funding Council) (2002a) Consultation HEC 02/ 2002. An enhancement led approach to quality assurance. Edinburgh: SHEFC.

SHEFC (Scottish Higher Education Funding Council) (2002b) Circular HE/29/02. An enhancement led approach to quality assurance: consultation responses and the way forward. Edinburgh: SHEFC.

Shulman, L. (2005a) Signature pedagogies in the professions, *Daedalus*, Summer, 134, 3: 52–9.

Shulman, L. (2005b) *The Signature Pedagogies of the Professions of Law, Medicine, Engineering, and the Clergy: Potential Lessons for the Education of Teachers.* Irvine, CA: National Research Council Center for Education.

Silver, H. (2003) Does a university have a culture? *Studies in Higher Education*, 28, 2.

Slowey, M. (ed.) (1995) *Implementing Change from within Universities and Colleges: 10 Personal Accounts.* London: Kogan Page.

Somekh, B. (1998) Supporting information and communication technology innovations in higher education, *Technology, Pedagogy and Education*, 7, 1: 11–32.

Sparrow, J. (1998) *Knowledge in Organizations.* London: Sage.

Sporn, B. (1999) *Adaptive University Structures: An Analysis of Adaptation to Socioeconomic Environments of US and European Universities.* London: Jessica Kingsley Publishers.

Stephenson, J. and Yorke, M. (1998) *Capability and Quality in Higher Education.* London: Kogan Page.

Sternberg, R.J. and Grigorenko, E.L. (2000) Practical intelligence and its development, in R. Bar-On, and J. Parker (eds), *The Handbook of Emotional Intelligence.* San Francisco: Jossey-Bass, pp. 215–43.

Tichy, N.M., and Sherman, S. (1994) *Control Your Own Destiny or Someone Else Will.* New York: Harper Business.

Trowler, P. (2001) Captured by the discourse? The socially constitutive power of new higher education discourse in the UK, *Organization*, 8, 2, 183–201.

Trowler, P. (2008 in press) *Cultures and Change in Higher Education: Theories and Practices.* London: Palgrave Macmillan.

Trowler, P. and Bamber, V. (2005) Compulsory higher education teacher education: joined-up policies; institutional architectures; enhancement cultures, *International Journal for Academic Development*, 10, 2: 79–93.

Trowler, P. and Knight, P. (1999) Organizational socialization and induction in universities: reconceptualizing theory and practice, *Higher Education*, 37: 177–95.

Trowler, P. and Knight, P.T. (2000) Coming to know in higher education: theorising faculty entry to new work contexts, *Higher Education Research and Development*, 19, 1: 27–42.

Trowler, P.R. and Knight P.T. (2002) Exploring the implementation gap: theory and practices in change interventions, in P. Trowler (ed.), *Higher Education and Institutional Change*. Buckingham: SRHE/Open University Press.

Trowler, P., Saunders, M. and Knight, P. (2002) *Change Thinking, Change Practices: A Guide to Change for Heads of Department, Subject Centres and Others Who Work Middle–Out*. York: LTSN Generic Centre Report.

Trowler, P., Fanghanel, J. and Wareham, T. (2005) Freeing the chi of change: the higher education academy and enhancing teaching and learning in higher education, *Studies in Higher Education*, 30, 5: 427–44.

Turkle, S. (1995) *Life on The Screen: Identity in the Age of The Internet*. New York: Touchstone.

Turner, V. (1982) *From Ritual to Theatre: The Human Seriousness of Play*. New York: PAJ.

Tuomi-Gröhn, T. and Engeström, Y. (eds) (2003) *Between School and Work: New Perspectives on Transfer and Boundary-Crossing*. Amsterdam: Pergamon.

Tyack, D. and Cuban, L. (1995) *Tinkering Towards Utopia: A Century of Public School Reform*. Cambridge, MA: Harvard University Press.

University of Oslo (2007) *Underveis: UIO's Interne evaluering av kvalitetsreformen*. Oslo: University of Oslo.

Van Note Chism, N. and Bickford, D.J. (2002) Improving the environment for learning: an expanded agenda, *New Directions for Teaching and Learning*, 92: 91–7.

Vibe, N. and Aamodt, P.O. (1985) Trengsel eller trivsel? Studentens bruk og vurdering av universitetenes tilbud. Oslo: NIFU Rapportserie 11/85.

Vygotsky, L.S. (1962) *Thought and Language*. Cambridge, MA: MIT Press.

Vygotsky, L.S. (1978) *Mind and Society: The Development of Higher Psychological Processes*. Cambridge, MA: Harvard University Press.

Watson, D. (2007) Academic identities and the story of institutions, in R. Di Napoli and R. Barnett (eds), *Changing Identities in Higher Education*. London: Routledge.

Watson, D. and Bowden, R. (2005) The turtle and the fruit fly: New Labour and UK higher education, 2001–2005. University of Brighton Education Research Centre Occasional Paper. University of Brighton, May.

Webb, E., Jones, A., Barker, P. and Van Schaik, P. (2004) Using e-learning dialogues in higher education, *Innovations in Education and Teaching International*, 41, 1: 93–103.

Weick, K.E. (1976) Educational organizations as loosely coupled systems, *Administrative Science Quarterly*, 21, 1: 1–19.

Weick, K. (1995) *Sensemaking in Organizations*. Thousand Oaks, CA: Sage.

Weiss, C.H. (1995) Nothing as practical as good theory: exploring theory-based evaluation for comprehensive community initiatives for children and families, in J.P. Connell et al. (eds), *New Approaches to Evaluating Community Initiatives: Concepts, Methods and Contexts*. Washington, DC: The Aspen Institute.

Wenger, E. (1998) *Communities of Practice: Learning, Meaning and Identity*. Cambridge: Cambridge University Press.

Wenger, E. (2000) Communities of practice and social learning systems, *Organization*, 7, 2: 225–46.

Wenger, E., McDermott, R. and Snyder, W. (2002) *Cultivating Communities of Practice: A Guide to Managing Knowledge.* Boston, MA: Harvard Business School Press.

Whitchurch, C. (2006) *Professional Managers in UK Higher Education: Preparing for Complex Futures.* London: The Leadership Foundation for Higher Education.

Yanow, D.J. (1987) Towards a policy culture approach to implementation, *Policy Studies Review*, 7, 1: 103–15.

The Society for Research into Higher Education

The Society for Research into Higher Education (SRHE), an international body, exists to stimulate and coordinate research into all aspects of higher education. It aims to improve the quality of higher education through the encouragement of debate and publication on issues of policy, on the organization and management of higher education institutions, and on the curriculum, teaching and learning methods.

The Society is entirely independent and receives no subsidies, although individual events often receive sponsorship from business or industry. The Society is financed through corporate and individual subscriptions and has members from many parts of the world. It is an NGO of UNESCO.

Under the imprint *SRHE & Open University Press*, the Society is a specialist publisher of research, having over 80 titles in print. In addition to *SRHE News*, the Society's newsletter, the Society publishes three journals: *Studies in Higher Education* (three issues a year), *Higher Education Quarterly* and *Research into Higher Education Abstracts* (three issues a year).

The Society runs frequent conferences, consultations, seminars and other events. The annual conference in December is organized at and with a higher education institution. There are a growing number of networks which focus on particular areas of interest, including:

Access	FE/HE
Assessment	Graduate Employment
Consultants	New Technology for Learning
Curriculum Development	Postgraduate Issues
Eastern European	Quantitative Studies
Educational Development Research	Student Development

Benefits to members

Individual

- The opportunity to participate in the Society's networks
- Reduced rates for the annual conferences
- Free copies of *Research into Higher Education Abstracts*
- Reduced rates for *Studies in Higher Education*

- Reduced rates for *Higher Education Quarterly*
- Free online access to *Register of Members' Research Interests* – includes valuable reference material on research being pursued by the Society's members
- Free copy of occasional in-house publications, e.g. *The Thirtieth Anniversary Seminars Presented by the Vice-Presidents*
- Free copies of *SRHE News* and *International News* which inform members of the Society's activities and provides a calendar of events, with additional material provided in regular mailings
- A 35 per cent discount on all SRHE/Open University Press books
- The opportunity for you to apply for the annual research grants
- Inclusion of your research in the *Register of Members' Research Interests*

Corporate

- Reduced rates for the annual conference
- The opportunity for members of the Institution to attend SRHE's network events at reduced rates
- Free copies of *Research into Higher Education Abstracts*
- Free copies of *Studies in Higher Education*
- Free online access to *Register of Members' Research Interests* – includes valuable reference material on research being pursued by the Society's members
- Free copy of occasional in-house publications
- Free copies of *SRHE News* and *International News*
- A 35 per cent discount on all SRHE/Open University Press books
- The opportunity for members of the Institution to submit applications for the Society's research grants
- The opportunity to work with the Society and co-host conferences
- The opportunity to include in the *Register of Members' Research Interests* your Institution's research into aspects of higher education

Membership details: SRHE, 76 Portland Place, London W1B 1NT, UK Tel: 020 7637 2766. Fax: 020 7637 2781. email: srheoffice@srhe.ac.uk world wide web: http://www.srhe.ac.uk./srhe/ *Catalogue:* SRHE & Open University Press, McGraw-Hill Education, McGraw-Hill House, Shoppenhangers Road, Maidenhead, Berkshire SL6 2QL. Tel: 01628 502500. Fax: 01628 770224. email: enquiries@openup.co.uk – web: www.openup.co.uk

Index